NORTH PHOENIX HIGH SCHOOL
LIBRARY

# *The Tropics:*
# WORLD OF TOMORROW

## Books by Charles Morrow Wilson

~ ★ ~

### FICTION

ACRES OF SKY

RABBLE ROUSER

GINGER BLUE

A MAN'S REACH

### NON-FICTION

AMBASSADORS IN WHITE

ONE HALF THE PEOPLE: DOCTORS AND THE CRISIS OF WORLD HEALTH

CENTRAL AMERICA: CHALLENGE AND OPPORTUNITY

MIDDLE AMERICA

NEW CROPS FOR THE NEW WORLD

ROOTS OF AMERICA

BACKWOODS AMERICA

AROOSTOOK

COUNTRY LIVING

TREES AND TEST TUBES

MERIWETHER LEWIS: OF LEWIS AND CLARK

EMPIRE IN GREEN AND GOLD

LIBERIA

THE TROPICS: WORLD OF TOMORROW

# *The Tropics:*

# WORLD OF TOMORROW

*by Charles Morrow Wilson*



HARPER & BROTHERS . PUBLISHERS

*New York*

THE TROPICS: WORLD OF TOMORROW



*Printed in the United States of America*



FIRST EDITION

C-A

*TO BYRON H. LARABEE*

CONTENTS

# Look South Again

~ * ~

TODAY and tomorrow the tropics are urgently, vitally important to us all.

For the tropics are earth-circling spheres of potential abundance for all people. They are the great and durable cradle of life. They are also a crucial sphere of decision between totalitarianism and democracy; and they are an inevitable basis for any far uplifting economy.

The tropics include most of the habitable frontiers that remain on earth. They are arenas of ever-increasing human populations. Tropical populations now total somewhere near one-and-a-fifth billion people, which is somewhere near half of all mankind.

At present there is good reason to believe that the tropical census is increasing at the rate of about forty thousand people every twenty-four hours. At this rate tropical populations could very well be doubled by the end of the present century.

Disciples of Malthus or Margaret Sanger might consider such a prospect calamitous. But the fact is noteworthy that whereas a probable two-thirds of the current increase in human population is taking place within the tropics, at least two-thirds of all tropical lands still have too few people for the effective or immediate development of their natural resources. As this far-scattered shortage of people is overcome—and that is clearly in progress at the present time—the world-wide importance of the tropics is certain to increase. The tropics were forceful and at times decisive factors in the empire-building world of yesterday. Today they are far more influential than most of us realize. Tomorrow the tropics can be the saving grace of a free world.

It is therefore well to consider the real meaning of "tropics," a tempting word and one almost traditionally engulfed in whimsey or fantasy. Plainly the time when we can afford to accept a definition of the tropics from the movies, or the Broadway stage, or the Memoirs of Lieutenant General Blimp, or Foreign Secretary Bullthrupp, or Ambassador Blotz, former president of Blotz Trolley Wreckers, Inc., and alternate national committeeman from the greater Scranton area, is now long gone.

We can afford no longer to envisage the tropics either as perennial green hells or palmy Utopias. For they are neither of these; and they are not Hollywood, nor Broadway, nor Shangri-la. The tropics are earth, air, rain, sunlight, and growth, and even more importantly they are people, in great part warmhearted, exciting, and admirable.

By minimum dictionary definition "a tropic" means either of two approximate circles of the celestial spheroid called Earth parallel to and north (Tropic of Cancer) or south (Tropic of Capricorn) of the equator and 23 degrees and 27 minutes from it, a measure marking the maximum directness of the sun's rays on earth. The maximum directness of sun's rays remains the real gist of the definition.

"Tropics," in turn, means those regions of land and water that are either between the two parallels just named or preponderantly close to them. Thus, practically, the tropics are the lands where sunpower is at a maximum.

The total land surface of our earth is about fifty-one million square miles, but as the atlases and almanacs and military planners keep pointing out, much of this total is expensively lacking in sunpower. The earth has continents, subcontinents, and principal islands which, though supposedly underlaid by land, are so effectively sealed off by hundreds or thousands of feet of ice and snow that the whole issue becomes academic, except to a specialized few.

Not all the tropics are friendly to people and not all the tropics are habitable. But proportionately and as a whole, the tropics, which include somewhere near one-third of the land area of the earth, keep proving their amiability toward people by providing homes for almost half the human race. And, as noted, the latter proportion is increasing so steadfastly that some of us may live to see two-thirds of all people living in the tropics or in closely adjacent subtropics, and our children may see the proportion raised still higher. The latter is a rational possibility, and because the magic of sunpower calls for immediate musterings of manpower, it is also a devoted hope.

## MANPOWER AND SUNPOWER

THERE are many tropical impediments, but there are still more tropical advantages. Unquestionably, the greatest of the latter is sunpower. This superior sunpower creates superior power to produce goods. It establishes the general and global proposition that a given measure of human energy capably applied to a given resource is more productive in the tropics than anywhere else on the earth. And to a world that is still preponderantly hungry, ragged or naked, and chronically lacking in tangible goods, "productive" remains one of the most cherished of all adjectives. Because of superior sunpower, vegetative and bacterial growth is far more rapid in the tropics than out. The tropical cousin of the tree that grows in Brooklyn will likely grow somewhere between two and nine times as fast in Panama or Honduras, or in Leopoldville, Belgian Congo.

Brooklyn, of course, though favored and exceptional in so many ways, is part of the winter-harassed temperate zones, and comparing its tree-growing aptitudes with those of the rich deep tropics is considerably like comparing the cookery of an old-fashioned off-and-on baking pan with that of an efficient pressure cooker.

But the fact is also noteworthy that the tree that grows, say, five times as fast in a fertile and humid valley of Panama as in Brooklyn, when dead and left exposed to weather will rot several times as rapidly.

For with maximum sunpower, acceleration becomes the word for tropical decay and disintegration as well as for tropical growth. It is inspiringly true, however, with superior sunpower and adequate manpower working together, tropical growth usually can overcome, frequently overwhelm, the forces of tropical death, decay, and disintegration, leaving the totals of tropical production strongly in the black—and the green.

Evidently, and naturally, farming is man's most effective means for benefiting from the momentous and seemingly eternal advantages of tropical sunpower. Appropriately, farming is the preponderant tropical trade; more than four-fifths of all tropical peoples today are agrarians of one kind or another.

Adding to the bounties of superior sunpower is the likelihood, in many areas a known certainty, that the greater part of the rich soils remaining on the earth are in the tropics. This may or may not remain the case; the decision here waits largely on man. Even the richest of soils are essentially a perishable film rarely exceeding seven or eight inches in depth. Tropical sunpower performs bountiful magic in building and rebuilding soils, but its alter ego, tropical rainpower, if not duly heeded can loot and destroy soils even faster with a force which frequently appears to excel that of sunpower, and with a speed and violence which are almost as difficult to compute reliably as the force of sunpower itself.

Most tropical farmers revere sunpower and retreat more or less stoically before rainpower without learning nearly enough about ways and means for benefiting from either or both of these momentous forces. Stating this more directly, tropical farmers as yet have actually learned amazingly little about the supreme trade and science of tropical agriculture.

But the non-tropical farming world is in no position to deride or condemn this almost fantastic lack of knowledge. For speaking very factually, we are only now beginning to learn the first smatterings about temperate-zone agriculture. Even in the United States where we lay claim to having one of the more advanced agricultures in the present-day world, and in many respects this claim is reasonably well supported, any realist knows, or can readily find out, that U.S. agriculture as a whole still laps and thumbs the pages of its primer and has not yet shed all its swaddling clothes. Many of our "safest" textbooks on farming, like Artemus Ward's long-delayed book about women, still require a boldface errata admonishing the reader to substitute *is nots* for *is's*, and *maybe, possibly,* or *God knows* for the *is nots.*

But if temperate-zone agriculture is in querulous childhood, tropical agriculture remains in toothless infancy. This statement bears no malice, for the truth stands that toothless babies are absolutely essential to this world of people. So, too, is tropical agriculture, which is the great warm hope for world abundance and the foremost productive use of the still supreme force of sunpower.

Among its many benevolences, sunpower relieves tropical vegetation, and other things tropical, of the ever grim actuality of winter—not so much the mere botanic function of leaf shed, which frequently occurs in the tropics, as elsewhere, but of the freezing, quasi-sterile months that are the hair shirts suffered by temperate-zone vegetation.

To endure freezing winters, perennial plants are obliged to endure and somehow survive the repeated forming and melting of ice crystals in their organs of survival—buds, leaves, roots, or bulbs, and to suffer the ever-disruptive physical law that every time moisture enters into the ice-crystal state it expands powerfully and thereby strains or tears the vital tissues of vegetation. Drought is another remorseless curse of most temperate-zone winters. As a rule, winter winds are dry winds. Greedily and stubbornly they suck out as much moisture as plant tissues are able to release. And verse and fable to the contrary, plants in the temperate zones rarely succeed in keeping warm under "blankets" of snow or dry leaves or grass, since during long intervals of most winters the alleged "blankets" are simply not there.

Luckily, most temperate-zone perennials have varied and ingenious protective chemistries that help them survive. Even so, winter freezing remains a momentous impediment, a very basic and dogging disadvantage which has done most to force temperate-zone people into the generally extravagant recourse of growing annual crops.

As a whole, perennial crops are far more economical and effective, since the growing of annual crops means plowing, seeding, and otherwise cultivating anew each successive spring. The resulting wastes of labor and soils, due to erosion losses that are the inevitable result of laying open soils to the wrath of rains and winds at yearly or more frequent intervals, are ever formidable. For men and lands alike, annual plantings are expensive.

By fortunate contrast, the tropics are the age-old strongholds of the great perennial crops which live and flourish without the penalty of winter killing, without the formidable costs and wastes incidental to annual seeding, and without the expensive hazard of leaving valuable soils uncovered during much of the year. Actually the great majority of tropical crops are perennials which require planting only once in several years, or once in a decade or quarter-century or half-century, or even once in a century. Nowadays a planting of such tropical staples as bananas, coca, or coffee bush is good for at least a quarter-century of recurrent harvests. Once started well, the great perennial crops of the tropics require little or no cultivation. Most tropical grasses, including the giant sweet grass called sugar cane, are likewise long-time perennials. In the U.S. South, sugar cane must be planted annually or biannually. In Cuba and many other tropical places, sugar cane requires planting only once in twenty to thirty years. It is therefore reasonably apparent that sugar, like many other world crops, is on its way back to the tropics.

An excellent appraisal of the immense advantages of perennial crops is being provided by the diligent, expensive, and sometimes inspired efforts now being made to develop perennial crops for temperate climates, for example, perennial wheat which, so far as the United States, Canada, and Australia are concerned, has gone no farther than the development of a rather promising series of range grasses.

Even so, the systematic study of tropical perennials is one of the most exciting and promising fields of current international research in agriculture. In addition to grains, grasses, and principal vegetables, so many of which came originally from the tropics, present-day agricultural research is taking heed, at long last, of some of the potentially great tropical crops which flourish in muck or mud.

Through the farming years, almost all the great crops of man, as thus far developed, have somehow acquired genetic prejudices to "wet feet" or annual rainfalls in excess of sixty inches or thereabouts. In the United States we have only one wet-land crop of any consequence, rice; and dry-land rice appears to be on its way in and upward. Otherwise all our principal crops today thrive only in drained soils. The methodical drainage of crop lands, now generally accepted as necessary for any successful farming in the temperate zones, is obviously one of the many great development possibilities that await hundreds of millions of fertile but swampy acres that are scattered in and across great sectors of the tropical earth.

But people are learning, too, that even greater areas of tropical wet-lands do not respond amicably to drainage, however competently devised. For these lands, and frequently already growing there, usually without benefit of cultivation, there are such potentially valuable root crops as taro, already used as a staple starch food by millions of people in the Pacific tropics, and dasheen, another great root crop of tropical mires which holds exceptional promise as an important international source of industrial starches, cellulose, alcohol, engine fuels, and animal foods as well; and there are many other wet-footed crops which are potentially great.

The development of such plants, indigenous to and already flourishing in tropical wet-lands, can very probably succeed in introducing a great new family of valuable and mud-favoring crops, thereby opening still another doorway to tropical abundance.

More emphatic and immediate promise is held for the many too-little-known tropical grasses including the herbaceous ancestors of our cereal grains and corn, now by far the most valuable of all crops. Far-flung tropical land surfaces such as the millions of square miles of Central and Eastern Africa or the immense and still vacant uplands of South America can very well become vast green pastures for the largest and most beneficial herds that ever walked the earth.

Plainly the tropics are the world tomorrow or, at minimum, a great and decisive part of it. No man can see tomorrow in all the vivid, tangible details in which he sees today. But even in our babyhood of precise knowledge we can see the tropics as the most variously productive farm area the world has yet known.

For with all that still waits to be learned, during the past quarter-century people actually and specifically learned more about tropical agriculture and the potentials of tropical soils and climates than they had learned during all the previous centuries. And although we have only begun to replace smatterings of ignorance with the first faint glimmers of knowledge, more and more people are learning to look south for the promise of abundance.

## ON THE NAY SIDE

THEY are also learning to look south for constructive definitions of the problems and impediments of our world tomorrow.

There are plenty of tropical impediments, past and present and, no doubt, future. We know some of them quite well, and we are perhaps too much inclined to infer, deduce, or arbitrarily fear others, and to peer about or even to open doors to imaginary hobgoblins.

The latter habit is all the sillier because there are plenty of actual impediments to the south. For one, and as my Uncle George used to say when somebody else mixed his drinks for him, there is too damned much water. As any map viewer discerns, there are thousands of miles of tropical waters for hundreds of tropical lands. One who reads history knows how these huge tropical spaces of oceans and seas have served as wet stadiums for exploration and empire building, and that they remain decisively important in terms of world trade and the employment of navies, air forces, land forces, and in the strategies and tactics of war.

As any map viewer notices, too, the proportion of tropical waters to land, though extravagant the globe around, in the southern hemisphere is excessive. The latter fact is immensely relevant to many of the great world stories of yesterday, today, and, no doubt, tomorrow; it is a basic reason for much of the globe-circling reality of tropical "backwardness," and particularly the backwardness of the southern-hemisphere tropics which, because they are so preponderantly of seas and oceans, through the centuries have been obliged to look to the north for wealth, credit, leadership, and, alas, for conquerors.

Tropical oceans and seas, though beautiful to look at and incessantly dramatic and varied to travel or to live by, keep on infringing the solvency of tropical lands. These infringements are atmospheric as well as aquatic. For as many centuries as we know even vaguely, the broad, stubborn, and violent belts of tropical trade winds, abetted by such recurrent and devastating tropical storms as hurricanes, typhoons, monsoons, and harmattans, have strafed and oppressed most tropical lands. They have also retarded, destroyed, or otherwise penalized tropical trade and the many beneficial developments incidental to trade.

These facts, though common knowledge, remain underemphasized, all the more so because the tropics are preponderantly farms, and a farm, wherever located, is by definition a planted or growing field, or a succession thereof, possessed of a road or a way to a market.

Whether the road is a sea lane, an air lane, a paved highway, a bumpy cart lane, or a dim and wavery bush trail, the reality persists that any force, natural or otherwise, which impedes or blockades the road is, per se, a noteworthy impediment to the comfort, prosperity, and progress of all peoples and lands concerned.

Tropical roads to markets are primarily sea roads, as they have been through the centuries. Century after century the trade winds and the more violent types of tropical storm have impeded and destroyed ships and shipping, thus wiping out fortunes, upsetting work schedules, and otherwise retarding tropical development. Winds, so the adage goes, blow as they please. Century after century they have pleased to blow contrary to the advancement and well-being of the tropics.

This reality, which persists, was particularly powerful during all the centuries of sailing ships. But even the present age of steel ships, powered by steam or Diesel or electric turbines, and equipped with radio, radar, and all the other gadgets of modernity, is far from being immune to the havoc of tropical winds and storms. The same applies to the great new age of air commerce. Though the superbly powerful and fleet airplane enjoys a somewhat greater degree of immunity to tropical storms than does surface transport, practical operation of aircraft remains considerably more difficult, erratic, and expensive in the tropics than in the temperate zones.

The impediments dealt by tropical seas and oceans, and the air above them, keep infiltrating into tropical lands in several ways. For one, there is the remorseless and largely inexplainable fact that tropical shorelines are hard to get at because they have disproportionately few harbors or other usable port sites. This reality is stubbornly set. Today, yesterday, and tomorrow good harbors are relatively essential to the birth and growth of cities and nations. Through the ages many of the world's principal cities have gained stature and greatness from their water resources. The tropics, in general, are desperately poor in terms of such resources. There are disproportionately few good ports on seas, oceans, bays, or major rivers of the tropics. Although there are a few great and successful tropical ports, the fact stands quite relentlessly that the majority of all tropical shorelines are not readily accessible by sea, because of shallows, reefs, protruding ledges, incompatible tides, virulent winds, or other natural impediment.

In the trading world as a whole, somewhere near nine out of ten of all tropical ports now in use must be listed as inferior from a standpoint of commercial navigation. Maritime records show that about 70 per cent of all cargo tonnage now originating in the tropics is penalized by inferior harbors which means that most ocean-going ships calling at most tropical ports are still obliged to ride anchor off shore and to discharge or recruit cargo by the costly use of lighters or other smaller carriers.

Historians have the best reasons to appreciate the global importance of this age-old scarcity of competent ports and harbors in the tropics. Even U.S. Congressmen have begun to awaken to this highly unpolitic scarcity. Even Navy brass has become aware of the somewhat insolent reality that along almost six thousand miles of West African coast, which could become militarily one of the most strategic of all coastlines, there is not a single harbor suited to the operation of major ocean-going craft. Hurriedly and no doubt wisely, beginning in 1947 the United States underwrote the building of a capable seaport at Monrovia, the ever picturesque capital of Liberia, on the great western bulge of Africa. No sleeve stripes are required to see that many other man-built tropical ports are urgently needed.

And no exhaustive study is required to find out that the largely unaccommodating shorelines of so many tropical lands are not the only barriers to man's easy entry into the tropics. Inherently and by stern geography, the majority of tropical mainlands and islands are hard to penetrate or occupy. They abound in big, abrupt and distinctly unfriendly mountains, in anti-social rivers, flatlands, and swamps. Heavy rainfalls and violent watersheds, common to most tropical lands, prompt hundreds of tropical rivers to become menacing and, at frequent intervals, destructive. During rainy seasons altogether too many tropical rivers bash and ruin with violent floods. And during dry seasons they are sordidly inclined to sink into sullen morasses or sand flats.

Also, the preponderant direction of tropical rivers (the Nile is the illustrious exception) is not north and south, the direction of flow of most of the temperate-zone rivers which have proved so effective in making world powers of certain peoples and abject vassals of others, but rather east and west, which demonstrates the wrong-way Corrigan as regards basic geography.

Had the colossal Amazon been destined to flow north-south like the Mississippi, the United States of Brazil, not the United States of America, might now be the number-one world power.

But God decided the directions of rivers and the placing and proportions of mountains, valleys, and plains. In these particular decisions, divine and fateful averages appear to be somewhat against the tropics.

The majority of tropical lands are still more than averagely difficult for man to move over readily or to populate evenly. Accordingly, tropical populations remain inconsistently placed, clustered or knotted in occasional dense groups or scattered too lightly over huge areas which still lack people enough to realize and develop their many natural bounties. It follows that about one-twentieth of all tropical lands is conspicuously overpopulated whereas about two-thirds are conspicuously underpopulated. It follows, too, and no less pertinently, that God has given bountifully and that it is both the opportunity and obligation of man to put His gifts to better use.

The building of roads, highways, railroads, harbors, airports, pipelines, power lines, telephone, radio-telegram, and other communication facilities in the deep tropics is usually difficult and expensive. So is maintenance. But there is proof both can be done and are well worth doing. The truth persists that transport and communications are substantially more difficult to build and maintain in the tropics than in the temperate zones. Here are two comparative instances, both factual, commonplace, and more or less typical.

Recently the State of Michigan completed 412.7 miles of "all-weather" gravel roads between what the reports term a succession of county and rural community centers. The job was planned and completed without fanfare or claim of being exceptional. Traffic experts made careful estimates of the needs of the roads, the probable traffic loads, upkeep costs, and revenues obtainable by way of gasoline tax and other sources. Experienced contractors dispatched surveying crews, assembled the necessary equipment, located railheads and storages as needed, made routine checks of local rainfalls, water tables, and flood levels of creeks and rivers; they also made routine samplings of subsoils and rock formation.

Then they went to work, as they had done many times before. Aware that there is no such thing as a "perfect" road, the builders planned and completed good roads of their kind and cost.

At about the same time (October, 1948) another road-building project of about the same size and specifications was begun in tropical West Africa, starting at a point near the mouth of the Farmington River 3.2 degrees north latitude, following inland about 112 miles across the low rolling hills and broad valleys of Liberia to a native town called Ybanga, and from there, via the easiest route, to join the right-of-way of the old French colony road in French Guinea. This, too, is, or is built to be, an "all-weather" road with specifications virtually identical with those of the Michigan roads just mentioned.

In West Africa, as in Michigan, the road-building equipment was first-rate: American-made and operated and repaired by American technicians. The African labor was about as competent as the Michigan labor.

Even so, the African roads cost about three and a half times as much as the Michigan road, and the building took almost four times as long. In Africa the costs of operating and repairing the necessary machinery were at least twice those in Michigan, and maintenance costs appear to be about four times as much.

Yet the actual traffic load in Africa is less than one-third that of Michigan, while direct revenue possibilities are hardly one-tenth as much. Even so, the African road is crucially needed. It draws cargoes from scores of ancient trader trails, and no comparable throughway is available. The point is therefore evident enough. The cost of building and maintaining or operating communications in the tropics is usually far greater than in the temperate zones. But tropical communications also must be regarded as essential resources and as noble efforts to make up for lost time and opportunities. For obviously the good of the tropics depends in great part on man's ability to enter and move across them, to stay or to leave as he chooses.

More and more each year, human migration is being reslanted toward the south. In great part this is a reversal of the past when temperate-zone man tended to move southward only under exceptional pressure or duress, or singly or in small groups to explore, seek easy wealth, serve properties of others, escape the sheriff or warden, or in despair or desperation to try beginning anew.

Until the present century, comparatively few tropical peoples were obliged or indeed able to move north. Even now most of those who come north are of trade or professional groups or come as recruited laborers. But for the most part populations have overflowed from east to west, or vice versa, much less frequently from north to south, only rarely from south to north. Accordingly, in the past, most tropical lands had little or no opportunity to benefit from a two-way traffic in peoples.

The latter situation, which has also added greatly to what is known as tropical backwardness, tends to abate. But other rather personal paradoxes remain. For example, as an all-too-evident detail of environment, tropical peoples have yet to comprehend or take advantage of the temperate-zone habit of thrift which is born of man's age-old struggle to store up for the cold and sterile winter ahead. To one who has never known a winter, this line of action strongly suggests insanity. Yet, ironically, this get-ready-for-winter urge so common to most nations of white men has had much to do with the latter's establishment of so many non-tropical colonies and trading fronts throughout the best parts of the tropical earth.

But all this has become as unnecessary as a case of smallpox. Just as any intelligent man or woman can appreciate the value of health even while healthy, tropical peoples can and do learn thrift and economic competence even though they may never be obliged to face a hard winter or an entirely empty larder. Furthermore, they can learn of thrift as it must be interpreted in terms of the tropics.

Other advantages of what the old-fashioned school books used to term "natural education" have been denied most tropical peoples. For example, the land masses of the temperate zones have been relatively easy for people to move over and to occupy. Accordingly, throughout most of the temperate zones a pastoral or nomad era has provided man with sound motives for spreading over and otherwise occupying the land and for establishing durable farmsites and towns.

But although the decisive pastoral world of tomorrow may very well be centered in the tropics, the best half of the tropical earth today never had a pastoral age and the profound advantages that come with it.

Thus far, too, and in some part because of the lack of a pastoral age, the working strength of the tropical farmer has tended to remain slight in comparison with that of tropical vegetation. "Colossal," which has now become one of Hollywood's hardest-worked and highest-paid words, is still about the best word for describing the variety and growth-rate of tropical vegetation. But when left untended, the latter has a way of bulging into giantism or being obliterated by other plants which turn to herbaceous giants. "Colossal" likewise becomes the suitable word for depicting man's necessary efforts to control and direct such rampant vegetation. The time is right for admitting squarely that man alone cannot realize tropical abundance solely with his two hands, his bare flesh and brawn. He requires neighbors and helpers. He must have mechanical support and technical help. He must have more than self-contained protection from other vast and more or less natural forces, which certainly includes protection from disease. All are basic portions of what one would like to term "natural education." But the truth is now too wholly evident that all do not just come naturally.

People are learning, for example, that health in the tropics can be attained when individuals, communities, and governments work as one. But the task is not easy, and it certainly cannot be listed as a free enterprise or a natural blessing. For the micro-organisms of ruinous diseases which, like tigers, leopards, and other animal predators, have gone south for better hunting and escape from winter are still far and away the most ruthless enemies of man in hot countries. The undersized predators bask and multiply in the year-round warmth and in the abundance of victim-hosts, and they succeed in shaping a vicious circle of human hunger, poverty, and sickness.

Very plainly in the tropics, even more emphatically than anywhere else, this tragic circle of disease and want can be broken only by the determined use of the classic weapons of knowledge, devoted work, authority, and money. Very plainly, too, "natural learning" cannot supply the all-necessary knowledge of tropical diseases (so many of them actually cosmopolitan) which number the still scrambled directories of viruses including those sardonic ones that inhabit dying cells, many dimly known micro-organisms such as spirochetes, bartonellas, and many others which medical texts continue to list wistfully as "malicious things"; and, in addition to all, the crawling, burrowing, and flying carriers of disease, many self-distributed disease organisms, or of many "exotic" diseases, such as intestinal worms which avoid the intestines, blood parasites that cling resolutely to artery linings or in lymph spaces and never show up in the blood, and too many others. Or of malaria, which is still deeply intrenched in the tropics and still the foremost communicable disease of man, or tuberculosis, still a serious threat to the tropics, particularly in view of oncoming industrialization. Or the many diseases of tropical livestock which is so requisite to the good of people.

Very fortunately, hundreds of medical workers and other men and women of the sciences have recently made memorable findings in many fields of tropical medicine and are hot on the trails of ever greater ones. The learning involved is preponderantly technical.

The total picture of disease and health in the tropics is far from roseate. But it would be avidly terrifying if it were not for the fact that there is already such widespread progress to report from so many places, some of them far-distant from the tropics. Though we have much left to learn and to do about tropical health, during the past twenty years more has been learned and more done than during many preceding centuries.

Every year sees medicine more able and facile in its defense of tropical peoples. Even more inspiringly, each year sees greater numbers of capable men and women of medicine who sincerely desire to help mankind by learning and doing more about the dark, fierce mysteries of tropical disease. Already medicine and public health administration, working together, have progressed far enough to know and to prove clearly in hundreds of varying and difficult locales that good health in the tropics is both possible and attainable.

## THE SEESAW GOES UP

THE fact of knowing and proving that people can enjoy healthy lives in virtually any type of tropical environment is, as I see it, this century's most memorable contribution to tropical development.

There are still other contributions deserving of notice. Some are literally new. Some, more or less age-old, have only now come into clear view. Others, though more or less apparent and clearly important, remain in the categories of maybe or perhaps.

One among the latter seems to call loudest for a hearing at this time. It deals with the place and part of the tropics in what the business journals rather awesomely term "Our Age of Synthetics." Quite logically this poses a direct question as to whether or not the productive awakening, or reawakening, of the tropics comes too late to benefit the world at large. This is one of those skulking and pouncing questions which eventually leap at every devoted student of the tropics.

Recently the question overtook me afresh at a gathering of importers, exporters, consuls, and consular workers from the American tropics. It was my lack of good fortune to be assigned a place next an overweight and otherwise expansive industrial chemist who loudly explained that the whisky he sipped had been distilled from petroleum, while the flask from which he drank had been fabricated of coal-tar plastics. Within a quarter-hour the chemist recited by name and catalogue number a list of twenty-nine other synthetics which his firm now manufactures and markets, every one of them a "replacement" for a present or former tropical product.

He closed his exposition with a tremendous swig from his plastic flask, then turned to me and all but whooped:

"So you see, Doc, while you and your playmates fumble around trying to breed and cross-breed and develop new crops for growing in the tropics, or to spruce up the old ones already there, me and my outfit are actually producing the end products—all the way from coconut oil to vanilla and back again—by sound chemical methods in good air-conditioned workshops. Today, we got more different tropical products to sell than the East India Company, United Fruit, and Lever Brothers put together, and *all* our tropical goods are actually started and finished this side of Trenton. . . ."

The total discourse, though neither original nor scintillating, directed me once again up a dark alley of reflections about the sometimes painful reality that technical progress in the temperate zones, especially in the United States, shows an almost fiendish talent for impeding, frustrating, or erasing many of the foundations and sill structures of tropical agriculture and the latter's synonym, which is better lives for people in the tropics and out.

Synthetic rubber, synthetic flavors of coffee, cocoa, vanilla, and scores of tropical spices, synthetic fibers, and so on are but passing entries in a synthetics list which begins to read like the Middletown telephone directory. Product after product that once graced sun-splashed tropic fields or the holds of tropics-plying ships is now being challenged as to basic source by more or less human characters in white smocks who, possessed of photogenic test tubes, glass boilers, and vacuum jugs, plus thick corporate bankrolls, streamlined laboratories, and plastic flasks appropriately and synthetically filled, keep bobbing up to "research and produce" substitutes from coal slag, fermented garbage, wheat straw, or virtually any other crass material currently in surplus.

The temptation to underestimate the hazard to tropical production incident to a real and impressive age of synthetics is rather formidable to most of the wishful and determined champions of the tropics. On the other hand, enthusiasts for the synthetics age are no less tempted to underestimate the challenge of tropical production to the synthetics age. The subject is first-rate for debating teams or for prolonged arguments between reasonably friendly rivals, and the chances are rather overwhelming that, quite regardless of argument, both tropical fields and synthetics laboratories and factories will keep on expanding, prospering, and fulfilling more and more needs.

Furthermore, whether one elects to speak for the affirmative or the negative, whole bevies of basic facts keep crowding the foreground. One of these is the very obvious truth that tropical sunpower still comes free; that lands and labor and tax rates in the tropics remain generally cheap as compared with those in the temperate zones. Another elemental truth, which can be used beneficially by either side, is that the very term synthetic implies one or more specific starting materials, and that granting certain memorable exceptions, such as "catching" nitrogen from the air, the starting materials are preponderantly tangibles.

Preponderantly, too, these necessary starting materials are harvests of field or forest, or long-time residues thereof, such as coal, petroleum, or natural gas. They are also the less valuable stalks and stovers of grains; they are sawdust, timber wastes, and the less valuable tree growths; they are roots, pith, pods, and seed that, prior to fabrication as synthetics, are of comparatively little worth. They include food wastes and ore wastes, slags and low-quality coal, refinery residues, or deep-well petroleum and gas which only a few years ago would never actually have been produced. The starting materials for synthetics also include by-products from many and frequently complex industries; also in use are soils, rotting vegetation, and manures. Yet the great majority of basic materials are still strongly dependent on the magics of sunpower, rain, soils, and the metals and minerals below them.

In terms of accredited sources of synthetic materials, the tropics continue to excel, since so many starting materials are most abundant and most rapidly producible within the tropics. Also, and importantly, neither the factories nor laboratories where synthetics are fabricated nor the power sources that propel them nor the hands and minds that keep them at work are bound immutably to such places as New Jersey, Delaware, New York, Connecticut, Massachusetts, or Illinois. More and more synthetic industries are quite literally moving south. Still more are turning southward to procure their starting materials. The trend is well defined and increasing.

Granting all this, the reasonably good but extremely hard-worked phrase, "synthetic age," must not be worked to death. For the world generally has already learned that such synthetics as vitamin pills, though gaudily advertised and sold at obese profits, are no true substitute for steak, chicken, fresh vegetables, honest butter or margarines. People have learned, even politicians have learned, that synthetics or no, several acres—at a minimum, about three acres of well-tilled, well-stocked field and pasture land—are still required to feed one adult person adequately the year around.

Many people observe, with growing certainty, that the really impressive farming and forest frontiers of the world today and tomorrow are in the tropics.

Otherwise important tropical crops can be synthesized and thereby, politely stated, terminated. But the calm, cool statistics prove that extremely few are being so terminated. Thus far, the most complete synthetic capture of any memorable tropical crop has been directed toward vanilla, an exotic and parasitic orchid cousin presumably native to Mexico. Many synthetic vanillas are excellent products which have gained wide acceptance.

Yet the growing and processing of real vanilla remains a valid, actually an increasing enterprise. A third-century ago or longer, it was a common published prophecy that with the advances of mechanical refrigeration the long-memorable spice trades, always predicated most heavily on the use of spices as meat preservatives, would stumble and presently die. Mechanical refrigeration has now covered a great part of the earth. The synthesizing of tropical spices remains brilliant and aggressive. Yet the tropical spice trade continues to grow. The United States, for example, now spends about twice as much for tropical spices and uses more than half again as many pounds as we spent and used half a century ago, and this despite the fact that we are the most refrigerated and the most synthesized nation on the face of the earth.

The flavor called cocoa or "chocolate," made from the thumb-sized seed that crowds the melon-like pods of a beautiful, silver-splotched fruit tree born of the American tropics, can be synthesized effectively. Even so, true cocoa remains an international crop of steadily rising importance and value; true chocolate is still the most sought-after flavor, and second only to milk, cocoa remains the world's most popular food drink.

In the United States and elsewhere, synthetic industries have excelled unquestionably in the field of specialized fibers. Yet specialized fibers from the tropics, including jute, roselle, piassava, abacá or Manila "hemp," raffia, and others are in greater international demand than ever before.

Coffee remains the largest tropical import of the United States and the dominant tropical export of South and Central America. Native to eastern Africa, it is still one of the least "scientific" of tropical crops, which, alas, is saying a great deal, and to date this has received deplorably little consideration.

"Outrageous" is too mild a word for the prevailing era of coffee-marketing and prices. Synthetic coffee flavors are soundly developed. Yet with every imaginable incentive for turning to them, the coffee-drinking world at large does not do so to any important extent. Instead we keep on buying more real coffee than ever before, and paying and paying and paying for it.

The most expertly publicized story of synthetic annihilation of a principal tropical crop deals with rubber. This story involves what is unquestionably the world's most memorable victory of high-fee New York publicity agents and perhaps the balmiest publicity field day ever enjoyed and later regretted, principally at the expense of U.S. taxpayers.

Much of the foregoing stems from the fact that rubber is inherently complex whereas public relations counselors, U.S. Publicists Numbers 1,2,3,4,5,6, and so on through 12,219 or thereabouts, are preponderantly simple.

Beginning somewhat more than a century ago when a Connecticut peddler and tinker named Charles Goodyear found out how to vulcanize the stuff, rubber—more literally the milk-like latex from the inner bark of an Amazon Basin forest tree called Hevea—climbed to foremost place as a world-influencing tropical export.

Even before the present century, the selected seed of Amazon rubber trees had been carried to the southeast tropics, particularly Malaya and Indonesia, where they presently became world-influencing crops. Meanwhile, by 1912 or before, German chemists had begun to produce the first synthetic rubber, more properly termed "substitute elastomers." The story of the latter was destined to make memorable news. But so was the story of natural rubber from the tropics.

During the middle and latter 1920's, Dutch planters in Indonesia and a few British planters in Malaya set out to develop superior strains of what had heretofore been wild or "scrub" rubber trees, lifted directly, by way of seed, from the remote reaches of the Amazon Basin.

Promptly, the development and introduction of these hybrid rubber trees raised average yearly yields from averages of three hundred to four hundred pounds per acre to from one thousand to sixteen hundred pounds. They further reduced disease losses and showed the way for changing one of the least efficient of tropical harvests to one of the most efficient. But changing over from the erratic though beautiful "wild" Hevea rubber tree to a high-yielding hybrid strain calls for time and for much local experimentation and adaptation. Accordingly, the majority of rubber growers, including American producers in such highly favorable areas as Sumatra and Liberia, were unable to bring any sizable plantings of the hybrid trees to yield until late in the 1930's.

By then a global war was begun, and because of crucial war needs for much greater quantities of rubber and, shortly thereafter, because of Japan's lightning conquest of the great rubber plantations in and close by Southeast Asia, the Western World, led by us, turned to synthetic rubber. Yet after World War II ended, the international demand for natural or tropical rubber remained strong. Synthetic rubber had been war-multiplied, U.S.-Treasury subsidized, and vociferously publicized, yet promptly U.S., British, Soviet, and other rubber industries began consuming almost double their prewar rubber tonnages.

Almost instantly, natural rubber regained its market preferences, and tropical rubber harvests were raised by about a quarter-million tons annually. By August, 1950, world prices of natural rubber had climbed to 58 cents per pound as compared with the quasi-subsidized price of about seventeen cents for synthetic rubber, and were crowding higher: an eloquent testimony to the relative merits of the two in the experienced hands of one of the most competitive of all industries. Actually, between the years 1937 and 1951, the progress and ingenuity applied to natural rubber production exceeded the impressive measure of progress and ingenuity applied to synthetic rubber wherein the spade work had been performed by German and other good chemists more than a decade before the first experimental development of high-yielding hybrid rubber trees.

## FROM BOUNTIFUL TROPICAL EARTH

MEANWHILE, entirely beyond the realm of controversy or man-maneuvered news or man-made substitutes, the fact stands certainly that the tropics have several specific and earth-circling advantages and pre-eminences in providing great and much-needed commodities. Foremost among all these are trees, which are far and away the most extensive of existing tropical crops. Considerably more than half of the great forests remaining on earth are in the tropics, and for this we can thank God who makes trees, since we cannot, with any real accuracy, thank people.

In the American tropics alone, from the Rio Grande south to the Plata and throughout the land-dots of the Caribbean, woodlands, in great part virgin, still cover an area larger than all the United States. They include several of the most heavily forested countries on earth, such as Honduras and the Guianas where about four-fifths of the land is greened-out by trees. About three-fourths of the land surfaces of Nicaragua, British Honduras, and the Dominican Republic still are forests. So are approximately half the lands of Colombia, Peru, Venezuela, and Trinidad. About 60 per cent of the lands of Costa Rica and Panama are forested. In Guatemala, the percentage is 41; in Bolivia, 37; Ecuador, 33; French West Indies, 32; Jamaica, 25.

The most denuded woodlands in the western tropics are those of Puerto Rico and the Virgin Islands, where barely one-tenth of the land remains in trees. The rest of the West Indies have an average of about 16 per cent; El Salvador, 11 per cent; Cuba, about 18 per cent; Mexico, about 20 per cent. These latter percentages are deplorably low. Even so, except for Soviet Russia, which has the most extensive forest resources of any one nation (its estimated four and a quarter million square miles of wooded lands are almost a third of all the forest lands remaining on earth), the American tropics remain definitive strongholds for trees.

Yet at the present time barely 1 per cent of their forests are in beneficial harvest, even though fuel wood and other forest products remain in chronic shortage in most countries. But neither this nor any other paradox can erase the unique and basic value of the great forest crops, or such proved and relevant realities as the fact that native cedars in Honduras reach their prime age for lumber-making in about thirty years, whereas similar hardwood in Finland requires two hundred or three hundred years, or that a teak tree in Ecuador reaches harvest age within twenty years, whereas a conifer in Siberia takes about one hundred fifty, or that in the tropics, as a whole, trees are actually crops which a man can plant, harvest, and profit from during a medium lifetime or less, whereas farther north few men live long enough to harvest the forests which they may plant.

Through the ages tropical trees, for the most part neither planted nor tended by man, have lived on, fighting for space and light, cleansing the air for man's survival, sheltering birds and other wildlife, conserving water, building soils and holding them in place, and otherwise providing and storing the materials of shelter, fuel (including coal and petroleum), and other power sources which become even more essential for survival. In time past, temperate-zone countries have been homelands for what is now somewhat optimistically termed "scientific" forestry.

Sweden, for example, is today the most heavily wooded nation outside the tropics; and through the centuries Sweden's forests have done most to keep Sweden prosperous. But Sweden happens to be the one temperate-zone nation that has done most to keep its great forests productive and otherwise valuable.

As noted, Russia, which thus far has done little about it, has more forests than any one nation of earth, including the unrivaled coniferous belt of Siberia, about three thousand miles long and six hundred to eight hundred miles wide, which is far and away the world's biggest center of evergreen forests. Russia has more forest land than any other nation or continent, and only the tropics, taken in combination, can surpass her.

Foresters, though generally a hard lot, still lack the stomach to take the tropics in combination. For the tropics include the best tree life on earth and the worst. For an eyeful of the latter, one need only view the tropical and subtropical Middle East, or the lower Sahara, to behold the ultimate boneyard monuments to the suicidal destruction of what were once great forests. Compensating, in some slight part, are the long-belated but exceptionally gallant struggles of Israel, one of the newest of nations, to restore some vestiges of its once great forests, and of the new republics of India and Pakistan, where some of the world's most devoted and competent forest services now struggle to restore and maintain memorable fragments of what were once magnificent and life-sustaining forests.

It is terrifying to view the forest loot of Burma, which is said to have the greatest variety of trees of any comparable area on earth. Similarly, even a quick journalistic view of present-day China, where a bare 5 per cent of the land is forested and where most people now lack wood for building houses, furniture, or even coffins, makes a rabid conservationist of almost anybody, and this on the entirely rational ground that the normal reaction to viewing the vast ruin of earth that results from the ravagement of trees is the rational urge to save and to use the great forests that remain.

That urge spotlights the tropics. It focuses appreciative interest on the natural strongholds of trees provided by many of the Pacific islands and most of Southeast Asia. It lends very real importance to otherwise lesser-known islands such as the third of a million square miles of Madagascar off East Africa, where more than four thousand varieties of tropical trees still flourish. Or the preponderantly wooded spaces of Ceylon, home of tree ferns and many of the most beautiful of flowering trees. Or the Malay Peninsula, about three-fourths of which still grows trees—principally tropical hardwoods. Or splendidly forested Sumatra, the great "frontier island" of Indonesia, or Borneo, where at least three-fourths of this third largest island grows trees, including some of the biggest anywhere. Or New Guinea, the earth's second largest island, where at least four-fifths of the land is still in forests.

Most particularly, the world spotlight of forest interest swings to Africa, by far the biggest of the tropical mainlands, which can certainly be the world's wood lot tomorrow. Even along its great East Coast, which is so largely barricaded by tidewater breastworks of mangrove swamp, there are immense treasuries of valuable forests that include both evergreens and deciduous trees. Great and valuable pine forests cover the mountain slopes of Kenya and Tanganyika. To the west and south are the far-flung jungle and hillside forests of the Congo Basin, one of the truly memorable reservoirs of trees remaining.

From the Congo, Africa's principal forest zones stretch westward and north and again south into the Niger, Farmington, and Gambia basins. At hundreds of places these forests are broken by cleared lands, and in other great woods the evidences of greedy pillage are many and formidable. Yet Africa remains a stupendous, potentially decisive stronghold of forests.

In Africa as in so many other great tropical lands the epic of tropical forests continues to unfold. Like other world-influencing epics, it is not easy to interpret or appraise. Many keep thinking of tropical forests as immense, impenetrable jungles full of snakes and wild animals. Some tropical forests are immense, but few are impenetrable, and fewer have any literal similarity to jungles. Unfortunately, general knowledge of tropical forests is at least as inadequate as general knowledge of tropical agriculture. Actually, the business world persists in appraising tropical forests in terms of a mere handful of the so-called precious timbers such as mahogany, cedar, teak, rosewood, and balsa, when the overall truth is that tropical forests in general have the essential values and fulfill the same basic functions as any other forests. One effective way of personally discovering the latter is to travel the new Inter-American highway and to view at close range the superb abundance of valuable temperate-zone trees which grow along the right of way, including, in the region of Cartago, Costa Rica, tens of thousands of acres of what is probably the most magnificent virgin oak forest that remains on earth: primeval oaks seven to ten feet in diameter with trunks that tower one hundred feet or more to the first branches.

There are many good reasons for the prevalent unawareness of what tropical forests really are. Extreme scarcity of roads and railroads in the forest areas is one. The immense variety of trees in the same wooded tract is another. As a rule, the more coveted of tropical trees, such as mahoganies, rubber trees, rosewoods, and the like, grow in widely scattered locales, rarely more than one or two to the forest acre. This means that the old-style procedure of total logging ranges from impractical to impossible and that new and capable ways for harvesting tropical forests wait to be discovered and proved.

But there is no need for arguing or proving the irreplaceable value of tropical trees in building and anchoring soils. And there is no need of debating the benefits derived from returning cleared lands to woods. Such far-separated tropical countries as India and Puerto Rico have set up *taungya* or *parcelo* systems whereby citizens can earn land by perpetuating the forests, on the ground that there can be no remaining doubt of its desirability, since the place of tropical forests in anchoring and developing soils, controlling floods and violent water erosion, and perpetuating bird and other beneficial wildlife is long beyond question.

But nagging reality persists that we still do not know nearly enough about the total value of tropical forests or how to realize them, locally or otherwise. Yet we know that international demands for tropical timbers keep growing, that the world today is faced with a critical shortage of timber, and that, in the tropics as elsewhere, man's need for timber keeps increasing.

Yet, ironically, forestry is a great and beneficial science which, tropically speaking, has not yet had a chance to become a science. There are no more than twenty accredited schools of forestry on earth today, and at this writing there is not one in all the tropics, though Mexico, Trinidad, Malaya, India, Siam, Honduras, and several African colonies are striving to make amends for this deplorable lack. Even so, all the accredited forestry schools today are in the United States, except four in Europe, two in the British Isles, and one in Australia.

This means, of course, that most of the too slender company of foresters now at work in the tropics have been obliged to study their trade in temperate-zone centers and thereafter to adapt and reapply what they learned to tropical needs, which at best is a costly trial-and-error process.

Even so, tropical forest practices, as now discernible in rubber groves, spice plantations, and other specialized tree farms, rank favorably with the best anywhere. There is monumental need for more of the same, and for widespread research and practical work on the harvest, milling, curing, and practical use of hundreds of tropical timbers, many still unknown to the consuming world. Also, we need to know vastly more about the natural enemies of tree life in hot countries, and more about the botanical classification of tropical trees, and a great deal more about the hundreds or perhaps thousands of valuable fruits, fibers, resins, alkaloids, and other useful products that can be harvested from tropical trees.

Granting all these needs, the momentous, inspiring truth stands that tropical forests are far and away the largest and most varied on the face of the earth; they are superior yardsticks for measuring tropical destinies—magnificent, world-influencing resources now and for generations to come.

## THE PALMS

THE same can and should be said of the palms, a stupendous tree family which is almost exclusively tropical. There are somewhere near three thousand known members of this huge warm-country family which continue to bear fruit, fiber, wax, or other valuable products in the wilds and without the formality of cultivation.

Several dozen varieties have been adapted to cultivation, and hundreds of uses for palm harvests are now well known. Palm products have long been world commodities: palm oils for cooking, shortening, and butter substitutes; palm waxes for floor, auto, furniture, and shoe polishes, for carbon paper and phonograph records; other palm oils for metal-plating, including the manufacture of "tin" cans and other food containers; for making better-quality toilet soap and many cosmetics; for various parts of automobiles, for dozens of specialized lubricants, varnishes, and weather-coatings; for the making of candies, syrups, flavoring, and scores of other food products.

But, for the most part, palm harvests are even more vital to tropical peoples than to us. For besides the uses just named and many more, they are the principal supplier of life-sustaining foods, of housing materials, including roof thatch, of fibers for making clothes, sandals, hammocks, and utensils, of fuel, furniture, wine, and liquors, salad greens, paints, and so on by the page. The coconut palm, with its proverbial 999 uses, is still the most versatile of crops, though nowadays other great palm crops are overtaking the coconut in terms of proved values and in many tropical places are erasing it.

But the most important of the palmy facts is that the present-day world is only now beginning to learn what the palm resources really are. We are learning, for example, that almost all the approximately three thousand known varieties of palm flourish in one or both of two principal tropical centers: one in east and central South America; the other in the Indo-Malayan sector of Southeast Asia. We have found out, at least in a general way, that considerably less than one-tenth of the palms that grow and bear today are harvested, and that less than 1 per cent are grown in tended groves or other cultivation. We have learned, too, that a single nation, such as Brazil, has at least four hundred fifty varieties or species of palm, and that the American tropics as a whole have at least twelve hundred.

We know that, although the coconut is still the most renowned of palms, other great members, including the African oil palm, the date palm, babassu, carnauba, muriti, raffia, buri, palmyra, and many others, are being graduated to positions of world importance. We know that in the world today palm harvests comprise man's first-ranking source of edible fats and oils and a premier source of vegetables and fibers; that palm oils now supply "baths" for iron, copper, and other metallic platings; that palms supply the basic materials for the making of baskets, nets, ropes, rugs, bags, furniture, brooms and paper, pipes and pilings, and many other commodities that are part of man's life today.

Palms, more than any other group of crops, have introduced the tropics to international trade. Since the times of Columbus, the eastern tropics, from India to the Marianas, supplied the bulk of palm oils in world trade, and since the turn of the present century, East Indies planters have employed methodical research, large-scale plantations, capable milling centers, and shrewd merchandising to change the once leisurely grab bag of palms to a billion-dollar commerce.

Yet edible oils remain in world-wide shortage, and palm fruits are far and away the most economic source of edible oils. This is stated with all deference toward the many other still too little realized values of palms—for building wood and pulp wood, for fibers, fabrics, dyes, waxes, and other uses yet to be developed.

The sources of palm oils include the nuts or seeds of palm fruits and the pulp which surrounds the seed. As a rule, valuable oils are imprisoned in both. In order to release the oil, the varying cell structures must be broken or softened, which means that palm oils are obtained by grinding, crushing, boiling the fruits in water, exposing them to the sun, by fermenting them, and by suitable combinations of these devices.

For the most part palm fruits are easy to grow, easy to harvest, but comparatively difficult to convert into oils. Through the ages, as today, tropical people have struggled to devise suitable implements with which to recover the ever-needed oils, and, more often than not, they have been unable to develop efficient machines. Amazon people still use the *tipiti*, a cylindrical sieve made from coarse palm fibers through which the oil, actually a meager fraction of it, is pressed. In other palm-growing countries one still sees various other Rube Goldberg-ish inventions of palm-oil presses, some operated by wedges, levers, screws, or by fulcrums weighted with heavy rocks or logs. Even so, many kinds of valuable palm nuts are too hard for any primitive or inexpensive cracking devices to process.

These difficulties are being overcome. Modern palm-oil mills are using hydraulic presses and elaborate screw presses which remove most or all of the nut oil. Chemical solvents and new types of centrifugal separators make possible the removal of most of the pulp oils.

The development of costly and highly technical mills for extracting the many valuable palm oils involves a sizable measure of irony—this because palm oils remain primarily subsistence crops for hundreds of millions of tropical peoples who cannot afford expensive and elaborate presses. The latter urgently need simply built, lightweight mechanical presses that can be used close at home as private or cooperative properties.

The feat of supplying such presses would contribute valuably to the tropical diet as well as to tropical earning power. Moreover, the local processing would supply pressed cake, meal, and other valuable livestock feeds which are also urgently needed. The long-distance shipping of palm nuts to pressing plants in Brighton, or Newark or Cincinnati, is absurdly inefficient and demonstrates merely another of the grim and ill-odored public jeopardies that are incident to real or attempted monopolies of tropical products.

More knowledge of the agronomy and horticulture of palms is also badly needed, since the palms as a great group remains the least developed of any of the principal families of crops, with many species, potentially valuable, that have never been classified botanically. Hundreds more, including most of the valuable fiber-bearing palms now known, such as piassava, which supplies the stiff, water-resistant fibers used for making hard brushes and rollers for street-cleaning equipment, and raffia, one of the most versatile and durable of fibers, have never been adapted to cultivation.

Tropical palms, like tropical timbers, are God's donations, not man's. The oldest and most revered of the palms is coconut. Yet the horticulture of coconut remains wretchedly incompetent. The African oil palm, at present the most productive and profitable of cultivated palms, has succeeded brilliantly thus far primarily because to date it has not fallen victim to any principal disease or other natural enemy, and here's knocking wood.

Accordingly, U.S. imports of African oil palm have increased about forty-fold in ten years, and the heavy bronze-red nut clusters are hanging high all the way from West Africa to Ceylon, Java, Sumatra, and Central America. Still more recently, other great palm crops are emerging, like tacum, bacaba, murumuru, pataua, licuri, macauba, corozo, and babassu, to name only a few of them. Cohune, the seed of a giant forest palm that is native to the Pacific slopes of Mexico and Central America, is another important contender.

Meanwhile, synthetic age or no, uses for palm products keep far ahead of production. In earlier times only the kernel oils were deemed valuable. First used to make candles, then as lamp fuels, these oils, because of their nonsynthesizable lather-making qualities, became essential to the toilet soap, shaving "cream," and shampoo industries which are still obliged to use palm oils at least in minor part; palm oils are also necessary to our Gargantuan candy industries.

Nowadays, however, uses for oils extracted from the pulp or fruit of palms are multiplying in proportion: for metallic plating "baths," for making inks, weather-coatings, cosmetics, commercial glycerines, fabric-printing, dentifrices, many pharmaceuticals, and other products. The immense leaves of the carnauba palm of the wet lowlands of Brazil continue to provide the only vegetable wax save beeswax. Thus far carnauba wax cannot be synthesized, which leaves it a more or less indispensable ingredient of good polishes, phonograph records, and carbon papers.

Meanwhile, too, more and more palm fruits are being used in the mass industries of cola drinks and fruit flavors. In West Africa, Brazil, and other tropical lands where petroleum remains scarce and expensive, palm oils are being used as fuel for Diesels and other combustion engines. Tens of millions of lamps in Africa and the South Pacific are still fueled with palm oils. The use of the latter as specialized lubricants is growing impressively. But the most memorable of palm uses is for human food.

As distinctive gifts to the tropics, the immense and prolific family of palms is handsomely capable of banishing tropical hunger for all times. It is distinctly capable of favoring the entire world with a new and improved definition of abundance.

## LIVESTOCK IN HOT COUNTRIES

GOD has endowed the tropics with the great palm crops and a majority of the great forests of earth. Thus far, however, God has not endowed the tropics with any very extensive wealth of livestock, another pre-eminent and definitive resource which, from all appearances, tropical peoples must develop for themselves.

This reporter is among the last to lament or deplore such an apparent decision. God keeps helping those who help themselves; and through the centuries, the keeping and tending of livestock has done much to make and establish the world's best farmers. No revision of this general statement seems necessary.

God gave the tropics trees and palms in multi-billion-acre quantities. Man has only to learn their conservation and uses. But livestock, as we know and use it today, is not a tropical crop. As noted, the great majority of tropical lands have never yet known or benefited from a pastoral age. The latter can be attained, and its attainment can raise tropical living standards and health standards to levels which as yet are not perceivable. But it can be attained only by the devoted enterprise and competence of many people, as well as many governments.

For the good of their lands and their great crops, present and future, and still more for the good of their people who desperately need more meat, milk, leather, draft power, and all other kinds of animal products, the tropics require livestock and a great deal more of it.

Any competent reporter or any discerning traveler knows that virtually all the way around the equator the absence or scarcity or inadequacy of livestock is a foremost blockade to good and secure lives for the people. Hundreds of millions of tropical peoples today have never so much as tasted beef or cow's milk.

Nobody can state the exact number of tropical babies who have died when their mother's milk gave out. Those of us who know the tropics can guess the number high into the millions, particularly if we have tended dying babies and dying mothers and if we have watched the frequent and occasionally successful efforts of tropical mothers to save their babies with green coconut juice or other inadequate substitutes locally available.

The student of the tropics also learns what the chronic lack of meat, milk, and other protein foods can do toward debilitating tropical workers and toward opening their skins, mouths, lungs and other doors to ghoulish museums of diseases. We see, too, what the lack of shoes, due to the lack of leather, due to the lack of animals, can do and stubbornly does to engender additional diseases and nagging incompetency in work.

All these observations and realities are beyond the realm of question or doubt. Yet the fact stands that most tropics lack livestock, and that this lack, though desperately serious, cannot be overcome quickly or easily.

Throughout the present-day world the age of the great roaming herd is finished. For the most part, too, livestock cannot be established by sudden splashes of outside investment capital. As a rule, citizen farmers must buy, tend, slaughter, or sell the animals, develop pastures and feed crops, supervise breeding and selection, learn and apply protective measures against animal diseases, adapt breeds of animals to specific tropical locales.

In the tropics, as elsewhere, the challenge of the animal continues to expand and to gain pertinency. In the tropics, as out, livestock is the superb instrument for converting grasses and other vegetation to superior foods and by-products for man and for keeping and enriching the soils. In the tropics, as elsewhere, livestock serves as basic conversion machinery and much more—an incessant and very vital challenge to develop from the mysteries of living cells and the magic of chromosomes more perfect and more useful animals than ever walked before.

The challenge is all the greater because throughout the populated world the age of the wild animal as a basis for man's subsistence has ended or is fast drawing to an end. The tropics have been the last great strongholds of the wild animal. But at present even in farthest Africa or deepest South America, the intricate cycles of wildlife population are breaking apart. There and virtually everywhere, the day of the professional hunter is ending. It is entirely true that great areas of the tropics and subtropics are still the best remaining reservoirs for wildlife. But it is just as true that even the most bountiful of these wildlife resources have ceased to be adequate for supporting all the people.

For throughout most of the earth people are increasing more rapidly than any others of the "higher animal species." This is true even in the United States, which has barely 6 per cent of the earth's people and at least 60 per cent or more of the earth's provable wealth. Even so we still do not have enough livestock to supply fully the meat-and-milk needs of millions of our people; our shortages of both beef and dairy cattle are more or less chronic, and our human population continues to outgrow our animal populations.

Yet our livestock resources are far and away the most plentiful anywhere. Such a small and casual state as Vermont is the only land surface now known that has a third again as many milk cattle as people. The United States is supplying most of the breeding livestock now in international trade, and we are not obliged to live by flimsy and largely phony fables of livestock abundance such as those which drift in from the Argentine, Australia, or the Channel Islands.

But out livestock tallies, like others, support the provable fact that for centuries the great developed or domesticated livestock crops have tended to veer away from the tropics. Especially during the past two hundred years, most of the valuable breeds of cattle, sheep, hogs, horses, and poultry have emerged from Scandinavia, the Channel Islands, the British Isles, and Western Europe, preponderantly from cold countries. In the western tropics, for that matter, in all the Western Hemisphere, the valuable livestock—with the rather minor exception of turkeys, llamas, and alpacas, the latter two Andes-born—has been introduced from the British Isles, the Channel Islands, and Europe.

In the great majority of tropical places, domesticated livestock have remained forlornly inadequate, which plainly enough is a prime reason why the tropics at large remain starch-eating countries with all the disadvantages and penalties thereof, including rotting teeth, bad eyes, misshapened bones, short lifespans, and a wretched and baffling abundance of deficiency and other diseases. The penalties levied against tropical soils because of the lack of livestock are hardly less severe or widespread. Painfully unfriendly jungles and deserts now erase what were once great tropical ranges, and billions of acres of possible tropical ranges are still without cattle or other beneficial livestock. The dilemma is formidable, and it cries out for solution.

Like people, most livestock can be adapted in time to drastic changes of environment. The adaptation usually demands work, planning, and other expense, but it is usually possible. Here in the

United States, for example, in the North, Midwest, and Far West, European breeds of cattle, horses, and sheep have flourished and prospered. In the South and Southwest, the heat-tolerant mule and more southerly cattle breeds, such as the Jersey and Shorthorn, also flourish. Significantly, in the far, hot Southwest today, one sees the beginning and crossbreeding of distinctly tropical cattle breeds, such as the Brahmin.

Traveling farther south into Mexico, one sees "grade" or mongrel cattle and sheep which, though belonging to no particular breed, have become securely adapted to the climate, altitudes, and vegetations of the locales in which they range. But here, too, one sees distinctive tropical breeds, such as the fawn or whitish short-haired cattle called Brahmin, or Zebu, imported originally from the hot grasslands of India.

Traveling still farther south, one notices, too, with considerable disillusionment, that the native or grade cattle become increasingly scrawny, smaller, and more degenerate—even as the plant life becomes larger. Thus one is prompted to guess that ten to fifteen degrees of latitude mark the jumping-off place for the better-accredited or currently popular breeds of livestock, and that the justly renowned pure-bred animals of the temperate zone are inclined to fall into evil ways when taken directly into the "deep" tropics.

This inference is rather well supported by home records. Any experienced milk farmer knows, for example, that dairy cows produce less milk during extremely hot weather than in medium weather, that as prevailing temperatures rise from, say, 50 to 95 degrees Fahrenheit, milk production drops one-third or more. Brazilian government experiments show that excellent pure-bred dairy cows from New England when first imported into the hot lowlands of Brazil, even when fed exactly as at home, produce a mere 56 per cent of their previous milk records.

Average year-round tropical temperatures range from 67 to 69 degrees Fahrenheit. The principal breeds of temperate-zone milk cattle are adapted to mean temperatures of 50 degrees Fahrenheit, or slightly less. This difference is potent, and tropical environments usually include lengthy rainy seasons which discourage grazing, and milk and meat production as well. Furthermore, in most tropics, animals breed inconsistently; hens lay poorly and eggs hatch badly. We still do not know all the reasons, but we do know that far better adaptation to the tropics is attainable.

For there is current and memorable progress in adapting livestock to tropical environments and developing new animal breeds that aptly fit the tropics. One illustrious example has risen recently here in the United States where the Klebergs, of King's Ranch in Texas, have developed the first truly American breed of beef cattle, the Santa Gertrudis, a successful cross between the Shorthorn, one of the better temperate-zone breeds of beef cattle, and the Brahmin, the greatest of tropical cattle breeds. Already the Santa Gertrudis cattle are thriving in many tropical countries, including lower Mexico, Ecuador, Brazil, India, and Siam. The U.S. Department of Agriculture is now developing a comparable tropical breed by crossing the Aberdeen Angus, another of the great temperate-zone beef cattle, with the Brahmin. In India, Brazil, the Philippines, and other tropical places, farmers are making distinguished progress in developing milk strains of Brahmin cattle.

Cattle are far the most beneficial livestock in the world today. The tropics, as a whole, are weakest in terms of cattle resources. There are noteworthy exceptions. India is one of the world's greatest cattle-raising nations and has been for centuries. In Alexander Hamilton's times the West Indies boasted some of the most valuable cattle herds anywhere, and during the past century some very important areas of tropical Africa, including major ranges of Nigeria, Kenya, and Uganda, have developed impressive resources of range cattle and, particularly in the Fulani country of Nigeria, of milk cattle. Both in terms of area and natural ranges, Central Africa could become the largest livestock range on earth. Now that impressive progress is being made in treating and controlling animal trypanosomiasis, or sleeping sickness, which is the most ruthless disease of African cattle, there is a real chance that tropical Africa may yet emerge as the pre-eminent cattle reservoir.

In the western tropics, Brazil is gaining stature as a cattle-growing nation; Venezuela is one of the last strongholds of the olden Criollo,

South America's counterpart of the now vanished Longhorns; Central American areas, particularly Costa Rica and Honduras, are adapting and developing excellent dairy herds, while the cattle resources of Cuba, Puerto Rico, and many of the West Indies are clearly upward-bound. These developments and others are encouraging. But they do not erase the more prevalent fact that tropical cattle as a whole are far under par both in terms of numbers, breed qualities, and general competence.

There is the timely and encouraging fact that a great deal of distinguished and effective work is now being done to develop and adapt better tropical cattle. In such feats as those of establishing heat tolerance, skin coloration, hair length, and many other physical and nervous characteristics, a new era of selective breeding is arriving.

Though comparatively few types of tropical cattle are yet at the pure-bred or registry stage (most of them are crosses or local strains), selective breeding continues to increase resistance to solar heat and sunburn by stressing light hair and deeply pigmented skins (as in the instance of the Africaner, an excellent tropical strain already developed in French Africa) and the development of laxer nerves and slower metabolisms, also a major benefit to tropical cattle.

Two courses for adapting livestock to the tropics are now well defined. The first, as in the instance of the newly developed Santa Gertrudis breed, is accomplished by the carefully planned crossing of pure-bred sires of one breed with pure-bred dams of another. Such an attainment requires much time as well as husbandry skill, since at least five cattle generations, covering a quarter-century or more of lifespans, must be propagated in order to "set" a durable breed or even a locally adapted strain. Furthermore, success cannot be assured in advance. Trial and error are requisite, details are exacting, and ventures in breed-founding are usually carried through at a high price.

The other and usually more economical course is that of methodically selecting and breeding desirable types or strains from a ready-established cattle population. An excellent example of the latter is the Caracu cattle of Brazil, or the Blanco-Orejinegro of Colombia, both rugged beef and grazing types developed by means of discerning selection of the offspring of pure-bred Brahmin bulls (for the most part imported) and selective native or grade cows. This course, much easier and usually more practical than the outright creation of new breeds, frequently requires that pure-bred bulls be imported and, in any case, that substantially good native cows be available locally. Fortunately, artificial insemination is reducing the usual toil and expense of importing and adapting pure-bred bulls.

But the really salient point is that good livestock, far better than the current tropical average, can be developed and established in most tropical lands. The task, though big, is completely overshadowed by the chronic and usually crucial tropical need for livestock. The greatest immediate benefits are obtainable from cattle, because cattle provide the best opening for other valuable and needed livestock, particularly hogs, sheep, and poultry.

Now, as in the past, the introduction of cattle is particularly strategic. It challenges and develops the best farming instincts because it demands the development of pastures, shade, water supplies, shelters, and the production of "solid feeds," such as grain or palm millings. By providing more or less immediate harvests of valuable and usually salable products, the growing of cattle promptly encourages many other agrarian blessings, such as better home nutrition, refrigeration (or, at minimum, the canning or smoking of meats), the wearing of shoes, the growing of feeds, and the building of fences, barns, and other shelters, as well as opening the way for other beneficial livestock, particularly hogs, sheep, and chickens.

There are, of course, king-size obstacles to be met in the introduction and development of tropical livestock. All who have ever worked in the tropics are aware of these, and entirely too many of us are prone to exaggerate them. One of my own earlier "human adventures" in the tropics consisted of urging Honduran plantation workers to grow chickens. The first reactions were almost as uniform as they were eloquent: "But Señor, we adore the chickens and eggs to eat, also the rice with chickens, and all the other most lovely things the chickens make when fried or boiled. But, first of all, how can we keep the *pollos* safe from the snakes and lynxes? Also, oftentimes, the eggs do not hatch when set under hens, all the more so when we take and boil the hen the next day. Furthermore, Señor, how will we feed the chickens grain, as you admonish, when we do not even have enough grain to feed ourselves and our *hijos* and *mujeres*? . . ."

There is a self-perpetuating abundance of difficult questions about livestock. Even so, in Honduras, as elsewhere, the growing and tending of livestock engenders a state of mind which is that of the good and lasting farmer. The task is hard, but its benefits are monumental. Since the days of Babylon and perhaps long before, livestock has built for tropical greatness; the southward trails of livestock are neither untried nor unproved; and regardless of latitude or longitude, livestock farmers have a way of emerging as the best farmers with the most adequate possessions.

For in the tropics, as out, livestock is more than a crop. Inevitably it is a co-ordination of crops, grasses, palms, grains, and the like, some planted, others obtainable from natural vantages. And it is a co-ordination of developed skills and services, ranging from those of the professionally trained veterinarian to the capable shearer or milkman. Livestock requires studied husbandry, diverse farming, incessant building, inevitably mechanics, and many other toils and talents and tangible goods that merge into great and durable agriculture.

Thus far, in terms of livestock, the tropics remain below second-best. As of today, with almost half the people of the earth, the tropics as a whole appear to have barely one-fifth of the livestock resources. But there is a good chance that tomorrow's picture in this respect will be different and better. The age of the animal is at last beginning to move south again, and the tropics may very well be tomorrow's green pastures to the world.

## THE FRONTIER CROP

TREES and palms are foremost crops which God gave the tropics. Livestock is a particularly vital and valuable crop which man, for his own immense and durable good, can give the tropics. There is one even greater tropical crop which endures and for which we can best and properly thank God alone.

The latter is the frontier crop. By the billions of potentially usable acres, frontiers wait in the tropics. They are not lush Utopias waiting easy settlement. Frontiers have rarely, if ever, been easy or entirely safe or painless. For the most part, frontier-taking in the tropics is more laborious and hazardous, and less suited to individual enterprise, than in the temperate zones.

But great frontiers wait in the tropics. They are highly visible at least from the air, and they are readily listable. There is not space enough in this particular book to list all of them in full detail. That would fill several books as big as this one, and these pages must be content with summaries and suggestions.

One could list the tropical frontiers alphabetically, which would be rather stupid. One could list them by size, which would be misleading because many of the smaller frontiers are more immediately important than some of the larger ones. Or one could list them in terms of nearness to the United States, which, though not necessarily a brilliant idea, has some small manner of a point.

Closest to U.S. boundaries is the remarkable Mexican territory of Lower California, a mild-climated, sparsely peopled, 800-mile-long subtropical peninsula into the Pacific. Among many other slightly known and little used resources, Lower California has the great Colorado Delta, which actually is the body and legs of California's renowned Imperial Valley, which by virtue of man-built irrigation is reputedly the most productive farming center on the face of the earth. Well over a million acres of equally fertile lands wait unused and waterless in Lower California's Colorado Delta. If water from the Lake Mead impoundments of Boulder Dam could be released across the border, one of the most fertile farm centers ever planted could be created—according to expert testimony, at very modest cost.

But Lower California has much more than rich lands without water. Its great port of El Alamo is one of the best fishing bases anywhere. A single central highway could open many millions of acres of excellent grazing and ranching lands to immediate use. The lake region of the peninsula is mild-climated, highly inviting, and almost without people, and the peninsula also has superb grazing lands still unused.

Most of Lower California is dry and subtropical. Accordingly, water is its greatest denominator of value. While this is true of many other tropical frontiers, an even greater number have abundant water. One observes this in numerous and almost peopleless wonderlands of Central America, which remains one of the most rhapsodically beautiful and the least known of all the tropical subcontinents.

Nobody, Central Americans included, knows nearly enough about Central America. There are still no reliable maps of great parts of it and no really competent geological or botanical surveys of the subcontinent as a whole. But Central America remains generously dotted with small and memorable frontiers. In some instances these make up the greater part of entire nations.

In Costa Rica, for example, barely six thousand square miles of the nation's nineteen thousand are as yet settled. And more than two-thirds of some seven hundred and seventy thousand Costa Ricans live in the airy and sleepy tablelands in and about San José, the highland capital where the *mesetas* contain less than 3 per cent of the land area of the country. Here, as in so many other tropical places, the choice of settlement sites seems strangely arbitrary. For within fifty to a hundred miles of the lovely *Meseta de San José* are at least three other similar areas, with excellent soil, weather, and altitude, and superbly suited to settlement. But they still lack settlers, even though all three are potential wonderlands for cattle, range grasses, and grains; even though their fertile valleys are excellent for growing sugar cane, vegetable crops, and fruits; and even though Costa Rica is traditionally a nation of land-loving farmers.

Below Costa Rica is Panama, where a heavily forested and immensely fertile south coast area remains largely untenanted and in great part awaits purchase from the Panamanian government at prices of five or six dollars an acre. The lands of *David* are the "little Iowa" of Central America; they are "deep" tropics—within ten degrees of the equator; they have plentiful rainfall, splendid forests, rich soils, and generally livable climates. But they still do not have nearly enough people, and in substantial areas they have no people at all.

The same general situation applies to much of Honduras, which is an immensely interesting, little known, dictator-ridden country of about forty-four thousand square miles (roughly the area of Ohio or

Maine) but with barely one million people, though its resources are sufficient to support at least double that number.

It is true that much of Honduras remains extremely remote and that it has no huge blocks of tenable and vacant frontiers, such as one finds farther south. But its present status of settlement is about that of the Cache Valley of Utah a century ago. Indeed, Honduras strongly resembles the U.S. West in many ways—including saloons and also pistols, the size of which indicate prominently the wearer's social importance.

The overwhelming majority of the American tropics remain chronically underpeopled. The most painful exception is El Salvador, a tired dot of a bare eight thousand square miles that is now obliged to support about two million people, most of whom are sadly degenerate Indians. But Guatemala, El Salvador's beautiful sister, despite regrettable blotches of eroded lands and small centers which are direly overpopulated, has many rich-soil areas that still wait without nearly enough people. In fact, Guatemala's Vera Altapaz, where topsoils range in depth from five to seventy-five feet, is one of the most attractive frontiers in the world today.

The latter is not entirely true of British Honduras, Guatemala's one-time Mayan littoral, which Britain took and, for still ambiguous reasons, fails to give back. British Honduras remains a British Crown Colony and a premier, dark-green paradox. Once an important banana-growing stronghold, the colony was abandoned by United Fruit and other exploiters during the early 1920's when an insidious root fungus began to ravage the once extensive banana planting in the rich lowlands back of Belize, which is now a moldering, decrepit, and largely forgotten ghost of a port capital. The withdrawal left several thousand jobless Negro laborers and no industries except a few feeble ventures in mahogany-logging which have now sluffed away.

Accordingly, British Honduras remains ramshackle, undeveloped, and isolated. Most of its sixty thousand Negro people survive within the limits of a few extremely purposeless remains of towns by the sea. Yet at least four-fifths of the country is heavily and, in some part, valuably forested. The northern half, most of which is fertile lowland forest, is still owned by dormant lumber companies which remain so "on His Majesty's Privilege."

Its western third, the "Maya Mountain Region," has at least twenty million acres of fertile lands (I know because I have helped make soil surveys of the area) waiting at altitudes from one thousand to four thousand feet above sea level and with highly livable climates. Yet the entire Maya Mountain country is virtually unpeopled. To the northwest is a far-spreading and fertile limestone plateau, which was a principal corn granary for the one-time great Maya Empire. At present it is a vast, sleepy woodland where one can tramp for a week without meeting another human.

So British Honduras slumbers on, a green-misted wonderland of potential but long unrealized abundance.

That dilemma is a long way from unusual in the tropical world today. South America, with its partially good five million square miles of tropical land, abounds in peopleless or sparsely peopled spaces, some of them immense, many of them promising.

South America also has oversize servings of tropical badlands, such as the three Guianas—British, French, and Dutch or (Surinam)—all of which are depressing, rain-forested spaces, virtually unsettled except along their narrow coastal belts and even there quite poorly.

But not far distant, the South American frontier situation turns brighter. There is Venezuela, for example, probably the most conspicuously resourceful of all the underpopulated countries remaining. Venezuela is somewhat bigger than Texas and even better-heeled in terms of oil. In the age when petroleum does so much to run the world, Venezuela is first among all the petroleum-exporting nations, and a majority of Venezuelans, including the national government, benefit considerably from oil and its royalties. Even so, Venezuela's population is still a mere three million eight hundred thousand, approximately that of the State of Indiana, though its resources are probably sufficient for thirty million. The majority of Venezuelans, more than two-thirds of them, continue to live in high Andean foothills on less than one-eighth part of the nation's lands.

Frontiers of great promise await settlement in the Andean foothills, within short distances of the fabulously rich Maracaibo oil fields, and almost a third of all Venezuela lies in the sparsely settled but exceptionally fertile grasslands of the great Orinoco Plains. To the southeast are the decidedly exciting Guayana uplands which are about as big as Pennsylvania and include immense iron deposits and tens of millions of acres of tenable ranch and farmsites. Yet, all told, the latter area, which is twice the size of New England, has fewer than seventy-five thousand people.

Undersettled Venezuela remains one of the largest and perhaps most resourceful of all the remaining frontiers. Second only to the United States, it is the greatest petroleum-producing nation, and its natural ranges are probably the best on earth. Yet Venezuela is only one of the many South American frontiers.

There is also Ecuador, which is almost incredibly underpopulated. In the past its great fertile lowlands have been direly afflicted by malaria and other endemic diseases. Though many of the latter persist, it is now common knowledge that they can be greatly reduced or removed altogether.

But the greater part of Ecuador, that is above the "over-sickly lowlands," also awaits settlement. Land costs are still almost unbelievably low, averaging barely one dollar per acre. The great Quito Valley, with elevations ranging from six thousand to ten thousand feet, is typical of Ecuadorean farmlands which are capable of growing both tropical and non-tropical crops.

The Quito Valley is at least partially settled. But similar topographies and soils remain virtually without people as, for example, Ecuador's West Andes slopes, which cover at least ten thousand square miles, and the exciting Los Alpes and the San Domingo de los Colorados lands. In the latter areas great quantities of government-owned lands are still free for homesteading, and great tracts of private lands are for sale at no more than a dollar an acre.

Ecuador, which the equator crosses squarely, remains a frontier tropical nation. So in principal parts do Colombia, Bolivia, and Paraguay—the latter more or less bisected by the Tropic of Capricorn. And the immense tropical conglomerate called Brazil, which has fewer than one-third as many people as the United States though almost a third of a million more square miles of territory, still has enough literal frontiers to cover all the United States west of the Mississippi, with land to spare.

As with most other frontiers, by no means all of the still vacant spaces of Brazil are suited to settlement. The most apparent and oversize wastelands include the huge flood-tortured, steamy wildlands of the Amazon Basin. But the fact is noteworthy that respected geographers join with experienced engineers in believing that no less than a million square miles of the now untenable "sun-less lands" of the Amazon can be made habitable, though such a feat would require decades or generations of inspired and expensive work, immense structural projects, perhaps a succession of Tennessee Valley Authorities, and a new era of soil-conservation practices.

For more than a century past the Amazon Basin has fascinated real or would-be tropical appraisers. But actually there are several more Brazilian frontiers which are far more attainable. For example, there is northeastern Brazil with an area of about two hundred thousand square miles, most of it very sparsely peopled and much of it fertile. This northeast province is preponderantly dry country, and thanks to the recent and brilliant work of the Brazilian government and the Rockefeller Foundation, it is now pretty well cleared of endemic malaria.

The Brazilian government has already spent about a fifth of a billion dollars for building impoundment dams and roads in the northeastern area and has demonstrated there that excellent farmlands can be placed under irrigation at costs averaging no more than sixty-five dollars per acre. There is excellent reason to believe that with adequate irrigation, hydroelectric development, and roads, northeastern Brazil could be made one of the most productive farming centers anywhere.

The largest of all tropical frontiers, and in total terms the least developed, are still to be found in the immense and underpopulated spaces of tropical and subtropical Africa. These include such ever-amazing picture-book lands as the Sudans, the great rain forests of West Africa, the huge and long-promising Congo Basin, the almost benumbing vastnesses of French West and French Equatorial Africa, the oversize island called Madagascar, the rich green Cameroons, and the huge prairies, valleys, and mountainside forests of East Africa, particularly those of Togoland (Germany's one time "model" African colony), Kenya (still the hunters paradise), Tanganyika, and others.

Africa as a whole simply cannot be "typed" or hastily summarized. It is stupendous in size—almost half again as big as all North America. It is intermittently overpopulated but on the whole amazingly underpopulated. African censuses are notoriously exaggerated as is the prevailing estimate of about one hundred seventy million people for the entire continent. Yet many of the most stubborn conservatives agree that tropical Africa alone has space, soils, forests, and other great resources sufficient to maintain half a billion people, plus immense exports to spare—this if only and if ever the resources could be developed.

These resources and their preponderant lack of development are enough to floor the most audacious and resourceful of all the thousands of press agents and other publicists who are so ripe for being floored and, indeed, buried. For example, though the waterpower potentials of Africa are greater than those of all the rest of the earth combined, less than one-tenth of 1 per cent of them are as yet used. For less than 1 per cent of the tillable lands of tropical Africa are as yet in use. Far less than 1 per cent of its forest resources are used as of today. And though the mineral wealth is unquestionably gigantic, for the greater part it has not yet been explored, much less developed.

On the other hand, and at first hand, I have learned enough about tropical Africa to appreciate something of its adversities: the violence of its recurrent storms; the erratic migrations or abrupt disappearances of game animals on which millions of tribal Africans are still heavily dependent; the vast, impeding blockades of desert, rain forest, jungles, and swamps; the flood-tortured river valleys; the persisting hell-holes of disease; the outrageous bullyings and conscienceless thefts and rapine still being perpetrated by white men.

I have learned, too, that to speak specifically of Africa's continent-load of frontiers involves a dilemma similar to that of the fruit peddler who is called on to hold up a sample of his wares. Peddler's instinct directs that he display the best orange or apple or tomato or plum that remains in the bed of his cart.

The same general dilemma confronts the reporter of Africa.

This reporter has viewed and pondered several of Africa's valleys of destiny: the great sprawled gardens of the Congo Basin, the tumbling plains and forests of the Niger, the rich soil meccas of the Sudan and upper Nile, the incredible beautiful Lake and Falls countries—each one a memorable gateway to still other great frontiers.

In any case, here are a few of what I believe are the medium and honest samples of prevailing African frontiers, though they are not exhibits at all, or even the best, of the contemporary frontiers of tropical Africa.

Tanganyika, formerly German East Africa, is currently a British territory of three hundred sixty thousand square miles and about five and a half million people, plus a fringe of densely populated Belgian territory called Ruanda Urinda. On the whole it is typical of Africa's great range lands: an ancient domain of grazing lands, cattle herds, of huge birds and other "big game." Like most of Africa it is Negro country (the resident white population is fewer than two thousand) and farming country; its people are preponderantly herdsmen and small-plot farmers. Yet less than one-sixth of its area is in cultivation or grazing, and the present crop list of peanuts, rice, cotton, coffee, and sisal could be expanded quite heroically. Unfortunately, this has not been accomplished as yet.

Instead, Tanganyika, like too much of the tropics, has been obliged to endure the blatant mishandling of inexperienced and alien fussbudgets, notably and recently the British Labor government's ludicrous and flamboyant ground-nut or "peanut scheme." But the really memorable resources remain intact. Thus far, most of Tanganyika's developed farms are in the lowlands. Enticing frontiers wait in the highlands, in the Usambara mountains, long a proud stronghold for cattle and cereal grains, and in the adjoining lands of the dead volcanoes, where herd grasses grow to man's height.

Tanganyika's southwestern highlands, though still direly lacking both in roads and people, abound in potential wheat lands, fruit lands, far-spread pastures, and fertile soils, much of them blessed with sufficient rainfall. Farther on, in the Matengo highlands and the Livingstone Mountains are many more green and still untenanted prairies. And beyond them are the great fertile though dryish spaces of Kenya and Northern Rhodesia, likewise significant frontiers of yesterday and tomorrow.

To the farther south and east is the great island frontier of French-controlled Madagascar, the earth's fourth largest island, with a land area about the size of Texas. The island has a population of barely four million people, practically all of whom are Negroes and lamentably poor farmers who cultivate, all told, a mere three million acres of the land. Madagascar's settlement remains erratic, as do many other characteristics of the island, such as, for example, the almost complete absence of family names among the natives and the fact that no less than twenty-five million acres of Madagascar's valuable forests and at least fifty million acres of tillable land remain entirely unused.

The island's interior is a succession of mountain ranges and lofty plateaus. The southwest corner of the island is semi-desert, but in the central and northern sections are little-used pockets and splotches of immensely rich volcanic soils, and the high plains of Ankaizina, which contain great areas of fertile land, still lack both roads and settlers. The northern highlands are among the rare tropical places where such diverse crops as cattle, coffee, and rice, both highland and lowland crops, flourish side by side. In all, Madagascar remains reasonably typical of the many underdeveloped and underpopulated tropical lands today.

The same holds for Africa's mainland Cameroons, the verdant entranceways to equatorial West Africa. Beginning in the 1880's these great tribal lands became a German colony; in 1916 the colony was taken up by the British and French, who together have done rather badly by it. The area of the Cameroons is about two hundred thousand square miles, slightly less than that of France; yet the almost completely Negro population is about three million eight hundred thousand, or barely one-eleventh that of France.

As already suggested, the Cameroons are particularly noteworthy because they demonstrate concisely such outstanding tropical advantages as the three rather distinct tropical zones of elevation: the lowland rain forests with great jungle tree-and-vine lands streaked by rivers; the open grasslands at elevations of three thousand to six thousand feet (which comprise about one-third of the territory) where rainfall ranges from thirty to fifty inches and where temperate-zone crops such as strawberries and peaches flourish at levels only a few hundred feet above those which grow such true tropical crops as bananas or oil palms; and the Thornbush Steppes, which are dryish, foothill country, well suited to cattle and coffee.

The Cameroons, as a whole, remain remote, undeveloped, and ill-used. The entire colony has a mere 275 miles of railroad which, like most of the 2,400 miles of permanent roads, are located in the French sector. Significantly, and as in other African colonies, the roads are built co-operatively by the native tribes. Meanwhile, the Cameroons comprise a challenging and definitive sample of the remaining greatness of Africa's frontiers.

Other tropical frontiers include part of the now fabulous South Pacific. There are memorable frontiers in and among the latter. For one, there is New Guinea, the world's second largest island (only Greenland is larger) with a land area of more than a quarter of a million square miles, and a mere one and a half million people, almost two-thirds of whom live in the 93,000 square miles that were formerly British mandate, though at present the island is adopted via "trusteeship" by Australia. Netherlands New Guinea, meanwhile, has about 165,000 square miles of land, with about two people per square mile, which probably would have seemed sparse even to Dan'l Boone.

As World War II veterans will recall, New Guinea is deep tropics, within ten degrees south of the equator. For the most part it is humid and downright hot in the daytime, in some part moderately endurable at night, and blessed, or much of the time cursed, with bountiful rain. Its settlement is remarkably inconsistent; some of its richest valleys are entirely without people, and its soils are almost as inconsistent as its settlement, ranging from deep and immensely fertile alluvial lands to lifeless shales. Some of the island's best lands are to the northwest, in the valleys of the Ramu and Markham Rivers and on nearby plateaus and prairies. But here again, people and fertile lands have failed to get together.

During World War II, U.S. Army personnel accomplished some noteworthy exploration work in farming some of the island's previously untried lands. Particularly in the Gusap area, the GI's proved for the first time and quite clearly that corn, tomatoes, and many green vegetables can be grown profitably and well; they also proved that the grasslands are readily cleared, and that tractor or jeep-drawn plows can quickly change wild-grown wastes to producing fields. The Army's work further demonstrated that cattle and other livestock can be raised successfully and that, in the more fertile valleys, forty to sixty acres is abundant space for a successful farm, provided the land is competently used.

New Guinea waits as another notable tropical frontier. So does the neighboring island called New Caledonia which, though a mere 8,500 square miles in area, is highly successful in terms of current pioneering. New Caledonia is French. Its colonial government grants liberal occupancy concessions to all settlers who are willing to homestead lands and develop them for a five-year period. The present population of the island is about fifty thousand, about one-third white immigrants from France. Developed crops include corn, wheat, potatoes, and other common vegetables along with such warm-country standbys as mulberry trees (for silk), rice, bananas, coffee, coca, and vanilla. Comparatively speaking, the space available for settlement is not great, though there is still room for many more.

New Caledonia supplies pertinent proof that pioneering in the deep tropics is still possible and desirable. So, in a somewhat miniature way, do the Philippines, particularly the island of Mindanao and the fertile plains and hillocks of Lanao, Cotabato, and Bukidnon, which abound in good grasslands and affable climates, as well as in versatile soils. Quite rationally, current laws enacted by the new Philippine Republic require that new settlers be citizens.

The tracing of tropical frontiers present and future leads back to tropical frontiers of the past which may again point the way to the future. The place of man's beginnings may have been somewhere in the tropical or subtropical Middle East. The latter spheres of ill-used earth include such heat-blasted true tropics as Aden and Yemen and the lower third of the great block of peninsula called Saudi-Arabia; also, a much larger swath of subtropics, including Upper Arabia, lower or southmost Iran, Iraq, Israel, the Trans-Jordan, and other fringes of earth which in the main are somewhat more tropical than otherwise.

Some observers view the lower Middle East as the ultimate boneyard of tropical creation. Others see it as an explosive hodgepodge of interminable hates, unrests, desperation, and degradation, all more or less self-perpetuating. Still others see it as one of the more inspiring frontiers—a great and vivid realm in which progress and better lives can be built up from the shambles of bygone failures. This reporter tends toward the latter view, but grants with more or less bewilderment that all three viewpoints as stated are powerfully supported by fact and actual happenings.

According to the maps, the contemporary vitals of the Middle East include about 160,000 square miles of earth's crust, which is populated by no more than ten million people, with less than one-tenth of the lands now in use.

Just as conspicuously, the foremost need of all the area is for water, and thus far this need has not been met. In Palestine, irrigation is largely dependent on wells. In Syria, Lebanon, and Iraq, river irrigation is well proved, and a few, though not nearly enough, hydroelectric dams are in work.

The ten thousand square miles of present-day Palestine, a mere eye-fleck of the immense "Arab lands," is particularly challenging as a frontier. Most of its highlands have fairly adequate rainfall, and the lime and volcanic soils of the Galilean hills include some of the richest soils yet tested. The Jordan and the Litani Rivers hold exceptional possibilities for irrigation and hydroelectric developments, and the 1,200-foot drop from the Mediterranean to the Dead Sea is a classic challenge to irrigation engineers. Furthermore, despite the shortage of water and electric power, present-day Jewish industries, which include chemical recovery plants, many textile and clothing mills, wood works, machine shops, leather factories, paper mills, and food-processing plants, are flourishing. So are many of the agricultural developments, with excellent records for citrus fruits, grains, green vegetables, olives, and other warm-country crops.

In a smaller way, the same is true of Trans-Jordan, which has only about four hundred thousand people and more than a third of a square mile of land per inhabitant. About half of the land is hopeless desert waste. But the Jordan Valley is an exceptionally promising irrigation base, and considerable areas of the western highlands have sufficient rainfall plus good soils, a livable climate, and, like the rest of the Middle East subtropics, an illustrious history of productiveness.

In the heyday of the Roman Empire the volcanic lands of southern and eastern Syria and adjacent Trans-Jordan were renowned grain lands. Capable students believe that a good fourth of the lands could be restored to their one-time greatness by efficient development of water resources.

Much the same holds for Iraq, which many observers believe could be made capable of supporting at least a dozen times its present population of about three and three-quarter millions. The latter possibility takes for granted that the delta of the Tigris-Euphrates could be irrigated to permit the growing of food crops along with long-staple cotton, citrus fruits, dates, and other valuable exports. It is a common estimate now that the Iraq portion of the Persian Gulf oil reserve is the richest anywhere. Hydroelectric possibilities in the same general area parallel the partly proved wealth in oil.

In all these fields, memorable if only beginning advances are being made.

But people remain the pre-eminent shortage in the most vital sectors of the Middle East. The same shortage applies with varying emphasis to the greater part of the tropical and subtropical earth and incidentally, to all the two-fifths of the tropical earth which with accuracy can still be termed frontiers.

In the tropics or out, frontiers with people to work and cherish them remain the age-old cradle of democracy, which is born not so much of theorists' dreams but of readily available lands in which and from which men can escape oppression and build themselves better lives.

By the millions of square miles, lands await settlement and development in the far-flung, life-restoring tropics. They are lands of problems and trials, liabilities and dangers. But they are also decisive sectors of our world tomorrow.

## THE OPINION CROP

HISTORY keeps demonstrating that the tropics cannot be made abundant and great merely by conquest, that alien nations can help only by helping the tropics help themselves. The greatest frontiers of earth remain in the tropics. They can be realized only by means of more people, not fewer; by less of alien prejudice; by more appreciation and a greater will to help. Men alone cannot stand against the giant's might of tropical growth. Many men must stand and work together. Many more man-hours than have as yet been generally mustered are required to keep a tropical acre in competent production. The tropical earth as a whole needs more people, and more urgently, it requires healthy, well-fed people who can therefore work effectively.

On Broadway or the Strand, or in Bombay or Canton or Singapore, where people do not appear to work, one is entitled to shudder at the sheer abundance of people. But these are exceptional places. I have learned at first-hand that in the toilsome and usually harassing accomplishment of constructive work in the tropics one spends much of his time in shuddering at the plaguing scarcity of people who are able to work.

Both in the tropics and out, I have found that the views of temperate-zone countries toward the tropics are changing, preponderantly for the better. So far as the United States is concerned, our figurative prospectors, trappers, and pelt-lifters are already in the tropics, as they have been for more than a century. But quite inevitably, too, they are finding themselves changing men in a changing world; for the tropics, too, are in mutation, much of it rapid and dramatic.

Some of the change is also cyclic, as United States viewpoint ably demonstrates. And since the immense field of American history is so stentoriously staked out by the bathhouse flag of Columbia University, these brief and respectful paragraphs will be limited to the past century of American history, since this writer's application into the skull-cracking union of American historians is only pending.

A hundred years ago the United States was being described by such respected commentators as Nathaniel Hawthorne as "tropics minded." There were reasons. One was that the uproar of petroleum development in Pennsylvania had yet to emerge. Petroleum was known occasionally as a "medicinal," and whaling remained a multimillion-dollar industry, since the lamps of America were fueled preponderantly with whale oil.

Productive headquarters for American whaling were mostly in the South Pacific, with bases ranging from Hawaii to the Carolines. Whaling was distinctly a tropical enterprise, and it had produced several exceptionally able reporters, including Herman Melville, later to produce *Moby Dick,* but who at the time was the amazed young author of four exceptionally popular travel books dealing with the Pacific tropics.

The latter books had sold lushly throughout a great part of the English-speaking world, and in treatise they were supported by other excellent and popular reports on even greater expanses of the eastern tropics. Mungo Park, Britain's most distinguished explorer-reporter of that era, was writing ably and well not only of the South Pacific (which was probably known more accurately by more English-speaking people in 1850 than, say, in 1940) but of Equatorial Africa, the West Indies, and the Amazon Basin. These and several other competent tropical reporters of 1851-55—men who had never met—arrived separately in an area of agreement which almost a century thereafter was to be publicized as "Point Four."

All agreed that enlightened selfishness on the part of temperate-zone powers required that the latter help tropical peoples to help themselves; that technical facilities and investment capital of the more prosperous temperate-zone nations should be placed at the disposal of tropical peoples and co-ordinated with opportunities for developing local resources; that the working policy should be one of live and let live on the broad grounds that intelligent and sympathetic work to help the "natives" better their own lot while living their own lives would reflect benefit to all nations. Mungo Park, in particular, outlined rather specific government or empire planning for the tropics which became substantially the British Colonial Welfare Acts of 1929-40-48, and Harry S. Truman's rather baffling first statement of Point Four seems to have been lifted from the text of the British Colonial Welfare and Development Act of 1940.

The various and unrelated authors of the Point Four of a century ago recognized the profound and durable qualities of tropical solvency. Business interests back home were in a position to agree. Britain of the 1850's was becoming the richest power on earth because of tropical trade, commissions, and colonies. The industrial revolution was a wealth-building reality, but the verdant tropics were much more so.

Britain was exporting "credit" to the United States and elsewhere, but many tropics were literally producing that credit. The United States, meanwhile, particularly the Atlantic seaboard, was still profiting immensely from such tropical bonanzas as whaling, spices, opium, medicinals, tea, and coffee. The latter, then being transplanted from East Africa, its indigenous home, to Brazil and Colombia was "taking like a house afire."

In terms of tropical relations, the Civil War marked the beginning of our great and long-continuing cranial black-out. While we fought each other, Britain, France, and the Netherlands proceeded to "take over the tropics and sew them in a bag," as Hawthorne put it. Other powers grabbed the crumbs and leavings, but the three just named not only raised flags but took over the promising crops, clinched shipping and selling monopolies, founded native oligarchies, and acquired vital facilities as outright properties. Thus our Point Four of tropical relations, as of the early 1850's, evaporated.

Fortunately there is an immortality about ideas. The Spanish-American War found us in the role of a gawky rustic bully who aches for a fight not because of viciousness but rather as a primitive sport. Fighting Spain and shortly thereafter building the Panama Canal brought us smack into the tropics again. Country-wrestler style, after we'd whipped 'em we were willing to leave 'em get up again. The fact that our tropical victims were so feeble and slow about getting to their feet appalled us. Even so, as early as 1910 there were clear evidences that the Point Four gospel, as recited by Melville, Park, and contemporary reporters in the 1850's, was being born again. In the words of the country bully, "My grandpappy was a reel gentleman!"

Our tropical policy since 1910 or thereabouts has been a memorable American scramble of noble sentiments and sharp practices. The auto age and its demands for rubber promptly established tropical trade as the biggest and most profitable part of all our foreign trade. It so remains. But by 1920, or somewhat earlier, U.S. foreign trade had developed an appalling lack of balance. About 88 per cent of its volume was centered in the cartel-dominated eastern tropics, a meager 12 per cent in all the rest.

Many observers were aware that we were by-passing the nearby American tropics, which had long been and still are our best and most loyal foreign customers. We were by-passing them commercially, and we were meddling with them politically—in numerous instances molesting their sovereignties.

Aware of this, a well-meaning Quaker named Herbert Hoover devised what he termed the Good Neighbor Policy which was in effect a theoretic Quaker meeting of U.S. business leaders, set up for pondering of good and pure thoughts about the nearer tropics. Shortly thereafter, with Cordell Hull as Secretary of State and Franklin D. Roosevelt, the chair-bound dynamo, as President, our first officially capable tropical policy was born as what we still label reciprocal trade agreements. Today our progress in tropical relations, even if somewhat embarrassingly imitative of Britain's, has teetered backwards and forwards, but in total it has clearly advanced. By now, indeed, we are officially almost as far advanced as reporters such as Melville and Park were a century ago.

Officially, the United States, Britain, and France alike have recognized, in one way or another, that the nineteenth-century version of tropical colonies can suffice no longer. Meanwhile and not always compatibly, the great generality of tropical peoples concur.

In the world today, with the sometimes apparent exception of Soviet Russia and the latter's kennels of heelers and hirelings, men of good will, quite regardless of latitude or skin coloring, are aware that justice and good lives are not attainable solely by means of flag hoistings. They also realize that the once-revered Victorian policy of "keeping the natives in their places" usually succeeds only in crowding the natives into untenable places and making additional and serious trouble.

The world at large continues learning, and rather painlessly, that many phases of tropical culture are actually interchangeable with those of the rest of the earth; further, the real and abiding interests of the tropics and the temperate zones cannot possibly remain far apart. Paralleling this is the spreading realization that one nation cannot keep on "carrying" other nations. Britain's recent "liberation" of India and Pakistan, followed even more recently by the Netherlands' "liberation" of Indonesia and preceded earlier by France's franchising of more than eighty million French Africans, are all memorable admissions that the white man is able no longer to carry the tropics as his particular "burden."

Apropos thereof, history continues to point out that the day is past when great tropical wealth can be grabbed or otherwise taken either by brutal conquest or insidious infiltration.

With the too-evident exception of Soviet Russia and its all too numerous satellites, most powers of the present-day world are learning that the feat of taking over great numbers of people, never easy, grows more and more difficult, and that the art of understanding peoples, though also never exactly easy, is almost infinitely easier than the feat of owning people. In fact, much of the present-day world, including the United States, is learning or has already learned that the feat of *not* owning people is, of itself, a great and attainable virtue.

Slave-and-master relations not only imply but actually require the interminable process of peoples living apart. The gospels of free men spell ready associations of the human kind and the willingness of one people to understand another and, preferably, all others. The latter gospel is of crucial, almost fanatical importance to the tropical earth today. It is the only real hope for breaking down the all too literal prison walls of tropical isolation. The tropics urgently need more and better trade with all nations of the temperate zone. But more urgently, in fact desperately, they require two-way traffic in those personal, folkish, and spiritual resources which we call culture.

Virtually all the tropical earth today is accepting salient phases of United States culture. It is accepting and absorbing our music—our popular music and our "jazz" (now the nearest world-wide medium of musical expression) and also some of our serious music and much of our folk balladry and religious music. The tropical world as a whole seeks our U.S. motion pictures and accepts our radio broadcasts where available. On the more casual side, during the equator-circling years of World War II, American cigarettes won a place, which in many tropical places they still hold, as the most acceptable medium of exchange or barter.

More and more extensively, the tropical earth is accepting American styles and fashions in clothing with results that are sometimes bizarre or even startling, at least in the beginning stages. More and more extensively, too, the tropical earth is accepting and eagerly acquiring, sometimes, alas, too eagerly, American autos, trucks, tractors, radios, plumbing supplies, and a huge catalogue of mechanical goods. More and more extensively, too, it is accepting our sports (particularly baseball), our mannerisms of speech and posture, our cosmetics, hairdoes, and barbering styles, along with our abiding love for gadgets. As the tropical traveler also notices, many millions or hundreds of millions of tropical peoples are being influenced by American newspapers and periodicals, not because great numbers actually subscribe to them, but because so much "native" publishing today is accepting or adopting our prevailing fashions in texts and make-up.

Granting that not all of these acceptances are entirely to the good, this reporter believes the total implies nothing short of the world's most widespread vote of confidence. For tropical acceptances of our real and everyday attributes is truly and vividly a proof of internationalism.

It is high time, I believe, that all of us realize and admit that the latter must be more than pompous rituals, sessions at Lake Success or swankier east side Manhattan, or stereotyped and otherwise corny speeches and publicity releases by United Nations politicians. To live, internationalism must have spirit and guts as well as blood and words; it must be human and specific and tangible.

Internationalism means noble intentions, or certainly it should. But it also means baseballs and baseball bats, bottled sodas, lipstick, ice cream, radio, television, community dances, and wrist watches. It means lovers in the moonlight or in the dark or in bed, old friends assembled for tea or highballs or lemonade, new friends meeting across the shop counters or at the filling station or at shipside or aboard planes or even, alas, on distant battlefields.

Internationalism also means freely given reciprocity in ideas, and confidences as well as trading goods. It is fitting and proper and immensely encouraging that the United States is noting and accepting most or all of these, along with varied facilities of culture from many different tropics. In more than one respect it is good, for example, that from Africa, particularly West Equatorial Africa, we have taken our now great heritage of "spirituals." From Mexico, Guatemala, the West Indies, Java, Brazil, Siam, and many other tropical or near tropical places we have taken great numbers of fashions, designs, styles, and innovations of dress; from the West Indies, Cuba, Bolivia, Brazil, the Plata lands have come many distinguished dance forms and rhythms including the calypso, rhumba, samba, tango, and others. From Indonesia, India, Ceylon, and Egypt the American stage has taken some of its memorable ballet and group dances. From Mexico, Cuba, the West Indies and East Indies, from Hawaii, Brazil, Peru, Bolivia, Ecuador, and Colombia, from many Pacific islands and Africa we are accepting and adapting more and more of tropical music, much of it excellent and most of it capable of adding warmth and grace and pleasure to our lives.

From Africa and the Middle East, usually without source credit, we are lifting many of the more interesting styles in women's hats, and from various tropical places we are adapting much of our so-called modern jewelry. Our medical pharmacy and pharmacology still lifts in great part from tropical drugs and medicinal plants and distinguished tropical knowledge of the preparation and uses of the latter. More than book-writing doctors or lecturing psychologists have yet told or, for that matter, have yet learned, substantial and perhaps decisive portions of "modern" psychiatry and psychotherapy have been lifted rather literally from the age-old skills, knowledge, or cult lores of Africa and other deep tropics which are not nearly so "dark" as they are too frequently and too cornily pictured by those who married or otherwise raped adventure.

There is also lingual reciprocity. Beginning with such a humble West African dialect word as *banana* and proceeding through scores of such Latin-American Spanish adoptions as *bolero, siesta, camisa, serape, frito, frijole, sombrero, hombre,* and many more, we have adopted literally and effectively into the living American language several hundred words taken from tropical languages and places. This is all the more noteworthy because virtually all the tropical world has adopted at least as many words from the living American language (beginning, inevitably, with "okay") and because a language is a vivid, living part of the nation that uses it. The United States is taking more and more words from the tropics, buying and selling more and more goods in the tropics, trading more and more generously with the tropics in terms of native talents, including music, folklores, crafts, and skills, and even more importantly in terms of understanding and appreciation of tropical graces and tropical needs.

Accordingly, the idea crop gains moment and beneficial values. It is a great crop, certainly the second greatest of all the many good harvests. But the first and very greatest crop and resource, in the tropics as elsewhere, is people themselves. Tropical people speak best and most revealingly of the tropics because they are the indispensable helmsmen, the prophets, the flesh, blood, bones, the vitals and the spirits of the tropics. People, indeed, make overpowering our incentives to look south again.

# Tropics Are People

# ISLAND MAN

AT PRESENT about nineteen thousand tropical islands are named, claimed, mapped, and inhabited by people—by a grand total of somewhat more than three hundred million people, or double the population of the United States. Now, as through the ages, and for several excellent reasons, islanders are a definitive factor in the ways and developments of the tropical earth as a whole. For the islands, despite many and more or less distinctive traits of environment, endure as man's stepping stones to mainlands, as his strategic outposts, and frequently as previews to the ways and moods of the mainlands.

In any case, knowing tropical islands permits one to better comprehend the tropics as a whole.

The last sentence is a sort of homemade proverb divulged by a well-featured, comfortably fat and gleaming black son of Madagascar who proudly lists himself as a tropical islander and who has made a career of being just that. He is Jlaru Yrabra Obusuhra, a name which reads like what might result if a robust cat kept bounding across a linotype keyboard. Though a native of the big island off lower East Africa, Jlaru is currently a resident of Fernando Po, the roundish hell-hole of a Spanish-owned island off the west coast of Equatorial Africa.

His name, actually his nominal allegory (people of Madagascar rarely have family names), means Flower in Sight of the Sea. Being one who reveres the good magic of allegories, Jlaru, the Flower, has spent the greater part of his life on ocean edges, for the most part on island edges within sight and sound of the deep blue. The Flower describes this as the proper destiny of an island man in contrast to that of a mainlander, and points out in reasonably good Spanish that his lifelong succession of island homes is entirely justifiable on the grounds that sea fronts of tropical islands are pretty much the same regardless of longitude or precise latitude and that a man can spend his days on a hundred or a thousand different islands without really changing his home.

On this premise and during his late teens, the Flower in Sight of the Sea took leave of the thatched fishing village that had been his father's home and joined the galley crew of a pre-World War I German fishing schooner. Toilsomely and in the main uncomfortably, he thus managed to see a great deal of tropical earth—from ocean edges. But presently the Flower began to look upon his state as an inversion, since as a deck sailor he was becoming a sea flower usually in sight of the land. Moreover, with passing time his esteem for tropical islands grew into a lush-green adoration of tropical islands and a succinct creed of internationalism by way of them. There were and still are reasons for the latter.

For scattered more or less haphazardly between the Tropic of Cancer and the Tropic of Capricorn are many thousands of islands, ranging in area from carpet-sized snags of coral or mile-high mountain peaks that rise bravely from the suffocating Pacific to immense near-continents. Island populations range from slightly animate human jetsam, countable by ones or at most fives, to fantastically dense populations, such as Java's, where about fifty million people are crowded together in a land area of only a trifle more than fifty thousand square miles. On the other hand, as already noted, some of the biggest islands of the tropics, such as Sumatra, New Guinea, Borneo, and Madagascar remain drastically underpopulated—in ironic contrast to the warm or hot islands which have become human incubators without frontiers.

Tropical paradoxes, which are always plentiful, settle easily on tropical islands. From vivid experience the Flower in Sight of the Sea grants this. With his own eyes he has seen small islands wiped out by monsoons or typhoons or hurricanes or tidal waves. He has seen others blown to smithereens by volcanic explosions or otherwise annihilated by the ever-greedy oceans. He knows as a first-hand observer that entire islands have vanished from the sight of man, and entire island populations have become casualties to a single natural calamity. But Jlaru's deference toward and affection for islands remain intact. He loves islands, and he has found this a rewarding love.

Evidently millions more feel much the same about islands. And most of these millions, like most other people, persist in breeding and multiplying. It follows that islands attract and hold considerably more than their proportionate share of people in terms of land areas. People multiply. But islands do not grow, which means that on them sooner or later the seekers after new lands can only plunge or stumble into the sea or ocean. As much as any living man, Jlaru Yrabu is aware of this. And as a long-time viewer of island edges, he continues to marvel at how comparatively tiny most tropical islands really are.

For example, as islands go, New York's Long Island is a big one; its some 1,680 square miles in area is almost as big as Britain's Crown Colony of Trinidad, one of the most strategic land areas in the South Atlantic. Long Island is half again as big as all the Samoan group, about twice as big as all the Azores (which foot by foot are the most decisive air bases in the world today), and more than twice the size of Jlaru Yrabu's present home, Fernando Po. Long Island is also about three times as big as Zanzibar, the great spice base, three times the size of Society Islands or Hawaii's Oahu or the Shetland Islands, and considerably more than three times as big as Guadeloupe, Grand Canary, Curaçao, or Rhodes.

The area of Manhattan Island is tiny—barely twenty-two square miles. Even so, Manhattan is bigger than Bermuda and almost as big as Hong Kong.

Rhode Island, with a total area of 1,212 square miles (of which about 1,058 square miles are dry land), is the smallest state of our union. Its length, some fifty miles, and its width of some thirty-five, barely permit the transient autoist time to notice that he is in Rhode Island. Even so, the tiniest of our states is bigger than more than nine-tenths of the populated islands in the world today.

As almost anybody knows (and is rarely permitted to forget), Texas is the biggest state of our union—about 760 by 620 miles, for an overall area of 267,339 square miles. Only three islands on earth are bigger than Texas. Frigid Greenland, whose land surface, if the ice and snow were cleared away which is not probable, is about the size of Western Europe. The other two are tropical New Guinea

(330,000 square miles) and tropical Borneo (306,000), both of them islands still blessed with frontiers and huge green markers to untried and unproved tomorrows.

But Texas is more than one hundred thousand square miles bigger than Sumatra, which is the lush green Goliath of the East Indies and a momentous key to tomorrow's tropical world. Texas is more than two and a half times as big as New Zealand, more than five times the size of Java, more than twice as big as all the Philippines.

Texas, of course, is big. But as the great Greeks of long ago pointed out, there is virtue, too, in considering the medium.

A medium-sized state of our union is Ohio, a President-foaling and otherwise far-influencing state, with a modest 41,222 square miles of land surface. In area Ohio ranks thirty-fourth among the States. Yet Ohio is almost as big as the island of Cuba; it is bigger than Luzon or Mindanao, almost half again as big as all the Moluccas or Hispaniola, Tasmania, or Ceylon, almost three times the size of the Solomons or Kyushu or New Britain or Formosa, nearly five times that of Sardinia or Sicily or New Caledonia, nearly six times that of the Fijis, and more than six times that of the New Hebrides.

In wealth and culture Connecticut is one of our richest states. In area (5,009 square miles) it is among our smallest. Even so, Connecticut is substantially bigger than Jamaica (4,450 square miles), the Bahamas (4,404), all Hawaii (4,015), Cyprus (3,584), Puerto Rico (3,435), Corsica (3,367), Crete (3,195), Cape Breton (3,120), or the Hebrides (estimated, 3,000).

In moments of fervent thinking the Flower in Sight of the Sea points out that the mere fact that the great majority of tropical islands are small does not mean that they are simple to comprehend or easy to lead or to push around. He suggests that Americans, particularly, should heed this because the United States is already at least hip-deep in the tropical island business and getting in ever deeper.

He adds that Puerto Rico, our oldest island territory, provides one of the world's most poignant examples of what not to do with tropical islands, and that the Virgin Islands have been among the worst-governed anywhere. Hawaii, our "doorway to the Pacific," swashes along as the stronghold of some of the world's most obvious and lushly political sugar-and-pineapple trusts which are known and smelled throughout most of the tropics and beyond.

The Flower in Sight of the Sea has recently learned, too, that the most recent and the most baffling set of islands now in United States' custody is "Micronesia" in the far South Pacific. Micronesia is Greek for "tiny islands," meaning, in this particular instance, about twenty-two hundred tiny islands that are scattered like green sawdust over the huge wet Pacific floor. Though Micronesia covers an ocean area about twice the entire land area of the United States, its surfaces pressed together, admittedly a most unlikely feat, would not be much bigger than Long Island. At most, all the known lands of Micronesia above high tide total no more than two thousand square miles, which means the average area of an individual island is somewhere near five hundred fifty acres or about the size of a medium Iowa farm.

The human population of Micronesia is believed to be about eighty-five thousand or an average of some forty people per island, provided Micronesians were to stay at home which, though remotely possible, is extremely unlikely, since most Micronesians, like so many other tropical islanders, are inveterate travelers; their canoes and sailboats and dories are everlastingly on the go and not without cause.

The Carolines, the Marianas, and the Marshalls are the nominal groups into which Micronesia is usually classified. Guam, immortalized by United States Marines, is the queenpin of the group, and far and away the most solvent and steadfast. Like Micronesia as a whole, Guam is in the deep tropics—mainly at or near the Philippines-Siam levels.

With Micronesia as with many other tropical islands the preeminent value is in strategic location. Otherwise the assured resources are dim and highly debatable.

Handmade products of the islands, such as grass skirts—which are not made of grass at all but rather of banana leaves or palm fronds—combs, purses, and beads, the latter made of seashells, and other examples of Micronesian folk crafts, are mildly interesting but not of sufficient value to win a secure place in world trade or even in inter-island trade.

All in all, the huge problems and handicaps of the many small land-flecks of Micronesia tend to typify those of island living or island hopping at its hardest. There is no very lucid hope for the resettlement of peoples because only tiny fragments of the lands are suited to agriculture, which at best has remained at the level of the most meager subsistence farming. Without agriculture, and even with it, the chances for developing discernible resources to support schools, stores, or medical services are too remote for encouraging words. Among the great groups of tropical islands, Micronesia is farthest from self-sufficient. If it is to be "ours," it is most certainly ours to care for and protect, not only against military aggressors, but against disease, hunger, and decimating poverty.

The Flower in Sight of the Sea has had only brief porthole glances at Guam and a few of the windrowed dots of land below. But he has spent time on similar land-dots, and he assures one that islands such as those of Micronesia can survive only as outposts at sea—"with blood cords binding them to mainland wombs." He doubts therefore that such islands can ever be possessors of the true spirit of the island men.

I asked him to name an island which he considers a reasonably typical begetter of the true island spirit. After some extremely wrinkling thought, the Flower named Jamaica, in the British West Indies. Long ago (the Flower has forgotten the year, except that it was prior to the First World War) the fishing boat in which he served as galley boy called at a small and particularly beautiful Jamaican harbor called Port Antonio. There the Flower smuggled ashore and beachcombed for almost three years or until a certain bright morning when an ink-black constable picked him up as being a boat jumper and loaded him on an oil tanker which was Africa-bound and short of stokers.

But the Flower in Sight of the Sea remembers Jamaica as it has long been, an island of crowds and "causes," social and otherwise, which encourage people to come together in groups. He remembers Jamaica as a crowded island where people seemed to spill out—like black sawdust from the ripped seam of a mammy doll—and where the spillings inevitably collected in the form of talkative, emotional crowds. He remembers Jamaica in terms of almost blindingly bright sunshine, of plowmen who use their younger sons as oxen leaders, of water boys and banana "headers"—staggery-gaited workwomen who get that way from carrying two or more bunches of bananas on their heads instead of one bunch as lawfully prescribed—and the "field women" who lean on their giant hoes or fondle their thick-bladed cutlasses; also he remembers the inevitable road workers, including the throngs of sweaty girls and women who during the sunlit hours sit beside the highways and tap small roundish stones with undersized hammers until the stones finally fall apart as if in weary disgust.

Affably and lucidly the Flower in Sight of the Sea recalls that the little, roundish, and beautiful island of Jamaica, at present the home of about one and a quarter million Negroes, keeps its now traditional place as a clinical instance of a tropical island with too many poor people for the available resources, yet with an admirable will for attaining a better life.

In 1944 Jamaica as a Crown Colony was formally granted what the British Colonial Office terms "sovereignty in self-rule." Even so, Jamaica's dilemma of poverty and overpopulation keeps growing. As the population bulges, with increases estimated as high as 3 per cent yearly, the great bulk of the island's soil remains ill-used. Yet as is the case with most tropical islands, whether with too few or too many people, agriculture is obliged to give employment and livelihood to about four-fifths of all the people. Sisal, bananas, sugar, rum, coconuts, ginger, and allspice have long been Jamaica's principal exports. All are distinctly hazardous crops. Most of the once great banana acreages have been stricken by plant diseases or failing rainfall. Sugar-growing and rum production are still tormented by severe British Empire market allotment quotas. Because of mediocre or incompetent management, the once-great coconut industry now stumbles into oblivion. Citrus fruits hold many bright possibilities which planters and island officials have drowsily neglected. Jamaican oranges, tangerines, and grapefruit are still as conspicuously badly grown as they are well flavored.

Jamaican livestock development is mediocre to poor. Plantation ownership, in the main native, is caste-ridden and preponderantly incompetent; only a comparative handful of Jamaica's plantations are well run. The majority are run badly. Tens of thousands of the "garden-patch" farms are barely a feeble scratch from extinction. Acre by acre and mile by mile, the island land is under increasing strain.

Barriers against emigration from Jamaica are raised ever higher. For the century ending about 1930, Jamaica's multiplying population could find exodus in the expanding labor markets of Central America, the Panama Canal, Cuba, and to some degree in coastal Colombia and Venezuela and upper Brazil. Since 1932, virtually every Latin American republic has banned the entry of Jamaican labor. Thus Jamaicans are becoming more and more direly bottled into their home island.

For more than three decades, even before the Flower was hoisted out, Jamaica has had ponderous labor and unemployment problems, featuring numerous riots and the drearily repetitious vulture-like inroads of Communism, infiltrating to exploit the suffering and despair of the overcrowded and the underprivileged.

In these and other ways Jamaica suffers or has suffered approximately all imaginable woes and disadvantages of tropical peoples anywhere. Yet, somehow, Jamaica survives, and in some manner the lot of its common man and woman appears to be improving.

Jlaru grants that, as one more overcrowded island, Jamaica can offer a scalp-crinkling preview of what mainland tropical life could conceivably and in time may become if people, aliens as well as natives, persist in using tropical resources as scurvily as they have been used in Jamaica. Even so, speaking both as a career follower of tropical islands and from first-hand experience and reliable hearsay in Jamaica, the Flower in Sight of the Sea submits that there is much of the hopeful and the inspiring about Jamaica today. The island still is preponderantly beautiful and its people still are preponderantly lighthearted. They remain real tropicals. They sing and dance and slosh pleasantly with emotions. They love good food, bright clothing, a little rum and gambling, and spare time sufficient for making love and resting in the shade at least for a couple of hours during the heat of the day.

Like most other tropical islands, Jamaica is a Negros land, bearing in mind that the word "Negro" is a mere Spanish-Portuguese colloquialism for a dark-skinned person. This is relevant in so far as most tropical islands have long been homes for the colored races (Robinson Crusoe was one mere paleface immigrant) and in so far as the skin color of tropical peoples throughout the world is tending toward the darker shades. The Flower views the latter as wholly rational. Direct sunrays darken skins—always have and most likely always will.

Significantly and appropriately, the Negroes who inhabit Jamaica are doing more and more to govern it. At present, Negroes head virtually all the departments of the Jamaican government. The magistrates, doctors, lawyers, legislators, school directors, planters, postmasters, public administrators, directors of public works, and crown solicitors are Negroes and native Jamaicans.

Another of the island's more hopeful resources is the accomplished reality that Jamaica very probably leads the Western World in the avoidance of "color lines," both publicly and privately, and excels in terms of racial amalgamation. Within its island limits, the blood of Africans has mixed completely and on the whole affably with that of the sons and daughters of the British Isles. Only the Chinese, who control some of the grocery trade, and the Syrians, who control a great part of the dry goods trades, have maintained any notable measure of "racial unity." In these ways, as the Flower points out, Jamaica demonstrates the long-proved prowess of tropical islands for the successful admixture of races within a clearly limited and inexpansible area of land. Jlaru does not deem the mixing of races inevitable. He merely points out that in Jamaica, as in other tropical islands, it has proved valid and beneficial to the people. He adds that in all the tropics, as in all the world, all the races must learn more of tolerance and justice, one to the other.

The Flower in Sight of the Sea further discerns that Jamaica was one of the first land areas of the Western Hemisphere to face squarely the equally global issue of woman labor. At least a third of Jamaica's day-labor population is female. In the banana, sugar, and coconut industries, women are a majority of the farm workers. Almost half of all the island's dock workers and at least a fourth of the labor employed in road-building and other public works are women.

Repeatedly the privately run Son-of-I-Shall-Arise style of labor union has discouraged the employment of women for manual labor.

But on the whole the island women have either evaded or defied the unions' admonitions to "go back to your homes and kitchens." The reasons are more than arbitrary. Tens of thousands of the women have no homes or kitchens to go back to; tens of thousands more have dependent and "fatherless" children to support.

In the competition of the sexes, Jamaican women have won their right to work; and this is still another trend that is widely prevalent throughout the tropical world. As economics become more grisly, both the need and the motivation for woman labor keep increasing. All too obviously a prevalent story in the tropical islands, the trend is immensely relevant to tropical mainlands as well.

The Flower in Sight of the Sea makes the point that in still other ways Jamaica's history has been a prolonged series of social, political, and labor experiments enacted against a background of highly inadequate agriculture. In view of the latter he is all the more favorably impressed by what he has heard—through the reliable tropical grapevine—about Jamaica's more than average success at the resettlement of excess people within island boundaries. From their beginning, in the late 1930's, these resettlement ventures have been supported solely by the colony government. They begin with purchase by the government of cheap farmlands in large tracts, which are presently divided into ten-acre or five-acre plots for resale—without profit and at low interest—to poor and needy farmers. The work is directed by the island's ministry of agriculture, and to date about ten thousand native families have been placed on tillable land in this way.

Climate favors the venture. Top-heavy investments in housing are avoidable. The settler has only to build himself a shack and to roof it with palm thatch. If the land is well situated he can rely upon hoe tillage to raise more than one crop a year, and he can direct his garden-farm toward self-subsistence. All this typifies one of the more profound advantages of tropical living. But unfortunately it cannot erase the fact that farming is no longer an easy game anywhere, and certainly tropical farming is grimly more than the plucking of heaven-sent mannas. Exportable crops are increasingly hard to raise. Plant diseases require more and more attention and preventive effort. Hurricanes and droughts remain perennial menaces to tropical fields and orchards.

Even so, in one way or another, Jamaica, the more or less typical tropical island, remains in the international trading picture and is involved in other memorable experiments as well. Among the latter is the innovation of voluntary taxation in terms of products profitably in trade. The first product to provide such a tax was bananas, until a few years ago Jamaica's largest export. The experiment was launched by Jamaica Welfare, Limited, a nonprofit limited liability corporation managed by a directorate of five non-salaried members appointed by the island's Governor General and authorized to raise money by means of the voluntary payment of one cent on each "count," or large bunch, of bananas exported from the island. Exporters paid the tax voluntarily and only on produce actually sold at profit. In return they received "forgiveness" from other taxes which were burdening non-productive resources. The Flower, speaking as a businessman, wishes that all tropical taxes could be limited to valid goods actually in trade. For this, as he sees it, would be "real and honest capitalism."

During the late 1930's, when the plan went into effect, banana exports, totaling in the vicinity of thirty million bunches annually, provided Jamaica Welfare, Limited, with almost a third of a million dollars. More recently the American banana companies have begun withdrawing from the island. Even so, Jamaica Welfare, Limited, well begun, is proceeding with its good work in behalf of the Jamaican people, using its funds skillfully to support badly needed and otherwise bankrupt country schools, to set up rural medical centers in parts of the island where no other hospitals or clinics are yet available, to build a model rural community center, and to buy books and other reading matter for distribution to the many communities on the island which have no libraries. Accordingly, Jamaica's experiment with voluntary taxation invites study and thought, and Jlaru, for one, has given it both.

Jlaru, the Flower, continues to live within sight and sound of the sea. At this moment, as for most of the past half-century, he is not especially busy. Fernando Po is a cocoa—in Spanish *cacao,* or at the soda fountain or candy shop "chawklet"—island. Harvesting cocoa consists of clipping the striated, melonlike pods from the smallish, silver-dappled trees, whacking them open with a heavy knife or cutlass, spilling out the chocolate "beans" and miscellaneous pulp, leaving the latter to dry in the hot sunshine, then presently collecting the "beans" or chocolate seed and toting or hauling them to a drying-and-sorting plant.

Rather pleasantly, but nonetheless really, cocoa smells strongly at first, then in a subdued manner until finally, with most of the scent removed, it comes out as candy or a sweetened beverage or cake icings or other tooth and belly worriers. Jlaru, the Flower, is blessed with sensitive nostrils. His present employment consists primarily of smelling the insistent stench of sun-drying *cacao*.

Aside from that, the Flower tenders fatherly advice in reasonably good Spanish, or in any one of the six tribal languages, to island growers of cocoa, who are inherently allergic to fatherly advice but occasionally are obliged to take it because they know the Flower speaks for a Spanish commission firm which now buys and resells at the greatest possible profits to itself about one-third of the island of Fernando Po's annual export of some thirty thousand tons of cocoa.

The Flower's sense of smell is professionally hard-used. Cocoa smells. So does Fernando Po. And so does contemporary Spain and its colonial policies and practices. Factually, Fernando Po stinks; it is one of the unhealthiest land surfaces on the face of the earth, and quite frequently the dead are not buried soon enough.

Politics, too, has its odoriferous part. Fernando Po, as the reader may recall, was the locale of the late League of Nations' denunciation of literal slavery in the twentieth century. Tribesmen from mainland Liberia were shanghaied and shipped to the hot low island to serve indefinite terms as cocoa laborers.

African sleeping sickness, or trypanosomiasis, was then rampant throughout the island. It is still epidemic. League of Nations investigations showed that more than half the enslaved Liberians died in their tenure of bounden servitude, that many more died in transit, and still others were returned sick to their native country to endure lingering and painful deaths while reintroducing the ruinous disease to mainland Africa.

Like this reporter, Jlaru, the Flower, remains very much bewildered by this. He has given it almost innumerable hours of deep thought as well as the considerable physical energy devoted to digging graves for several of the last of the enslaved Liberians. He has never met the colored and handsome Charles B. D. King of Liberia, this because Charles B. D. King has never seen fit to visit the hot, wet island of Fernando Po. In this the Flower, even while performing his occasional chores of lecturing cocoa growers, smelling the cocoa, and now and then the human casualties thereof, beholds a parable, which is that only the islands can endure the perennial infamies of the mainlands.

The Flower in Sight of the Sea admits that he has cynical moments, in the manner of most men and women, tropical and otherwise. Along with these cynical moments he has numerous grateful moments. As a habituated dweller on ocean fronts he has realized more lucidly than most men that the world today and tomorrow is inevitably one world; mundanely and specifically he has become convinced that the differences between one and another of the approximately nineteen thousand tropical islands as a rule are considerably less than decisive.

As the Flower sees it, the latter is true largely because tropical islands, though eternally separated by the blue and salty brine, cannot live and have not lived as remote and isolated entities. He points out that observation is contrary to most of the thought-provoking romanticisms about island Utopias and Shangri-las. Actually, throughout most of the earth the more extreme and remarkably brainless romanticisms about the beatitudes of isolation and nationalism are credos of the mainlands. The Flower has learned from long and intimate observations that throughout most of the tropics, as beyond, island people, even though blessed or cursed with the opportunity for living alone, are more than averagely inclined to make visits, agreements, treaties, federations, and other vital associations with neighboring islands and mainlands as well. This is still another reason why tropical islands and their peoples are so memorably relevant to the ways of the world today and tomorrow.

Simply and lucidly the Flower repeats that as a rule island boundaries are set by the gods (or by fate) and are not the arbitrary political boundaries which harass the mainlands and serve as causes or excuses for so many bloody and running mainland wars. He notes, also, that although the tropical islands are still principal strongholds of what white men call the primitive social structures, such as clans, totems, tribes, cults, and other normally disparaging terms, the long-time records of island governments are in many ways outstandingly enlightened.

"For many lifelinks the island peoples have tended to lead all others in getting along with their fellow men," the Flower declares. He adds in rather grim Spanish: "It is the mainlands that have most befouled the islands. It is islands that do so much to cleanse and whiten the souls of the mainlands. Islands have left intact the blood cords that lead to mainland wombs. . . . When people speak of islands as mere children of the mainland, I remind them that the child is father of the man."

Though certain white men and other mainlanders charge him with being partisaned in favor of islands, the Flower in Sight of the Sea continues to point out that in a world which relies more and more heavily on laboratories, testing plots, pilot plants, and other preview devices, tropical islands keep serving as all of these, as established, ordained, and paid for by the gods. He points out, too, that like the little island, the prevailing mind of tropical man has a way of gauging and interpreting life in terms of the miniature. While the American mind, for example, depicts its history in terms of vast and sprawling murals or on rocky mountainside bluffs as big as the west end of an auto factory, the tropical mind tends to carve its story and its aspirations in the bend of an ivory tusk or a napkin-sized drapery, a tiny statuette or a hand-sized mask. He cherishes the islander's very natural talent for encompassing greatness or other excellence in a small space. He is convinced that the latter will prove to be one of the more decisive talents and treasures in the world tomorrow.

Thus the Flower believes that the most memorable farm in the world today (he submits that farming is and ever will be the greatest of mortal work) is the typical tropical island farm that fits easily upon a single acre or, as people say on Fernando Po, the smaller half of a hectare! A garden-sized planting of corn or cassava, a few rows of peppers and beans, an elevated pen of chickens sagaciously protected from snakes, a pig well fed and tenderly guarded from leopards or other vermin, a modest planting of rice or millet, an aisle of oil palms, a few clumps or stools of bananas or plaintains, three or four cherished fruit trees and perhaps a grazing cow or two, and a small thatch-roofed house with doors and window sills painted blue.

As the Flower sees it, from such homes and garden fields, and only from them, people can find the modest yet all-essential tranquillity and security that make possible the good and durable life or what certain white men call "culture."

The Flower concludes: "Mainlands build tall houses and high smokestacks and heavy riches. But islands build and keep immortal the souls of men. . . . Mostly tropical islands can become paradises in miniature. Already they are the little worlds of tomorrow. . . ."

## BANANA MAN

AS YET, there appear to be no dictionaries for the native languages of Madagascar, though there is always the ripe chance that about nine such dictionaries will appear between now and the publication date of this book.

In any case, from conversations with the Flower in Sight of the Sea and other Madagascarans I gather that their flow of speech, whether in island dialects or Spanish or French (Madagascar French has a rather pleasant plurping quality, like the sound of walking barefoot in sticky mud, which is in pleasant contrast to, say, Harvard French, which grinds away like a hard-used cement mixer with a dirty spark-plug), abounds in allegory, poetry, and the moods thereof.

Even so, the Flower's use of the term "island" seems to abide the usual definition of a body or speck of land surrounded by water, in most instances by sea or ocean. But speaking as one who would rather use dictionaries as ballast for speedboats or plugging large holes in walls, I contend that the word "island" deserves to include such continental subjects as islands of Hearst newspaper circulation or islands of illiteracy or islands of beer drinking, bourbon drinking, or fancy cocktails, or islands of prosperity, poverty, rich lands or poor lands, or overalls or lounging slacks, or "dinner" versus "supper." In terms of the tropics, there are also memorable and land-bound islands of foreign penetration.

The United States has established a number of such islands in the tropics. Probably the most notable and certainly the most widespread of these U.S.-made islands inside tropical mainlands are those sired by American banana companies. The latter, and more or less figurative, islands are not the most productive of wealth; petroleum comes first in the latter designation; iron, aluminum, uranium, and other valuable metals crowd for second place; and rubber holds third place.

But like our foreign-duty armies, these latter great enterprises tend to carry their home environments with them and to remain forever transplants.

The banana trade, on the other hand, has established islands of tropical penetration, and some of these have lived as essentially tropical if not entirely noble enterprises. Certainly these are the nearest to tropical colonies yet attained by the people of the United States.

At any rate, the foregoing is the well-pondered viewpoint of one of the last of the first U.S. generation of banana chasers. The old man's name is Jules Bramble. Banana-chasing remains his trade, as it has been since the rainy season of 1896, shortly before which Jules pulled stakes and headed south from Circleville, Ohio. Since then banana-chasing has grown to be a comparatively big-money business. But Jules Bramble, who was christened Julius Caesar Bramble, never got any of the big money and not much of the little money. As an old man who neither boasts nor apologizes, he talks from the shadier deck of his hip-roofed shack on stilts, having first shed his shirt so that he can get a better bead at the mosquitoes which for reasons best known to mosquitoes prefer to work on the undersides of his forearms.

With proper encouragement and about half a bottle of Dewar's White Label Scotch Whisky, Jules Bramble sometimes admits that, though he is personally and definitely unimportant, he is perhaps slightly significant for just one or two reasons. He is one of the few survivors of the first rough wave of Gringo pioneers in the near tropics. He still represents the personal and reasonably human link between the old and new schools of U.S. behavior toward and in the tropics.

Jules is confident that as a banana chaser with over half a century in the wetter and lower tropics, he can be forgiven for talking a bit about old times, since the latter, like the rest of history, have ways of repeating themselves. Accordingly, having again condemned the climate and the mosquitoes of Bluefield, Nicaragua, Jules pours a round of stiff and warmish highballs, wipes the sweat from his still clear china-blue eyes, and uses his pocket comb to take the snarls out of his frontal halo of snow-white beard.

Jules begins by pointing out that the banana trade links the past with the future by means of its remarkable ability to produce, distribute, and sell a bulky, erratic, perishable crop quickly throughout approximately half of the earth, and in so doing to create profits where they never existed before and otherwise might never exist. Speed is the memorable maxim of the banana trade in a world which appears to desire to live or perish in a thunderous marathon of speed.

Jules is no champion of the banana as such. He has never enjoyed eating the damned things, and he never expects to. He has never listed bananas as a great tropical fruit, and he pledges that he never will.

As age settles upon him, Jules spends more and more time at reading and sleeping. In the course of the former pastime he has noted that bananas were formally named by Linnaeus, a Swedish botanist, *Musa sapientum*—"fruit of the wise men," because Pliny said that olden wise men of India lived on them.

For this and other good reasons Jules is thankful that he is not an olden wise man of India. Preferences notwithstanding, he has become convinced that in great part the history of the banana is also the history of tropical man.

Certainly the banana is one of the oldest of crops. It probably originated in the wet, hot, valleys of Southeast Asia. The name *Musa* is from the Arabs, who evidently carried the "bits" or rhizomes, the bulbous, highly portable roots of the plant, from India into the Holy Land and northern Egypt, and far beyond. For there is evidence that the Arabs had most to do with introducing bananas to continental Africa, by way of Morocco and the Sudan and, thereafter, by way of ivory trade across hot, wet Central Africa.

In any case, the banana crop was well established in West Africa when the Portuguese made their first voyages to those parts at the turn of the fifteenth century. Indeed, the name "banana" originated in West Africa; it is from a tribe dialect still current in what is called the French Guinea Colony.

By the time of Columbus' death, the name "banana" and its Spanish and Portuguese versions, *bananera* or *platino,* had come into rather general use as the Portuguese, then able navigators and maritime traders, extended their root trade most of the way around the equator—certainly as far west as Brazil and as far east as Moluccas.

The advantages of bananas as an easy and effective food crop for tropical peoples, who even then were harassed by ruinous famines, appealed to many of the earlier missionaries. For example, the need of relieving famines in what had been Columbus' own bailiwick of Santo Domingo prompted Friar Tomas de Berlanga to bring banana roots to that island, from the Canaries, during 1516, and later to introduce the roots to the warm green country which we now call Panama. In the rainy season of 1896, just 380 years thereafter, Jules Bramble began banana-chasing in Panama. In the beginning he regretted that Friar Tomas had ever gone missioning.

Friar Tomas brought red bananas, "Madieras," to the American tropics, and bananas still ripened red when Jules first went tropical. But today, as then, there are all of twenty-seven species or subspecies of bananas, a compact, rather dryish, yellow banana which one sees in the Guianas or Malaya or Brazil; the plantain, the starchy, green-skinned, cooking banana; the red bananas or Madeiras; the tiny, sweet "ladyfingers" of the Carribbean; the sloggish "water bananas" of Equatorial Africa; and the big, yellow Gros Michel, which has become the standby of American, British Isles, and most European markets.

The latter appears to be a "sport" or a botanical accident, which "just happened" on the island of Martinique some two and a half centuries ago. This fact, like many others, stresses the immense age of the banana, which has not been self-seeding at any time in recorded history and thus can be propagated only by digging up and dividing its bulbous roots. This calls for an immense output of labor, as does the abnormally toilsome harvest and the shipping and distribution of the crop, which are still more reasons why the entangled, fog-ridden, in many respects ludicrous success story of the banana may be apropos or symbolic of other tropical crops in time to come.

Jules Bramble ponders the future but rarely predicts it. He has learned, however, by the hard and long way that today as through the years the banana chaser, on land or sea and regardless of language or skin coloring, remains among the hardiest and fleetest of all dirty-shirt brotherhoods.

Jules' first and most effective tutor of banana-chasing was a Carib or "black Indian" from the swampy Honduran coast. Alfredo's working equipment included a stubby canoe or *cayuco* hewn from a Ceiba log, two patched canvas sails, and a double-bladed wooden paddle. He also owned and wore a homemade water jug fashioned from the butt of a banana stalk, a solitary gold tooth, a battered derby hat, and a ragged pair of white duck breeches, the legs of which had been hacked off about eight inches above the knees to assure ventilation.

Alfredo had been a fisherman in the Almirante Bay off Panama, and with time and experience he became known as the best boatmen on all the dangerous schools of *Bocas del Toro* or the Bull's Horns. That was why the banana *hombres* selected Alfredo to carry messages down the rocky, storm-beaten coast between the old banana outpost at Limón in Costa Rica and the then new United Fruit banana headquarters at Bocas del Toro in Panama—a seventy-five-mile run among the many surf-smashed reefs and treacherous inlets.

On his runs Alfredo carried slips of paper in a rubber belt tied around his neck. The papers gave instructions for cutting the fruit to fill the steamships which two or three times each month nosed into Almirante Bay from the outer channels.

The banana men at Limón paid the Carib twenty-five American gold dollars per run. Alfredo would slip the small and beautiful golden disks into the pouch about his neck, massage his one lustrous gold tooth, remove his breeches, and throw them into his six-foot *cayuco*, then paddle the latter to sea. When the weather was calm he could make the run in thirty hours, setting the yard-square mainsail and paddling furiously through the blistering day and chilly night, dipping among the flying fishes, pushing on without food or rest until he shoved his *cayuco* into the green-shadowed Bocas inlet.

That was Carib's supreme moment. He would pull on his breeches and trot up the beach to the thatched-roofed hut which was then home to Jules Bramble. There the Carib would remove the money belt from his neck, lift out the all-important scrap of paper, and deliver it with silent eloquence to the boss man, who would whoop loudly, whereupon dark forms would begin shuffling out from adjacent patches of shade: the banana reapers and mule men and stackers.

Within five or ten minutes several hundred sleepy mules and almost as many half-naked men would be on the trails to the outlying crescent of banana fields. Into the receivers of dozens of wooden-box telephones the gun-toting *Yanqui,* newly arrived from Ohio, would shout orders in profane Spanish, and virtually every able-bodied man of the colony would be cutting fruit for the promised steamship—and all because Alfredo had paddled and sailed the final seventy-five perilous miles to deliver a message which from Boston, or New York, had been sent by land telegraph wires to Galveston, Texas, from there by land and sea cable across eastern Mexico, down to a frontier port in Nicaragua, thence by land wires to a banana company's headquarters at Limón, Costa Rica, where Alfredo took over.

Thus were the ways of an earlier era of penetrating the tropics. Alfredo Cerrares lived dangerously, proudly, and well until one day during the late summer hurricane season of 1902 when Alfredo, for the first time, failed to appear at Bocas del Toro with the important scrap of paper. Another Carib runner went out to look for him and after days of searching found Alfredo's overturned *cayuco* high on the beach and half filled with sand. Some distance beyond the boat the runner found the drowned Alfredo, the money belt still tied around his neck, the gold pieces and the precious cutting order sealed safely inside the pouch.

In banana trade talk, Alfredo had "supplied the fruit." So by increasing steps did Jules Bramble who, having survived three years in Panama and three sieges of malaria, was transferred to Old Ceiba, on the swampy coastline of Honduras.

At Old Ceiba Jules became a banana "agent" with the conventional fixtures of a manaca-thatched shack, many bottles of highly stimulating chills-and-fever tonic, a cot with two sheets and no blankets, a tin bucket with several dippers, a wash pan, and a small arsenal of sidearms. The agent issued the *avisos* or cutting orders, which as a rule were nailed to the trunks of coconut palms by professional runners. Native farmers grew the bananas, and the agent "supplied" them to the ship.

Since most of the banana plantings were small fields rarely larger than five acres or two *hectares,* collecting a mere thousand-bunch cargo required that *avisos* be delivered to several dozen farms or *fincas.* Jules hired native runners to "post the orders," in particular one Toro Juan, who was the fleetest mercury of all. Toro regularly ran or dog-trotted a fifty-mile route and tacked the *avisos* on the prescribed coconut palms.

Until at sixty-four, when his large and filial-minded wife, Parmaleta, cut him down with a double charge of buckshot fired at close range, Toro Juan remained the fastest of all the little honored banana chasers, running a twenty-hour stint through storm and darkness, through mosquito-infested swamps and thorny jungle edges, posting the *avisos,* the while gulping an occasional *frijoles* or the briefest possible morsel of love-making, which frequently goes with the fast-motioned trade of bananas.

Jules Bramble makes no boasts of love-making. He has remained a steadfast bachelor. But he admits having been a fast man in a fast trade.

A great part of banana history has been written on the sea, and still is. Jules points out that the same is true and will remain true of tropical history in general. The nearest thing to a legitimate father the American banana trade ever had was Captain Lorenzo Dow Baker, a schooner master from Wellfleet on Cape Cod. The American banana trade was substantially born on Monday, April 20, 1870, when Cap'n Baker, returning his eighty-five-ton three-master, *The Telegraph,* from a long sailing up the Orinoco River, with a Yankee crew of eleven, put in at Port Antonio, Jamaica, for repairs and cargo. While waiting, the young skipper succeeded in collecting ballast of Jamaican bamboo and a few bags of ginger and allspice. While soliciting further cargo, he saw on the Antonio pier a rick of fat green bunches of bananas wrapped in straw. He bought all one hundred and sixty at a shilling a bunch and set out to reach an American market port before the bananas ripened and spoiled.

Luck and weather were with him. After eleven days at sea, *The Telegraph* "came to anchor at Jersey City, all well." Cap'n Baker succeeded in selling the bananas for a net profit of two dollars a bunch. That was the actual beginning of Boston Fruit, which became United Fruit, now the biggest of the banana companies, and it was the beginning of what thesis writers call the systematic international commerce of bananas.

By the turn of the century the latter was changing from a hazardous summertime trade to a hazardous year-round trade. By 1899 bananas were on sale much or most of the time in fifteen U.S. port cities or towns and in ever-growing quantities were being shipped inland, during cold weather via stove-heated box cars. By 1910 the swinging banana stem had become almost as familiar at the crossroads store as the cracker barrel or the monkey stove; bananas were being sold the year round, and banana-jobbing and huckstering had become proved passports to wealth and eminence for thousands of Italian and Greek immigrants, and their relations and descendents.

But this was rarely so to those who were in the tropics to toil, sweat, fight off the fevers, and otherwise supply the fruit. Jules Bramble learned this at first-hand. As the trade grew, its expanding tropical ends grew ever rougher. Plug-uglies, hired by rival jobbers and importers, hacked to pieces one another's fruit and performed other sabotage and mayhem with carefree, uninhibited abandon. Forthrightly, banana companies and banana railroad companies recruited jailbirds and police-roster names from New Orleans and other port towns, doing this on the grounds that it took "tough guys" or desperate men to hazard what were then the banana lands. Even so the trade kept growing, bigger, richer, more powerful.

Jules Bramble had abundant opportunity to ponder all this and to view and feel its tropical roots. Beginning with his first hot, mosquito-bitten, whisky-soaked year in the hells of Panama, he adjudged that the future, indeed the survival of the banana trade, depended most of all on shipping.

Sound ideas are usually contagious; this particular idea percolated into the seemingly grim, certainly non-tropical controlling minds of the trade.

For a third of a century or longer the latter had relied on "naturally ventilated" ships, for the most part rented or chartered, and known quite pertinently in the tropics as the Mosquito Fleet. Finally, in

1905 Andrew Woodbury Preston, the fat, shuffle-gated produce clerk from Boston who had made his way to the presidency of United Fruit, saw the chance to institute refrigerated ships on American banana runs.

Prior to 1905 British lines had held what amounted to a world monopoly on refrigerated shipping. By 1905 the latter monopoly was leaking badly, and the thickening Mr. Preston of Boston, as one of the very first banana millionaires, was resolved to sink it completely. By so doing, United Fruit could double or triple the shipping range of the already bulging banana trade; it could, indeed, ship Central American bananas into British Isle ports.

So Preston directed that one of the better banana ships, *The Venus,* be drydocked at New Orleans and there be "converted" into the first refrigerated steamer in the American merchant service. After several costly trials and errors, the conversion worked. From Boston to Quito and beyond, banana men looked and listened.

Lee Christmas, the renowned tropical revolutionist and former locomotive railroad engineer, at the time deeply involved in Central American revolutions, conspiracies, and the dubious winning of land concessions for rival banana companies, also in rapid bursts of gunfire, viewed the peculiar overhauling of *The Venus* in the port of New Orleans and once more aired his almost sparkling genius for vulgarity. "So now they refrigerate *Venus* by stuffing her stern with asbestos and straw!" he whooped. "Only a goddamned blue-bellied Yankee from Boston would ever *think* of that!"

Granting the latter, the banana trade, with the advent of refrigerated shipping, began soaring—to twenty million bunches a year, then successively to forty million, sixty, seventy, and eighty million; by the 1920's it had soared to a hundred million bunches, and on to two hundred million, as the British Isles, Western Europe, Scandinavia, and at least briefly Russia came into the orbit of the American banana "advantage."

During 1924 Andrew Preston died a multimillioniare, all of it banana money. Fourteen years earlier Captain Lorenzo Dow Baker had died a multimillionaire, leaving a progeny of great wealth, surrounded by immense Baker-owned cranberry swamps in the area of greater Cape Cod. Bananas were supporting the foremost refrigerated fleet owned by American capital: United Fruit's Great White Fleet, or, more properly, *Gran Flota Blanca.*

Banana agriculture, though far from competent, had grown to be somewhat less incompetent than the mill-run of temperate-zone agriculture; by 1920 the average yields of 1900—about a hundred bunches per tended acre—had doubled; by 1940 they had doubled again. By the latter date, one company, United Fruit, was supplying about 65 per cent of all bananas in international trade whose grand total was somewhat more than four million tons per year.

By 1950 United Fruit was a half-billion-dollar, fifteen-nation company with reported profits exceeding sixty million dollars a year, preponderantly banana money, with almost one hundred thousand employees, with more than six hundred thousand owned acres in tropical crops including about one hundred seventy thousand acres in bananas, about one hundred thousand of sugar cane, almost fifty thousand acres of cocoa or *cacao* orchards, about twelve thousand acres of African oil palms, plus such empire accouterments as fifty thousand head of cattle, twenty-two thousand mules, eighty-six refrigerated ships, and fifteen hundred miles of railroads operating in Central America plus accompanying towns, ports, wharves, and mills. But bananas, with fifteen operating "divisions" in Central America, Jamaica, Colombia, and Ecuador and, by way of United Fruit's British affiliate, Elders and Fyffes, three more banana divisions, one on Grand Canary, one in Nigeria, still another in the Cameroons of West Africa, were paying the tabs for the largest integrated farming enterprise in all the Western Hemisphere. Most importantly, the success story of the American banana trade stresses the likelihood that many other tropical crops, far more beneficial to mankind, are destined to write other success stories that are vastly more important.

Jules Bramble is the very last man who would deny the latter point. He has never had any sharp appetite for success stories as measured in money. As a banana man on the sweaty and at times perilous supplying end, he never made much money; neither did any one of his confederates. Matter of factly he lists himself as a typical transplanted *tropico.* Along with his own kind, Jules has been befriended by many "natives" or "nationals" most of whom he admires, likes, and terms, perhaps a bit sentimentally, the smiling people in the smiling countries.

He does not say the same of those whom he calls the banana barons. More or less inevitably he has followed the ups and downs of scores of the hefties or V.I.P.'s of the trade: the conspirators and revolution-hatchers, such as Lee Christmas; the able and glum location engineers, such as Louis Doubleday, last of the great railroad builders.

Jules likes such men. He admires a few of the "Company greats," big, tough, but thoughtful guys like Samuel Zemurray, the towering Bessarabian immigrant who got rich by peddling "ripes" out of local freight cars, then started his own shipping line and a superb banana company, called Cuyamel, on the Ulua in Honduras, then sold out to United Fruit, then took over United Fruit, and continues to run it. Or the Spanish scholar and Mexican Indian, known as Walter Turnbull, who proved to be the big winner as Zemurray's tropical manager. Also Harry Laiser, the beloved Honduran philosopher who was Zemurray's long-time thinker.

Jules approves such banana greats as these, but he loathes the big-shot banana lushes from New York and Boston. He approves such memorable banana innovations as refrigeration for ships, overhead irrigation for the plantations, modernized railways and ports, air-conditioned bars, concrete swimming pools, Diesel-driven equipment to replace the traditional banana-toting mules; he also approves the tractors that replace the hard-used oxen of earlier years, and the giant draglines and earth movers which shape the vast drainage canals that not long ago were a multiplicity of ditches dug by naked, sweaty men supplied only with picks and shovels.

All the foregoing epitomize progress. Jules Bramble accepts what younger men term progress, yet ponders its true meaning. Granting all the banana-born cavalcade of banana progress, Jules notes that fierce, seasonal storms continue to flatten the best of banana plantations like a giant might strew toothpicks; also, in several very basic respects, banana agriculture remains direly inefficient.

Meanwhile new generations of banana chasers keep appearing,

many of them the perennial, youthful romanticist who back in Keokuk met a Wonderful Girl who, being engaged to a Packard salesman using Vaseline Hair Tonic and a temporary membership in the Osmugoswola Country Club, would not marry him but would think of him always as a Brother.

So he becomes a boy banana chaser and sets out on a well-worn trail of eventualities. Maybe he quits and joins the Marines or a Petroleum Company. Maybe he drinks himself into a permanent coma. Maybe he substitutes sexual might for all other enterprises, thereby going insane, changing to a beachcomber, or more purposefully blasting his brains. Or perhaps, having served his initial contract, he returns to the States on leave and there marries the first remotely human female who will even consider such an entanglement, whether the tall and sympathetic waitress at the Majestic Café or the plump and smiling checker-outer at the White Swan Super Starch Hand Laundry.

The latter, in time, becomes another Gringo Señora of banana land. The alternative, of course, is to remain single and alive, if not entirely sober. Jules Bramble followed the latter course. At seventy-six he remains single, definitely alive, sufficiently sober, and a well-detached American.

The latter materialized quite gradually. In the old days a banana chaser drew home leave once in three years or five years, depending on where he was and how badly he was needed. Jules got his first leave after seven years.

That was in 1905 and springtime in Circleville, Ohio. His younger sister was being graduated from high school; his older brother had just won a job as relief dispatcher for Postal Telegraph. His mother and father were celebrating their thirtieth wedding anniversary. All told, it was a happy and highly communicative three weeks.

By 1910, the time of Jules' second leave, both his mother and father were dead, his brother languished with tuberculosis in a sanitarium near Tucson, and his sister had married a drunken druggist in a nearby village. Jules visited his parents' graves, did his best to console his sister, who had bruises, anticipated twins, and planned a divorce, then entrained for Arizona where he was barely in time to attend his brother's funeral.

On his third leave, during the autumn of 1916, Jules began to feel out of place and "unbelonging." He knew virtually no one in his home town; his visits to old high school cronies who then ran filling stations, funeral homes, a florist shop, and a drug store were not especially rewarding. The family home had been sold and converted to a mechanic's tenement.

His younger sister, fat and divorced, had moved to Columbus and was clerking in a department store to support her girl twins, who for no reasonable cause seemed to detest their Uncle Julius.

Awkwardly, in a Woolworth store, Jules encountered his high school sweetheart who had married a ne'er-do-well bank clerk and grimly had settled down to teaching in a suburban school. At that point Jules said, "To hell with all this!" hurried to a nearby saloon, did his best to drink it dry, then packed his bag and headed back to Honduras, granting audibly to all who cared to hear, and to a number who did not, that he was just a damned banana chaser and to hell, to hell, to hell with anybody who didn't like it. He has not been back to the United States since. It isn't that he dislikes his country. He feels that he belongs there no longer.

Among banana chasers, the latter inference is by no means exceptional. Jules has never been a helmsman for the arduously publicized new and streamlined era of bananadom. Bluntly and effectively he resents and repudiates the myth of the latter as it is perpetuated by New York publicists. Factually speaking, there is no decisive change, only a dogged increase in size and amounts, as in the seventh and eighth months of human pregnancy.

Bluntly, but not bitterly, Jules describes the continuing game of supplying bananas as the same old medicine show. For the past quarter-century he has viewed it from the superior vantage of a rear-guard follower. For that many years he has served as follow-up man—one who terminates growers' contracts and buys the final, feeble harvests of dying plantations; one who puts to bed and otherwise liquidates great company plantations which have failed, such as Almirante in Panama, or old Limón in Costa Rica, or once prolific Bluefields in Nicaragua, or Truxillo, in Honduras.

In such cases and places one buries the dead, comforts the dying, removes the rusting water tanks and railway rails, and gazes sentimentally at what were once splendid dance halls (employees clubs) and once superb, Boston-designed golf courses, now grown thirty feet high in rank jungle bush.

While carrying on as banana undertaker, Jules doubles as tropical prophet, as an American gone tropical, and as a lifelong and decidedly sympathetic student of tropical peoples and places. He believes in the tropics. He continues to regard himself as a living link between everyday people in the United States and the eternal yet death-shadowed life in places south. He reads a great deal, and, more importantly, he thinks a great deal.

From his long-time reading Jules gathers that the great past civilizations of man have grown out of fields of cereal grains and that the three premier grain crops—corn, rice, and wheat and/or rye—were born of the tropics or nearby subtropics, as were the premier civilizations.

Corn, indigenous to the American tropics, is the number-one crop in the world today. Wheat, presumably native to the lower Middle East and the Nile Valley, was the foundation of the long dominant civilizations of that part of the earth, in time made Rome the world's mightiest empire, and, abetted by cereal relatives such as rye and barley, made Europe a preferred habitat for people. Rice, born of tropical southeast Asia, still underpins and underwrites most of the Far East civilizations. Jules takes for granted that the decisive crops of tomorrow will also come out of the tropics.

From years of reading Jules Bramble has noted that for centuries past man, dreaming of Utopias, has given those Utopias tropical settings. There are bound to be reasons for this. Certainly it demonstrates the world-circling power of opinion. In terms of the latter, Jules is convinced that in the world today, United States opinion or viewpoint is the mightiest force in molding tropical destinies. As the most powerful commercial nation on earth, and possessor of the best half of the earth's established wealth, the United States is now the decisive factor in tropical trade, which means tropical living standards.

Quite personally and somewhat painfully Jules began his really studious acquaintance with the tropics during the Spanish-American

War. During that time the United States viewed the tropics much as a mouse views a cat. We granted we had to live in the same world, but we were not particularly happy about doing so.

As of 1900, coffee was, as it still is, our largest tropical import. But the United States bought most of its coffee from Brazil and minor quantities from Java, while other great coffee-producing nations such as Costa Rica, Colombia, and Guatemala continued to ship most of their decisive crop to Liverpool, Hamburg, Bordeaux, and Scandinavia. Shiploads of hides, tobacco, ivory nuts, and wild rubber from northern South America usually went to European ports. On the whole, "trade relations" among the Americas stank.

United States industries had not faced any really decisive need for "going beyond" home markets. Only a handful of industries, practically all of them operators, builders, or suppliers of merchant ships (which included the swaddling banana trade), sensed any real need for trade with the western tropics. Broadly stated, the United States tended to abhor the American tropics, and the sentiments were mutual. In general, U.S. business had no capable knowledge of what goods the American tropics needed or how to sell, pack, and deliver them; U.S. banks had no branches in the American tropics, where U.S. credit was about as easy to reach as the moon.

Shipping services made most of the American tropics only slightly more accessible than the moon. U.S. consular and diplomatic services remained mediocre to deplorable since U.S. State Department assignments to the American tropics, or for that matter any other tropics, were viewed as nothing short of extreme punishment. In those times not a single tropical nation rated an ambassador.

Americans who went to the tropics were generally looked on as the final dregs or barrel-scrapings, and too frequently the latter view was uncomfortably accurate. Jules recalls that in the course of his last home leave, back in 1916, a loud-speaking, barbering cousin roared at him: "Why, down in them monkey swamps a man can't be an *American*. . . !"

Jules recalls, however, that this point of view, or lack of a view, began abating somewhat as the murky 1920's galloped along. Back in Ohio, as in most other parts, some of the people began to awaken to the fact that Main Streets no longer ended in nearby cornfields or cow pastures; Main Streets were beginning to lead across national boundaries. From the far outskirts of the banana places, even in the dire Nicaraguan or Truxillo swamps, Jules watched more and more U.S. merchandise pouring south—granting, of course, that much of it was not what the "Southern Neighbors" wanted or could use. Repeatedly U.S. manufacturers dumped ill-chosen surpluses of goods into tropical ports, where much of the dumpage just waited on wharves or rail sidings. Rather abruptly, too, U.S. banks began raising credit antennae in Central American capitals. Power and light and petroleum companies and varied agencies began nosing and stumbling southward. There were numerous disappointments and mistakes. Jules noted that the old-style German peddlers frequently succeeded whereas the trade routine then known as "American high pressure" frequently failed.

During the latter 1920's Jules traveled just about all the 2,500-mile banana front, from badly lost Ecuador far into the green valleys of lower Mexico. As one who ponders while looking, Jules Bramble sought to find out the reasons why U.S. business, excepting bananas and petroleum, was not faring better in the near tropics. He deduced that U.S. business was simply not doing its half of the necessary getting along.

The fact was evident, too, that the "trusts" or cartels were dominating most of the great tropical exports: coffee, rubber, tin, copper, nitrates, petroleum, palm oils, and, alas, even bananas. Jules had never held a grudge against big business as such. But any onlooker could see that the continued growth and pyramiding of trusts and cartels was blocking useful development and the essential growth of tropical enterprises.

Cartel-run crops kept crowding out the all-necessary subsistence crops. Big business kept upsetting necessary local enterprises. Brazil was being made the coffee state, Honduras the banana state, Malaya the rubber state, the Netherlands Indies the palm oil states, Cuba the sugar state, and so on, even though just about any damn fool knows that crops are inherently common resources which cannot be patented or monopolized any more than sunsets.

Jules estimated that the whole greedy fantasy was injurious to the United States and more or less ruinous to the tropics. He further estimates that the 1920's represented one of the darkest intervals in tropical history.

But he kept predicting, even to the most sensitive and skeptical of the *Americanos del Sur,* that surely the United States and its people would begin to see light. Jules never regretted that prediction. He was delighted with Hoover's first statement of the Good Neighbor Policy; even more delighted when the first New Deal set out to erase at least part of the nagging U.S. interference in the home affairs of the American tropics. When F.D.R. recalled the U.S. Marines from the Caribbean, Jules Bramble could think of no way to celebrate except to retire to his shack and drink a straight fifth of Dewar's. He survived it, but hopes that the recourse will not be necessary again.

Jules read with heartiest approval, about the Roosevelt-Hull succession of reciprocal trade agreements with some twenty-eight tropical countries, including most of the American tropics, and the equally able succession of non-intervention treaties with eighteen American nations to the south. The then graying banana chaser admired immensely practically all of the "Good Neighbor Program" of the first Roosevelt Administration. But he recognized one ponderous drawback. The noble work had been begun too late for adequate results. By 1937, when the second Roosevelt Administration took over, the blights and grim shadows of Nazism were already trespassing on most of the tropical earth, not excepting the banana lands of Central America.

Promptly, and inevitably, the Roosevelt policy toward the American tropics began its working theme of "Hemisphere Security," supported by the very factual doctrine that the Americas were obliged to hang together in order to avoid hanging separately; that democracy or reasonable facsimiles thereof can endure, or indeed be born, only if and as living standards can be kept at tolerable levels. Jules agrees cordially in principle. He still feels, however, that the Good Neighbor policy, because of time, fate, Nazism, Communism, and other forces of darkness, became rather inevitably a shotgun wedding. Personally, Mr. Bramble lacks enthusiasm for any kind of weddings. Most particularly, he does not like shotgun weddings.

He grants, however, the immediate effectiveness of the shotgun marriage. Within a month after Pearl Harbor, ten nations of the American tropics had joined the United States as allies; Costa Rica actually declared war against Germany before the United States had time to; Brazil and Mexico followed suit, and completely around the equator, the overwhelming majority of all tropical countries swung to the side of the nominal democracies, in some instances at profit to themselves, in more at formidable losses.

However, as Jules Bramble had thoughtfully predicted, the Good Neighbor Policy as labeled by Hoover and materialized by the earlier New Deal, died with Franklin D. Roosevelt. With the Truman-Byrnes regime, it stumbled and bumbled. As Jules sees it, in an entire half-century of rather avid competition in diplomatic stupidity, Spruille Braden's Get-Tough-with-Argentina policy was the most abjectly asinine of them all. The resulting injuries promptly spread throughout all the American tropics and far beyond.

The Marshall regime was not afflicted with Mr. Braden nor cluttered by the Edward R. Stettinius kennel of Precious Youths. Yet the good and politic General Marshall was also unable to implement effectively the United States' sworn policy of financial and economic co-operation with the western tropics and much of the eastern tropics where Soviet power plays were and, alas, still are for us most uncomfortably effective.

As Jules observes, the first Truman Administration, unavoidably preoccupied with European "recovery," looked more to the east than the south, failed to support the establishment of an Inter-American Bank, took no very effective steps to make available the resources of the World Bank or the International Monetary Fund to valid tropical countries, even though many of the latter needed bank credits more acutely than ever before and engaged their best opportunities for repaying the loans.

Speaking personally, Jules has never been a borrowing man. But he recognizes that practically all business, and practically all nations, which are the biggest businesses of all, are at one time or another obliged to borrow in order to survive. Throughout the nineteenth century the United States was in precisely that situation. All Central America and the greater part of the tropical earth remains so today. Since the close of World War II, as before, many have been gravely penalized because they were unable to *borrow.* In the American tropics as elsewhere far south, the resulting penalties include rough and smashing waves of inflation and depression which continue to stir violent political uprisings and revolutions in many tropics, including, close at hand, Colombia, Costa Rica, Chile, Venezuela, and Honduras, and the rebirths of tyrannical dictatorships, as in Peru, Bolivia, Paraguay, and Guatemala, not to mention bitter and dangerous strife in more distant tropics.

Quite willingly Jules Bramble grants that not all the foregoing adversities could have been avoided merely by handing out credit. However, as a career *tropico,* a thoughtful observer, a painstaking reader of several of the best New York, London, and Central American newspapers, and a devoted listener to short-wave radio broadcasts from many capitals, he submits, as a generally accredited fact, that recently and currently the United States shows dangerous favoritism toward Europe and dangerous neglect of the tropics, including many close at hand.

Speaking as a banana chaser, which, after all, is one more kind of a farmer, Jules Bramble agrees that the opinion crop is the most important crop of all. From his somewhat unique place of vantage, he grants that U.S. opinion toward the tropics shows encouraging growth and improvement, though unquestionably it can stand a great deal more of both.

Jules Bramble is an old man now. He has gained a very gradual and rather costly victory over the perennial human fault of impatience. He remains a banana man, this without regrets or apologies. If he had his life to live again, he believes he would live it just about the same way, save perhaps for the omission of that third and final home leave. He believes the tropical world is only now at dawning, and in general he sees its new horizons as bright. He hopes to see many more fuzzy-faced youngsters from Ohio, Michigan, Texas, Arkansas, Montana, Pennsylvania, and all the other states coming to the tropics with bright dreams and bargain-buy cameras and eager inquiries regarding the friendliness of the natives and chances for "developments," though he does not offer to answer all their queries.

In part Jules' interests are personal; in part they are exceptionally objective. He has learned at first-hand that the tropics are the great and decisive frontiers remaining in our world today. He is wholly convinced that democracy can endure and flourish only so long as it has a background of tenable frontiers. He believes that the youngsters with the bargain-price cameras are the same Americans who rode nags or drove oxcarts to open the West a century ago and, much more importantly, built a nation dedicated to the survival, the freedom, and the integrity of the common man.

Jules Bramble grows eloquent at times. He cannot see why an old man, even a damned banana chaser, shouldn't.

## THOUGHTFUL FARMER

THE banana chaser endures as a rather memorable borderline tropical, a geographic and environmental in-between who inhabits islands of U.S. penetration into the tropics. Quite evidently the best half of him is farmer; the other half is variously partitioned as observer, co-ordinator, conspirator, critic, arbiter, and unofficial diplomat in a banana-inked shirt under a whisky-scented breath, with, more than occasionally, the mind and spirit of a philosopher.

But the fact is always relevant that banana lands, like other great and changing tropics, also have memorable, native-born farmers who love and serve agriculture, this most basic of tropical trades, thereby helping all the tropics. Such men, by their works as well as their beliefs, are particularly able internationalists.

Don Antonio Ramirez of West Guatemala is such a farmer. I met him a dozen years ago, and since then I have followed his expanding works and his noteworthy convictions with immense interest. I am obliged to admit, however, that a touring dentist from Dallas found him first.

The friendly tourist admired the tall, blackish-green banana plants, some of which towered to a height of forty feet; he also admired the cleanly tended, silver-splotched cocoa trees, and the several fields of lush tropical grasses.

A professional man who made a superb hobby of plant introduction, the friendly tourist had come a long way to see this particular Guatemalan plantation, and he was eager to meet the proprietor—in tourist guidebook Spanish, the *patrón.* So the *turísta* stopped at a newly built wooden bridge that spans an irrigation canal and called *buenos días* to a crew of field workers who labored naked except for sombreros and British-style shorts. The greeting was answered in English by a big, sun-reddened, broad-shouldered man whom the tourist took to be the field foreman.

The tourist inquired, "Where did you learn English?"

"In Philadelphia, Señor!" The speaker lowered his machete and smiled. The tourist, who is a dental surgeon, noted the head worker's clean, well-shaped teeth which, except for a small gold framing on an upper incisor, were immaculately white. The vacationing dentist nodded approvingly and inquired further, "Where do I find the *patrón*?"

The worker smiled again. "By the left-hand road, up the hill, Señor. A white house with blue trimmings. Walk into the front door and make yourself entirely at home. He will come shortly." The tourist thanked the worker and followed the road up a steep hillside to a yardway of orange trees and flowering bougainevillea, behind which stood an attractive white house with bright blue trimmings. The heavy, blue door waited open. The tourist entered and saw standing before him a big, broad-shouldered man dressed in shorts and a gay red jacket.

Again the traveler spoke good morning. "I take it that I have the honor to address the *patrón*?"

*"Si, Señor!"*

The host smiled, and again the touring dentist duly admired his well-shaped teeth. Then his expression became one of sheerest amazement. All the teeth were glistening white except the upper left incisor which was framed in gold. Bewildered, the touring dentist sank to a leather-thong chair, still gazing at the gold-framed tooth. Then he asked, "How in creation did you get from that field to this house so quickly?"

"There is a shorter way than the one you followed, Señor."

"And how did you get to be a quick-change artist?"

"I am only a farmer, Señor!"

Still somewhat dazed the visiting dentist, inquired, "But you must be Don Antonio Ramirez—the proprietor of this *finca!*"

The host nodded. "That is right, Señor. I have been so since the passing of my esteemed father." He added, "The fields which you noticed on your way to this house show some part of our toils to make useful what only a few years ago was one of the most hopeless of jungles."

The tourist asked, "And what was that you said a while ago about learning English in Philadelphia?"

Don Antonio opened a blood-red package of Guatemalan cigarettes. "At sixteen I went away from home to learn about the Colossus of the North that is called the United States. But instead of going to school, as my father intended, I got a job—first, as a bellhop in a Philadelphia hotel where I learned what is called the American language. From Philadelphia I went to Detroit and worked in one of the automobile factories. I was able to save part of my wages, and after seven years I came back to my own country and began running this farm. I used what little money I had saved and all that my father had set aside for what he thought of as my education and began building up the *finca* here. For the lowlands I hired men to build drainage ditches. For the high parts I built an irrigation dam and about two miles of cement canals. Also I bought tractors and scrapers. From that time on I have worked in my own fields and helped my workers learn about the new machinery and also about what is called modern or partly modern agriculture.

"I am the *patrón,* but I am also the worker. Accordingly, when visitors stop beside the fields and ask for the *patrón,* I show them to my home, then I hurry up the hill by the short path. That way I reach the house ahead of them, and coming through the back door, I slip my machete into the wall scabbard, then take off my hat, comb my hair quickly, and slip on a jacket. That signifies, Señor, the maximum difference between a Don, or what you quite grammatically call a *patrón,* and any other farmer."

Antonio Ramirez also personifies an especially noteworthy and hope-inspiring development in tropical life and work today: the revival of the enlightened, hard-working proprietary farmer. Don

Antonio is constructively typical in that he is one who has proved to have the moral and intellectual courage to discard the crippling equator-circling tradition of "planter" aristocracies and to work effectively and at first-hand to diversify and otherwise advance farming in the tropics.

Señor Ramirez is not working as a designated factor or comrade in any regimented or broadside "movement." He is found to be simply a tropical farmer, one among tens and hundreds of millions of tropical farmers. By inherent talent and deliberate design he is one of the many millions in the tropics who continue to prove most practically that they have "green fingers"—the talent for placing seed or other planting stock in suitable grounds and encouraging them to grow and bear harvests which supply valid uses and markets.

Green fingers (the term, of course, is not literal) belong to no particular race or "class" of people. They belong to Indians, Negroes, brown men, white men, and the interminable mixtures thereof. They belong to small farmers, large farmers, and hobby farmers, to scientists and other experimenters, even to politicians. They are the flesh, bone, and blood faculties for discovering, adapting, and improving new crops and for bettering the old. Since his return to Guatemala, Don Antonio has been determined to try new crops. Like many other good farmers, he is a devoted student and fancier of grasses. Thus, some ten years ago, in the course of a vacation trip to the West Indies and in Trinidad, he noticed a broad-bladed, heavily tufted grass which local country people called "Sarah." He noted that the local herb doctors (for the most part old Negro women) cut the "Sarah," put it in crude kettles, and thus distilled a strongly odored oil used for massaging sprained joints.

Promptly Antonio recognized the "Sarah" as citronella grass—called "sereh" in Ceylon and various South Pacific producing areas. He carried a bagful of roots of the grass back to his farm in Guatemala, planted them, and so developed a first half-acre of West Indian citronella. The following year he was able to expand the planting to four acres. After Pearl Harbor, when United States importers became eager to buy the unique oils that are distilled from several species of tropical grasses, Don Antonio devised and built a distillation outfit of oil drums, an earthen furnace, and a few lengths of copper pipe. He mowed the grass with a hand scythe, and when it was partly dried he filled the three drums with it and fired the distillery. Presently the citronella oil began to drip from the discharge end of the pipe. He sent first samples to a New York importer and received a favorable report. Then, by well-planned stages, Don Antonio increased his plantings of the oil grass to about one hundred acres and so played a part in developing one of the great new crops of Guatemala.

This, admittedly, is just one more passing example of the sort of agrarian enterprise which, when duly multiplied, co-ordinated, and otherwise "made natural," can change tropical lands from verdant wastes to cradles of abundance. Time, devoted work, skill and planning, intelligence and devotion, all are needed, and even with all of them the failures are many and more or less inevitable.

But with the failures come beneficial and world-influencing successes which reiterate the calm, persisting truth that the tropical earth is still preponderantly a farmer's earth. Its durable history keeps being written on the scrolls of fields and gardens.

Señor Ramirez is entirely convinced that the dogged and deplorable lack of variety is the most formidable stumbling block to the all-important development of tropical agriculture. He has read that no fewer than six thousand useful crops can be grown in the tropics, among these several hundred that are common to the temperate zones. Yet the great tropical crops to date are most conspicuous for their exasperating lack of variety, a lack which nature toils to overcome, and man docilely permits.

Don Antonio is certain that tropical agriculture—actually life to the great majority of all tropical peoples—pleads and languishes for variety which by natural decree is its primary destiny.

However, from intimate and diligent experience he has learned that a crop is much more than a collection of useful plants, that primarily a crop is a human phenomenon, and this because people must select the species or family of plants, prepare or adapt them for cultivation, plan, plant, cultivate, and harvest them. Mere plant life changes to crops only as people, living, hoping, sweating, cursing, praying, but no less importantly working, acquire the plant and set out to make it useful. By definition, crops are plants or animals selected by man. Just as basically, crops are the beliefs, the toil, sweat, blood, and tears of workaday people who gamble their time and their lands in proving or disproving them.

Antonio Ramirez has learned to respect the odds against the immediate success of new crops. But he is no less aware that winners' stakes are high, that the value of great, successful international crops climb, ever higher into the hundreds of billions of dollars or pesos or, as people say and use in Guatemala, *quetzalies*. But money estimates are not adequate for crops any more than they are for other lives. In the tropics crops *are* life.

Also, as Antonio Ramirez sees it, crops are history, and they are roads to survival. Meanwhile, the actual development and perpetuation of crops remains a human challenge within the minds and hands of people, mainly everyday and unsung people who by the millions and hundreds of millions, because of their work as farmers, are the brightest hope of the tropics today and forever.

Don Antonio is no professional philosopher. He is a man of action, specifically a farmer. But he believes that study and experiment are primary obligations of the latter. Accordingly, as a relevant hobby, he continues to study and experiment with some of the drug and medicinal crops which are among the distinctive heritages of tropical agriculture. The tropics have provided mankind most of the great and durable medicinal crops, and hundreds of these medicinal crops, or botanicals, hardly fewer than twelve hundred, have by now been adapted to cultivation.

Though Guatemala has particular aptitudes for medicinal crops, no one area could produce all the twelve hundred. Señor Ramirez has no desire to do so. He is not a pharmacist, and some of the botanicals he rules out on purely moral grounds—the narcotics, for example, which have dealt formidable injury via the opium poppy to lower China and many of the South Pacific islands, and the coca or cocaine bush which has dealt ruin to great numbers of Andes Indians.

But Guatemala, with its exceptional variety of altitudes, climates, and soils, all within a comparatively small and contrasting space, is one of the best arenas in all the tropics for growing medicinal plants. Great numbers are indigenous, and in Guatemala as in many other tropical places, the outside world has barely begun to appreciate the wonders and effectiveness of what is called folk pharmacy. However, as regards medicinal crops in Guatemala, various North American institutions, including E. R. Squibb Laboratories, the Harvard Medical School, and the Carnegie Institution of Washington, D.C., are accomplishing exceptionally perceptive research. Even so, the field is barely scratched, and in his own studiously determined way Don Antonio has set to scratching.

Throughout the tropical earth the medicinal plants are scattered with a rather splendid impartiality. Don Antonio has demonstrated, for example, that the thorny little tree called acacia, or gum arabic, presumably native to the dryish lands of the Anglo-Egyptian Sudan, will thrive in certain of the dryish midlands of Guatemala where it yields generous harvests of the medicinal inner bark.

The same is true of the *liliacea* bush, whose leaf juice provides the long-used laxative called aloe. Most aloe still is produced along the east coast of Africa and Arabia, though the shrub can be grown in Guatemala and many other dryish tropics. The shrub now gains importance because its green leaves are particularly valuable for treating X-ray burns.

Camphor, the distilled sap from a tree related to the cinnamon, is native to the hot, dampish tropics of Southeast Asia and Formosa. Commercial camphor is obtained by felling the tree, chipping the wood, and subjecting the leaves, chipped wood, and twigs to distillation, then in time, dissolving the gum in alcohol. The tree is apparently adaptable to many tropical and subtropical areas. Its recent introduction into Guatemala has been highly successful.

As a practical as well as an experimental farmer, the Don is more interested in adapting and growing fungicides and insecticides which can be used to safeguard other crops in the same general area. He points out that whereas about five-sixths of all the principal medicinal plants are growable in the tropics, where the majority are readily movable from one continent or island to the next, practically *all* the "natural protectors" against harassing insects and fungi are tropical.

The latter list begins with such well-known, widely used standbys as pyrethrum, rotenone, and nicotine, all of which Don Antonio has adapted successfully on his Guatemala *hectares.* Pyrethrum, one of the longest used of the vegetable insecticides, is related to the common garden chrysanthemum; its dried flower provides the insecticidal agent, and its principal sources include Britain's Kenya Colony of East Africa and important and comparatively recent plantings in Peru, Brazil, Venezuela, and Guatemala. Nicotine-bearing plants, preponderantly native to the American tropics, continue to provide valuable plant sprays, and several of the latter plants are "naturals" in Guatemala.

Meanwhile, rotenone, which is a semi-toxic powder made from the roots of several perennial tropical plants belonging to the widely spread, much-varied bean family, is native to upper South America in the form of the classic "fish poison roots" (which kill fish without injury to those who would eat the fish) as taken from such forest floor perennials as barbasco or lonchocarpus. However, during recent decades from the Malay Peninsula has come the generally preferred crop called derris. This is a sort of ground vine with slender, deep-burrowing roots that frequently provide the most economical source of rotenone, an ever-valuable "agent" which destroys sucking and crawling insects without poisoning people or other animals.

When he was a little boy, Don Antonio once traveled to what then seemed the distant and eternally beautiful Guatemala City to visit an aging aunt who dealt in spices.

His Tia Josefina read tropical history in terms of her shelf-fuls of hand-painted square clay spice boxes, and young Antonio was immensely impressed when Tia Josefina explained how spices, more than any other great group of tropical crops, have done most to bind together the tropical earth and write great pages of world history. The frail old lady illustrated her discussions with the sights and smells of many different spices, which she assembled from the far corners of creation and sold to the more discerning restaurants and inns throughout the great *mesetas* or highlands all the way from San José, Costa Rica, to the ever magnificent Mexico City.

She showed him clay jarfuls of red pepper brought from the distant Belgian Congo and lower India, and many more jarfuls of caraway seed from Syria and Morocco, paprika from Argentina, Portugal, and lower Mexico (to which the plant is native), bay leaves from Brazil, Turkey, and the nearby Indian lands of Guatemala.

There was also thyme from Spain and the Argentine, sesame from Brazil, anise from Cyprus, Paraguay, and Peru, and sage leaves grown in the Guatemalan highlands.

Tia Josefina took particular pride in the classic spices such as cloves, which are still imported principally from Zanzibar and Madagascar, cinnamon from Ceylon, allspice from Guatemala and Jamaica, and cured ginger root from India and Jamaica. Her list of locally grown spices included dill, chili peppers, mustard seed, garlic, basil, cardamon, and marjoram, all grown in Guatemala and now growable in such bizarre and distant places as California or India. She also sold the seeds of fennel, coriander, and poppy from India, oregano from Mexico, and cayenne peppers from Mombassa and India, and so on, more or less completely around the equator. The story of the spices has always been a good and contagious one, and long after his Tia Josefina returned to her preponderantly Quiche and Maya forefathers and mothers, Antonio has continued to follow the great story. He has read about pepper, for example, beginning with common black pepper, the mill-ground ripe seed of a hardy tropical vine, and white pepper, the finely ground immature seed of the same vine. Five centuries ago, the international pepper trade had grown at least as influential as the international petroleum trade is today. By the sixteenth century the value of pepper was more staple than that of most national currencies, with the result that it was eagerly accepted for payment of colonial taxes or as pay or bonuses for soldiers or civil servants.

By the hundreds and thousands, British and European trading firms grabbed for tropical domains, not because they particularly liked the tropics or sympathized with them, but because they knew the monetary and strategic value of peppers and many other great tropical spices. The Don has noted, too, with considerable astonishment, that the present world consumption of at least ten of the principal spices, including peppers, cloves, nutmeg, and allspice, keeps increasing.

Don Antonio is one who ponders the future in terms of the past. He has read how the demands for and the profits from spices did most to lure the white man into the tropics and to open the first great trade routes. He has read how his own country first gained memorable old-world interest by its spices, vanilla, and indigo. Also he has learned how in the United States, long before Lexington and Concord (perhaps, symbolically, forty-eight years before), such Yankee sea pioneers as Captain James Hannum, sailing from Salem, Massachusetts, blazed the most direct sea route to the prized vine pepper of the Moluccas.

He has read how the dominantly tropical spice trade has perpetuated globe-circling sagas of adventure and how Britain took over mighty India with the intent of making it a spice and tea bank and how twenty centuries before Christ, Egyptians had carved in stone their own formalized records of the preciousness of spice, how the Pharaohs staged regal celebrations at which spice was burned as proof of their infinite wealth. He has read how the Goths, conquering Rome, demanded ransoms in pepper, since Rome for centuries had been a world capital for the even then lushly profitable spice trade.

In his varied travels Don Antonio has viewed many of the great spice crops and pondered the chances for growing at least some of them on his own well-used lands. He has successfully transplanted, from Ceylon, the handsome tropical tree whose inner bark yields the great spice called cinnamon, and he finds that the tree flourishes on many well-drained and wind-protected tropical soils.

Don Antonio also experiments with planting clove trees. (Commercial cloves are the dried flower buds of this magnificent tropical tree.) The venture is not yet proved, but he notes that there is no successful synthetic or synthetic flavor of cloves thus far.

The no less classic nutmeg (*noix muscade*) tree, whose hard nutmeg kernels are separated by a lacelike membrane which supplies mace, also thrives in parts of Guatemala, as it does in some of the West Indies and parts of Brazil, particularly along the ocean fronts. The Don is also experimenting with the Caribbean-born pimento or allspice tree whose crop tends to combine the tastes and fragrances of cinnamon, nutmeg, and cloves, which explains the name "allspice."

Don Antonio has heard and read how nations of the past have

grown great and rich from spices, and how memorable spice monopolies have been gained and held at least for a time by means of whips, guns, and fire, then quite inevitably have been lost, because producing earth rarely tolerates manmade monopolies. He has read, too, how one after another the great tropical spices, like most other great tropical crops, have been carried completely around the globe from their places of origin, and thereby made valuable immigrants.

Within his own district Don Antonio has come upon several spice crops, and, as noted, he has planted, grown, harvested, and cured excellent spices for his own table and for the plainly expressed satisfaction of his Indian workers, who now number about forty good and loyal men. He has begun cultivating several types of edible peppers, which he regards as one of the more important indigenous food crops, and he continues to expand his experiments with the spices, not that he plans to go into the business, as Tia Josefina did, but rather, first, to satisfy his own farming curiosity and to demonstrate the crops for the benefit of his workmen and neighbors. When and if the latter are interested, he gives them planting stock. This, as the Don learned to say in English back in Philadelphia, is how crops get started. In a broader sense he also believes it is how the tropics gain self-realization.

Don Antonio would like to make a success of some of the spices, as his bellhop companions in Philadelphia used to say, "just for the hell of it." Much more ardently he would like to become a good orchardist of the tropics. After lengthening years of working and looking, Antonio (known in Philadelphia and later in Detroit simply as Tony) is convinced that tropical fruits remain the most tragically neglected of all the great tropical crops.

When the North American or the European thinks of tropical fruits he usually thinks of bananas—now that oranges, lemons, and other great citruses have ceased being tropical. Antonio knows several reasons for this. As a banana grower, and his banana "cuts" duly sold to United Fruit keep on providing a substantial part of his farm-sustaining profits, he is *simpatico* with the credo just mentioned.

However, like most Central Americans, Don Antonio loathes both the flavor and the sight of bananas; he grows and sells them for necessary money, not love; and he points out that the banana is not and never was a real fruit.

The foregoing is mildly technical and perhaps slightly debatable, but Don Antonio insists there is nothing debatable nor technical about the reality that people in general, including altogether too many tropical people, simply have never had a chance to learn how superbly delicious real tropical fruits are.

As one worthy instance he points to the mango, sometimes called the apple of the tropics, whose epicurean virtues place it among the best three fruits that grow from earth. Don Antonio explains in detail that flavorwise, the mango is truly superlative, this even though it continues to grow from scrub or seedling stock. Tersely and convincingly, Antonio points out that if temperate-zone peaches, apples, pears, and other standbys were treated as scurvily, the entire list of deciduous or temperate-zone fruits could barely qualify as pig feed.

The same holds for dozens more of the deplorably neglected tropical fruits, including the avocado or butter pear (which Guatemala and Mexico combinedly have given to the world), the litchi, the most revered of the many great fruits of lower China (and direly maligned by the dehydrated wreckage commonly served in Chinese-American restaurants), the kaki, misnamed the "Japanese persimmon"; the guava, one of the most magnificent of all the natural flavors; the papaya, the great tree melon of the American tropics; the superbly delicious zapote or *chico-zapote* fruit (from the chicle or chewing-gum tree which is also native to Guatemala); the truly magnificent tropical grapes; the superlative "peach palm" fruit; the deliciously podded bacaba, the cherimoya, which many Guatemalan Indians still believe was the chosen fruit of their olden gods, and the mangosteen.

Tropical fruits, according to an old Guatemalan proverb, are a particular gift of the lesser gods to the greater gods. Not one who contradicts proverbs, Don Antonio believes that tropical fruits were also meant for the good of people.

He can name many other great tropical crops which people need even more urgently. Grains, for example, the first great children of tropical agriculture, and the edible fats are the next most necessary progeny.

Like the lingering majority of tropical countries, Guatemala has never yet produced enough grains or enough fats to feed its own people. Plainly rice and corn are the most feasible hopes for fulfilling its need for grains, and cultivated palms are the best hope for a homeland sufficiency of edible oils or fats.

At present Guatemala, like several other countries in the American tropics, is making notable progress at planting palm crops, particularly the African oil palms, and even the comparatively slight first harvests are helping to overcome the customary home shortages of edible fats by producing edible oils and soap ingredients.

But the nagging tropical dilemma of grain shortage stays on, dealing avoidable hunger and the crippling expense of importing grains and impeding and penalizing livestock growth, which with sufficient grain would probably succeed.

Guatemala is one of the memorable homelands of corn or Maya maize which, as noted, has now become the most valuable of all crops. But the ancient strains of corn which sustained earlier eras of *Guatemalticos* have become degenerate. Average yields of native highland corns have shrunken to rarely more than five or six bushels per cultivated acre. Like other thoughtful farmers, Don Antonio is convinced that restoration of tropical corn crops is possible by means of hybrid types which in the United States have proved to be the greatest agricultural advance of the century. But the tasks incident to developing and adapting strains of corn that are suited to the ever-varying altitudes and rainfall rates of the tropics are far from easy. Time, work, trial, and error at wholesale are prerequisite to attainment and the particularly valuable goal is still somewhat distant.

On a few plots Antonio Ramirez has succeeded in producing promising hybrid corn, but the venture is still experimental and the thoughtful farmer is by no means certain that he will live long enough to complete all the succeeding experiments which are evidently required.

The Don also experiments with rice, the second greatest grain crop of man, which continues to provide primary subsistence for more than a billion people and for no fewer than half a billion tropical people. Yet strangely rice has never gained any widespread foothold as a crop for the western tropics, even though many types of rice can be grown effectively in this sphere of earth.

Don Antonio has viewed excellent rice cultivations in nearby

Honduras and more distant Ecuador. He knows that from Cuba south to the Amazon, rice is one of the most cherished of staple foods, yet he knows that for generations, indeed for centuries, the American tropics have imported rice by the millions of tons from the other side of the earth, from Siam, Indo-China, India, Indonesia, Ceylon, and lower China.

*Arroz con pollo* remains one of the most cherished foods of Caribbean peoples, even though the *pollo* is frequently monkey meat or iguana (because as likely as not chicken is not available) and the *arroz* must be imported expensively from lower Asia or, in these times of upset currencies and trade balances, from the expensive flatlands of Arkansas and Louisiana. Don Antonio has pondered this bewildering fact, and he has made test plantings of rice on his own *finca.* To date his most successful harvest has been of the red, dryland rice from the nearer west fringe of Equatorial Africa. This finding encourages the thoughtful farmer. But he believes that the "right kind" of rice may remain in the doubtful borning for a long time to come, since it is likely to involve the toilsome merging of several distant strains of rice.

The Don points out that the latter recourse, though frequently expensive and time-consuming, is certainly not impossible, since other great crops are being "passed around from half-way round the globe"—Philippine abacá or "Manila hemp," for example, from the hardy banana cousin called *Musa textilis.*

Don Antonio believes steadfastly, that if tropical farming is ever to realize its destinies, a far greater variety of crops is absolutely necessary. He holds no grudge against the word "necessary." Most of his life he has been viewing and striving to answer one necessity after the next. In Philadelphia he heard and memorized in English the fine old adage about necessity being the mother of invention. He had memorized a parallel Spanish proverb during his first uniformed term in a Guatemalan grade school, and still earlier, from his Indian mother he learned a closely similar proverb in the old and unwritten language of the Quiches.

As an able tri-linguist, Don Antonio prefers English for strength and directness, Spanish for poetry, the old Guatemala Indian tongue for philosophy. Yet above all he prefers farming which, all in one, is business, poetry, and philosophy, plus motion and mutation.

He sees the tropics, his own land and similar lands, as the great and enduring cradle of productivity, the waiting womb of abundance.

He tills and plants, harvests, judges, and plants again with the facile conviction that once adequately learned and put to use, the mighty facilities of tropical agriculture, both local and globe-circling, will erase want throughout the world, make strife and warfare as futile and uncouth as Gringo comic books or hat styles, and provide business, poetry, and philosophy for all mankind. As Don Antonio sees and feels it, no thoughtful farmer can believe otherwise.

## MOZO

IN THE tropics, as in the temperate zones, there are increasing numbers of thoughtful farmers. In the tropics, more markedly than in the United States, the principal kinds or types of farmers are readily classified. There is a growing and particularly important minority of working, proprietary farmers such as Don Antonio Ramirez.

There are the large-scale planters and ranchers who are rather more likely to be encountered in New York, Paris, London, Lisbon, Estoril, or the South of France, wars and politics permitting, than at home. And, inevitably, there are the farm workers, who are rarely tenants, usually underpaid laborers, and still too frequently peons, vassals, or quasi-slaves. More or less uniformly, and frequently cruelly, the people of the latter group are poor. For the most part, poverty and prejudice have given them little chance to be good farmers even though many have very real agrarian talents. Unfortunately, the tropics, more markedly than most other spheres of earth outside the regimented steppes and slave camps of the U.S.S.R., remain cursed with the hobnailed but otherwise bodyless legend of classes and masses.

Speaking as one reporter, I suspect, distrust, resent, and seek to dispute all such legends. Certainly, no reporter worth his salt can talk of classes and masses in the United States. We simply do not have classes and masses, and with extremely few exceptions, save for the sorrowful stain of Negro slavery, we have never had classes and masses in any durable reality. We remain a people of Jefferson, the shrewd but sympathetic lawyer; of Lincoln, the rail-splitter who became President; of Johnston, the blacksmith who became President; of Mark Twain, Cal Coolidge, Will Rogers (far more shrewd than witty); of Harry Truman, (perhaps more successful as President than as proprietor of a men's shop in furthermost Missouri); of office boys become business leaders, of rich men's sons gone screwball or otherwise; of laundry checkers turned movie queens; of peddlers changed to heads of corporation.

All this is fitting and proper, since nations with frontiers of space and spirit, with malleable economics and great resources in use, have neither room nor reason for classes and masses. The latter words are illusionary, and in these parts remain profitable only to warped brains and inveterate phonies, such as gossip columnists with phony names and so-called "society editors" with phony intentions and jobs on city newspapers which themselves could stand a small bit of integrity.

Yet in many tropical countries there appear to remain classes and masses. As one reporter I question both the validity and the durability of the classes or masses in the tropics. But for the time and for these few pages, suppose we grant there are tropical masses, meanwhile holding the term classes for sober verification.

There are many local or regional names for the masses: tribesmen, bushmen, and carriers, as granted by Belgian, French, Spanish, Portuguese, and, alas, British exploiters, the great majority of whom stank strongly; also *brutos, ladinos, cholos, peons, Mozos,* and so on, as taken from colony-sucking Spaniards who still smell and, from present as well as past indications, always will.

For the most part, names for the poor farmer workers in the tropics are neither eloquent nor accurate. But they are names in common usage, and anyone who lives and works in the tropics inevitably learns the local label. He learns a great deal more than that. Almost invariably he learns the likelihood that human and bona fide relations with tropical peoples tend to follow an arithmetic progression. If you hold them in contempt they hold you in at least twice as much contempt. If you openly hate or despise them, they privately hate and despise you at least four times as much. If you revile them, privately or otherwise, they revile you at least eight times as much. On the other hand, if you like and respect them, they like and respct you at least sixteen times as much. In the nearer tropics one meets the so-called Mozo. Almost invariably he speaks for himself. And as a rule he speaks for the too-little-privileged people throughout all tropics.

The best of good mornings to you, Señor, and *muchas gracias* for speaking *buenos días* to the Mozo. For I am that Señor, a Mozo—child of the banana flood plains—swinger of the machete—in Colombia, Honduras, Nicaragua, Costa Rica and Cuba, and other places all so very much the same. Just at this time I am helper to the head mule man of this banana plantation and I no longer swing the machete. But I remain a Mozo; that is my life, which I do not regret.

We Mozos are pretty much the same wherever you find us. Blood of Indian, Negro, or Carib, of Spaniard or other white men. Remember, Señor, South America and Central America and perhaps most other warm countries are melting pots the same as your country. All of us alike are what you call conglomerate peoples. A few drops of this blood and a few drops of that. In some part our Spanish blood and Spanish ways are real, Señor. But our Spanish blood is thin, and underneath the skin runs the same red animal blood of all men and the thick, good blood of the Indian or the Negro or the two mixed. In my way I am humble; much of the time I am kindly, and I am silly in the way of all people. Like so many others everywhere, I oftentimes play the game called cheating the tortilla.

The game is like this. A Mozo takes a tortilla and wraps it around a strip of beef. When dinner time comes he sits in the shade, squeezes the wrapper of tortilla to make the hard beef slip up into his mouth. Then he slips another piece of meat into the same tortilla and squeezes it into his mouth. That way the same tortilla lasts two days, three days, or until all the meat is gone, and only the wretched tortilla remains. The game is called "cheating the tortilla."

Plainly a silly game, Señor, very silly. Yet I have seen it played many times, Señor, and I have played it myself. I'm a simple man, yet even I know that the Mozo isn't cheating the tortilla at all. He is cheating himself—out of the tortilla which belongs with meat in order to make a better fare than the meat alone can give. Yes, Señor. These *Américas del Sur* are tortilla-cheating countries; also Mozo countries. But not all cheating the tortilla is done by us Mozos. You Gringos are doing it, too, and also the Britishers, Germans, Italians, Japanese, also the Russians—all come here and cheat tortillas in their own somewhat silly ways. . . .

Forgive me, Señor, while I go start frying some rice and beans and eggs for our breakfast. Señor, you Yanquis are not the worst tortilla cheaters—nor the stupidest. But oftentimes you are the rudest. Germans and Japanese, even Italians behave better, sing more, and cuss less than you Gringos. The British are what you call smug muddlers. They help themselves first. The Russians they are mainly solemn, self-helping, and also crazy. They learn Spanish and mix among us Mozos. They speak our language. They pat our shoulders. But their brains are shut tight, and they will not learn how we think. To them any country is a loud-talking religion without shrines. They preach not about God but about politics. They serve a master, but, strangely, that master seems to be themselves—their own very personal welfares and egos.

Pardon, Señor! The rice is scorching, and already the eggs are hard like old donkey dung. . . . Yes, Señor, and there is also Mexico which is close and to us much more real than the United States. Mexico is also big—the biggest thing we know for certain. Also Mexico raises up her fists quick and snarls even when she is not really mad. Indeed, Mexicans are somewhat different from the rest of us *Americanos del Sur,* quicker to learn and to grab. . . . In new banana operations Mexicans come down and take jobs like driving the steam locos and coupling the cars—the big and exciting jobs. Nevertheless, when they call us their brothers as after tequila and beers, we are somehow proud. That is why when we get mad at your Gringos we holler "*Viva Mexicanos!*" Only because we like Mexicans a little better than we like you. But not too much better. . . .

*Gracias,* Señor! I'll take the machete now—the sharp one in the leader scabbard. It is Yankee-made. The others are German-made and no damn good. Long ago Germany made good machetes. Then German steel became shoddy and dull—almost as shabby as the Japanese kind. It is evil to send bad knives, Señor, since knives must cut well. Yes, *Amigo,* the sunshine already grows warm.

But now, before siesta comes, again let me tell you another thing about Mozos. We live in our own world. We don't want to be roped and bound by what you Gringos call "isms" or any other foreign causes. In these you, or nobody else, can count on us for lasting loyalties. It is not that we are disloyal; only that you keep calling to us from another world.

That is what Communists also do. Don Modesto Gonzales, a very wise lawyer and poet, tells me that, to the North American or Russian or European, "Communist" means something quite apart from what it means to us here where it is warm. Here, *Communist* is hardly more than a word in politics—what one party calls the other at election time and between elections what the ones who are in office call the ones who would like to be in office, or the other way around. Anyway, Señor, Communism simply does not belong in lands such as ours. Don Modesto says that Communism is for big cold countries that have many big cities where poor people can easily starve and where men must work close together in factories or shops or stores or lounge together on sidewalks and cobblestones where corn and beans will not grow.

I think that is perhaps right, Señor. Men do not truly nor quickly starve in these countries—at least, not just now. When one is hungry and cannot earn his beans, he can take over a bit of land and borrow or beg or maybe steal a few handfuls of corn or beans to plant a *milpa* or garden. He can take his machete and whack down palm trees, and in a few days he can build a shack that is forever free of rent. Then perhaps he can borrow or take over a pig or a few hens and plant a few more eyes of seed. Also catch fish, and if he has a gun he can shoot deer or waterfowl. He can live—in one way or another—at least till sickness strikes him down or there come to be too many people to act accordingly. By law and by use, the land here is still for people. The rights of what you call squatters are most real rights in all our countries here, though maybe not in other tropics.

So when Russians or *Norteamericanos* or others who call themselves Communists come here and tell us that we must join the Party and carry green cards to keep ourselves from starving, we do not believe them, Señor. We have never joined the Communists before, and we have never carried green cards before, and we have never yet starved, for here in our tropics the summer thus far is forever. . . .

*Sapristo!* It grows late, Señor! Already almost too late for work! . . .

Like the Communists keep forgetting—we Mozos can live without working forever. We hire ourselves to work only when we want to have money in our pockets to buy ourselves clothes and fancy things, or make love to women or to drink fancy licker, or to hear sweet music played. When we work we want pay in money for buying, not in "isms" or printed cards. For we honestly wonder if the "isms" come and the money ceases to come, what, or whom, will we then be working for, if we work? And will we like it? Maybe we would like it better not to work at all—just to go back and live from our *milpas* and woods and rivers and boil our salt from sea water. Yet all the "isms" I have yet heard, Señor, all of them say "Work!" but they do not tell exactly why or for what or whom.

The breakfast is now coolish, Señor. The rice is a little greasy and the eggs are quite hard but still good for the hunger, Señor, the hunger of plain men. So while plain men eat plain food let us talk of less plain men, Señor: the grand dons who live in the so-much-talked-about Spanish or top-crust way. Well, if you are wondering, then I will tell you that these Spaniard ways are only a floppy, thin cloak worn to cover what is called by the Gringo a very immense inferiority complex.

It takes a Mozo to know a don, Señor, and so I will tell you what our don, "our high-caste Latin," really is. . . . He is one who thinks first of his own dignity and ease. That is what causes him to pay his debts, wash his body, and give his wife a new dress for the *fiera* or *fiesta*. Yet he is rarely ever loyal to anybody or anything, except possibly himself, though more likely, in the truthful way, not even that. He will lead his own parade, Señor, even if he must march alone. But he cannot live entirely alone because usually he is neither wise nor strong nor busy enough for that. So he comes to depend on his woman or women.

They say of your country that those United States is a man's country. Maybe, to that I say, only *maybe.* I doubt and I am not too sure. But these Americas of the South are mostly women's countries. For here the women usually do the running for all of the dons.

Here in the *Américas del Sur,* the don, the high-caste *hombre* is a guest in his own home; he never really lives there. So long as there is food he can eat it any hour of the day or night. He is petted and babied. Yes, Señor, the don is spoiled from babyhood up. Indeed, from the start the son is adored and pleased by the mama, the sister, the grandmama, urged to make love too soon for his natural time, let to grow up soft and flabby with petting. Usually it is the sister, not the brother, who feels the whip or the spanking hand, who learns to work and to serve others as well as herself.

That is why, down here, the señora is usually stronger than the don and not so silly, why the don is too often a spoiled man who can like you deeply for five minutes—then in half an hour hate your guts and speak wickedly behind your back. The Mozo is no don. And the Mozo will not believe in the foreign "isms" for any great number of minutes or hours. Of course it is true here that too many of our few roads lead only to the country estates of the *Presidente* or one of his high-up Ministers. But no "ism" from other lands will change this either, and kindly remember, Señor, that whatever loyalty we have to give must not be spread around too far.

This is the Mozo nature, Señor, and human nature as well. The don has it also. Like on the coffee *fincas,* when a landlord gives a tenant just one tiny electric light to hang in his hut, or half a cartload of dead coffee bush to feed his cooking fire, or possibly a partly spoiled pineapple to eat, then very often the *patrón* wishes to whoop and shake hands with himself and tell all the world of his own immense generosity and wonderful openhandedness.

But mostly the don *patrón* does not choose to tell the world that the coffee-growing Mozo must swing a machete or strip bush or heave berry baskets and heavy bags or shovel away in the *beneficios* or drying plants for six or eight hours for a very few centavos daily. Indeed, when coffee is priced like of today, Señor, you pay for one pound all of as much as the coffee-growing Mozo is paid for four long days of work, which is barely enough to buy his rice and beans, never enough to lift him out of debt.

So, plainly, Señor, it is not more "isms" but more monies paid out and good things bought and sold more freely that will do good for all of us, for us small ones and those big ones alike. So remember, accordingly, that when you hear talk of North America and South America and Central America falling forever apart, please remember our liking for and our need for what you call the greenback—the pesetas—the folding money. That last we like and need much more than we like or need these "isms" brought here from those many far places.

The sun grows hot and the shadows get fatter. It is almost noontime and still we sit and talk. *Poco a poco!* But there will be other days. There will always be tall weeds to slash with the machetes. Besides which, philosophy is sweet, Señor—sweeter even than the salty sweat of banana fields.

The ways and thoughts of men change, Señor; but in hot countries they change maybe not so fast as in the cold countries. That is another thing many of you *Norteamericanos* do not truly comprehend about us tropicals.

You see airplanes flying above the jungles. You see Mozos sliding from the backs of packmules or the beds of bull carts and climbing into new and shiny airplanes and you say, "Latin America she changes from oxcart to aviation overnight!"

On the smooth surface, and in one small way, she does change, Señor! But not nearly so much changing goes on underneath that smooth surface. Deep inside most of us *tropicos* it stays much like our fathers were.

Look at our countries more closely and for a longer time and still you see most of what you saw a lifetime before. You see the same kind of palm shacks with many clay chamberpots and fat pigs which the children lead on leashes and let sleep in the houses when they are good. And you will still see the peddlers who come to sell tangerines strung on raffia cords. Indeed, Señor, you see that the Caribbean moon and the other tropical moons are yet beautiful and bright. There are still no hammers and cycles painted on the moon and no drapery of foreign flags there.

And you will note, too, Señor, that the new brides and grooms can still be happy on dirt floors; also that the *mujeres,* our women folk, still hang their washings flat on the ground and pound the hell out of them with clubs like olden times. And we still keep our Bakeries of Divine Providence and our Butcher Shops of Sublime and Holy Peace.

The true blossoms still look very bright and beautiful in the moonlight. There is also great age, here, Señor. Particularly our cities stay wrapped with the centuries and washed with the mists of long ago—this even though the tin or tile roofs may be cluttered with radio wires. Our old women still wear black. Most of us still go barefoot, and to this very day most of us have kept our strength of back and arms.

You still see our country women with hindparts built like those of prizefighters, our burden carriers with shoulder slings and forehead straps who can lift their own weight and half as much again and carry it all day.

You still see the cobblers who strip off the beef hides and carry them straight to their shops. You see ox teams with drivers that rest beside the dusty mountain road and while resting take the time to smell of the wild roses. And you see our happy soldiers who take off their shoes and pick shady places and prop their feet to the level of their chins and quickly go to sleep. For here the world is at noontime.

Ah, noontime! Pardon, Señor, while I go call the mule boy to put on saddles. I will holler *"Chico!"* like that. And he will not answer. Then I will holler again. And then I will walk out and find that no-good *hijo* snoozing in the shade. So then I will smack him and shake him, and he will tell me that the mules are all busy packing in bananas and that the machete swingers have already cut overmany *hectares* and there is no reason why we should bother with the banana fields now. I know that boy, *Chico.* I know what he will say. Indeed, yes, and what he will say is true. No doubt it is better, Señor, that we ride to the fields tomorrow and that just now we sleep. . . .

## MALAY MAN

THE Mozo is a man of many races with considerable definition and some degree of steadfastness. He is a product of environment, far more than racial or "blood-line" factors.

I thought out the foregoing in Spanish and I have tried to reassemble it in English for better or worse, possibly the latter. The real point is that the admixing, crossing, and interbreeding of races within the tropics has now become the usual and the preponderant. Between the Tropics of Cancer and Capricorn there are comparatively few long-time pure-strain peoples remaining. For the most part these few have remained "unmixed" for more or less exceptional causes, such as extreme isolation or fanatical credos of caste, as usually allied with fanatical religions.

In the broader sense, the rarely literal racial boundaries of the tropics continue to fade. Tropical skins tend to grow darker. Close at our own doorways, for example, great Cuba is rapidly changing to a black man's island, and, second only to Africa, the Caribbean has become the great black incubator. Despite all the national statutes to the contrary, its black people are pouring ever farther into Central and South America. Brazil has changed to a preponderantly and exceptionally promising nation of colored peoples.

The loose talk of races meanwhile, like the even looser fables of social registries and other wishful studbooks for human breeding, has stumbled and sprawled into sheerest babble. The "yellow race" tends toward brown while the "brown race" tends toward yellow or black. Such jabberwocky as "Polynesian," which never meant precisely anything anyhow, means even less today. "Negro" is a one-time Spanish and Portuguese colloquialism meaning black man or dark man and, by implied usage, an African.

But, as any amateur anthropologist knows, there are many different African races, some featuring the whitest of all peoples. Meanwhile, the word "Negro" has become so wretchedly meaningless that some of the most astute of African courts, such as the distinguished Supreme Court of Liberia, for example, have given up all hope of ever defining "Negro" competently and therefore are obliged to substitute such dodge phrases as "persons of African descent" which, of course, would include Egyptians, Arabs, Portuguese, Spaniards, English, French, Chinese, Syrians, Americans, Swiss, Turks, and only God knows who else.

The word "Indian," which began as a misnomer when Columbus found Santo Domingo which he hoped would be India, continues to expand and multiply as a misnomer. The poor old flimsy label "Caucasian," meaning peoples originating west of the Caucasus mountains, obviously and as a matter of judiciary and other records includes all known degrees and types of skin pigmentation. And the designation of races in terms of mere nations, land surfaces, or ever-changing religions is showing the laxity and looping whackiness of a post-midnight session at an inexhaustible bar.

As I stated the foregoing which, however trite, is the way it looks to me, the Malay man, in a white linen suit tailored in downtown New York, clapped his brown hands to summon the waiter and took another Camel from his hammered silver case. "The great trouble," he confided, as he lit the cigarette with a Ronson lighter and gazed out at the languid waterfront of Singapore, "the great trouble with you reporters is that you believe too much of what you hear."

I agreed with his general treatise but hurried to point out that a great many reporters, in time, cease believing anything they hear; that I, as a graying tyro and tropical tramp, strive for the medium, the golden mean of Plato, meanwhile keeping my erasers dry.

The Malaya man smiled wearily. "I am a mere historian. It is customary in your country to believe a historian for a few months or a year or so, then to discard him altogether. Personally, I prefer to have people believe only a small part of what I say and to believe that little for a long time."

He tossed away somewhat more than half his cigarette and continued: "History is truth and truth is like the pearls that come from the Penang oysters which have fed some of my not too distinguished forebearers for the past ten thousand years; it is precious and it is eternal. However, only once in a year or several years, and millions of oysters, does the true pearl appear. But when it does," he lit another cigarette and blew an almost perfect smoke ring, "it is both precious and immortal."

Turning to the blue-robed waiter, who was one of the rather amazing fuzzy-headed pygmies from the farther inland mountains, the man of Malaya ordered two double Scotches and soda without ice, then tossed away his almost unused cigarette and began telling me why and how Malaya has become the most classic demonstration of the mixing of tropical races and why it therefore remains the most memorable of all tropical lands.

The historian began drinking his double Scotch and opened his lecture by naming a highly tentative date, perhaps about 5,000 B.C., when Negroid Papuans and the cannibalistic ancestors of Australian aborigines lounged, fought, and fished on the southernmost bridgehead between the continent of Asia and the Malay archipelago, this prior to crossing to the great fertile island of Sumatra and thereafter to New Guinea and Australia.

He paused to explain that he takes his facts from archeology, anthropology, liberal history, and the mountains of oyster shells that his forefathers left. He made way with his first drink and ordered another which turned out to be almost exactly the color of his skin. "On the heels of these Papuans—" he continued—"and by that I mean about three thousand years later in calendar time, another great migration followed from Yünnan, these a Nesiot or Indonesian people—forebearers also of the Sakai of the Malaya mountains, various hill tribes of Indo-China, Formosa, Borneo, even South China. . . ."

He consumed his second drink while amplifying the latter statement and obtained a refill. "Duly blended with a Mongol strain, these people became the Proto-Malay. Along with them, or within a few centuries of them, came the curly-haired Pygmies called Negritos, a few of whom still are in the north of Malaya and continue to taint the blood of so many, perhaps most, Malayans. But the Malayan today—" the historian took up his fourth Scotch—"the civilized Malay is a descendant of the Porto-Malay mixed with modern Indian, Chinese, and Arab."

The whisky-brown historian properly squelched my mumbled suggestion about getting to a point by stating that he had already got to one and was rapidly passing it. . . . "The point is that Malaya today as yesterday is far and away the most cosmopolitan cluster of countries on the face of the earth—the consummated wedding and welding of many nationalities and practically all the great races and religions of earth. It is a merging and welding not only of people but of time. For here in Malaya ten thousand years are as one with today, and the migration and merging of peoples is as one with life itself. Furthermore, Malaya is the most typical of tropical countries. . . ."

My informant finished his drink, smacked his lips discreetly, and added: "The ready migration and mixing of peoples now and in time to come is the best hope for tropical salvation." This historian admitted that through the centuries many leaders and usurpers of states have become converted to the need for the resettlement and intermingling of people in order to sustain empire, nations, or even colonies. He added that Malaya today is the world's best example of a federation of nations as created by migrations of people and kept alive by transfusions with newcomers. He names it, therefore, a tropical model for the present and future. Its history of resettlement and racial admixtures began with wars, intrigues, conspiracies, opium, and violent lusts for profits. What historians call modern Malaya was born of these, plus shameless exploitation.

Specifically, in 1641, the Dutch captured the rich Malaccan port colony, having first dug in at Batavia on the Sunda Strait, to build the working headquarters of what was shortly to become the mighty Dutch East India Company. But Britain's East India Company likewise demanded consideration. In 1795 Britain grabbed Singapore, with Malacca included, for use as a naval base against an impressively hostile French fleet. Then in 1818, with Napoleon out of the way, the British restored Singapore to Holland in keeping with the terms of the London Convention, but ten years later, by another turn of power politics, Britain took over Singapore again and some of the lands behind it and alongside, notably Penang and Malacca, all of which became in time the Straits Settlements, which for several decades thereafter remained the opium stronghold of the world.

The Straits Settlements promptly became a foremost military outpost of the British lifeline, a first far garrison between the Indian Ocean and the South Pacific, and this because Singapore snuggles closely to rich Sumatra, provides sea outlets for many great exports of Southeast Asia, and guards the way to Australia. The first British Governor of the Straits, appointed in 1867, assumed the title of Commander-in-Chief and headed an Executive Council which included the local commander of troops. The original legislative council for the Straits Settlements included the Commander-in-Chief as president and a well-stacked group of twenty-six members, thirteen officials and thirteen "unofficials," the latter including Chinese and Indians, but all British subjects and certified yes men.

This structure remained little changed for three-quarters of a century, and grew to be an almost classic example of arbitrary, makeshift colonial government. As recently as 1941 His Majesty's "historians" explained that the "unofficial members" of the Straits Settlements' legislative council were nominated and not elected owing to the difficulty of compiling an electoral roll from a floating population of many races and the impracticality of distinguishing between British subjects and foreigners at a polling place, adding that "Only a few Europeans and Straits-born Chinese inclined to democratic self-government. . . ." The latter statement, never very convincing, stands completely disproved by more recent Malayan history. But impressively, and for the best part of a century, the exceptionally noteworthy tropical melting pot remained under the vigilant eye and spoon handle of a distant and determined stirrer.

Britain tolerated the native chiefs and Sultan and certain other local "rulers," permitted them to collect taxes from their vassals and other victims, but paired each one with a British-appointed "Resident" whose advice had to be asked and acted upon on all questions other than those touching "Malay religion and customs."

Meanwhile, between 1874 and 1880, four more Malay states in the nearby hinterlands were taken under British "protection," and in 1895 they were "federalized" under a Resident-General who was Her or His Majesty's official ball-and-chain to the respective Sultans. Later, in 1909, when Malayan resources in rubber and tin had grown to world importance, Britain's "Governor" became High Commissioner with a superbly stacked federal council.

Even so, Malaya remained a particularly noteworthy example of a tropical melting pot with an unrivaled talent for coagulating almost fabulous wealth. As the archipelago became both a tin and rubber stronghold of commanding importance, the almost incredible profits that poured out of the slender and somewhat fragmentary horn of Southeast Asia left a discernible trail of local improvements: a first postal service, a Malayan civil service, an institute for medical research, a manual training school, a normal school for Malay teachers, one medical college, scatterings of separated elementary schools for Malays, Chinese, and Indians, one principal railway, valuable docks at Penang, and a fairly well-mechanized port at Singapore.

It became entirely evident that a heterogeneous people, assembled in a tropical area of exceptional resources, can produce tremendous wealth. But the latter slipped all too easily out of the overly trustful hands which actually produced it. Aggressive Chinese merchants swarmed into even the most remote of the provincial capitals. As the rich earth of the little archipelago yielded ever greater wealth to the plantation and mining companies, most Malays, even though they were being sunk ever deeper into peonage, remained loyal to their enfeebled Sultans and to their miniature homelands.

Despite all its mix-ups of peoples, Malaya had become a nation, and despite its super-exploitation, it somehow remained one. The whisky-tinted historian stresses this fact as an inspiring wall writing for the tropical world tomorrow.

He notes, also, that as a matter of known and proved reality, the British and other self-rationalizing exploiters gave the country very little which it did not already have. They brought in the great Amazon Basin Hevea rubber tree. But private enterprise and native planters, either singly or together, have introduced that crop throughout many eastern tropics and great areas of Equatorial Africa, and the likelihood stands that Malays themselves could and would have introduced Hevea rubber and made it a successful and important crop.

Certainly the British opium monopoly, which earlier had made the East India Company wickedly rich, did not help Malaya. The tin resources had long been known; five centuries before the British came, Malaccan Sultans had minted coins made of tin, and by 1780 such enterprising American financiers as Alexander Hamilton were apparently itching to invest money in Malay tin.

Agriculturally, long before either the Dutch or British came and took, Malaya had become outstanding. Numerous valley clearings already bore pineapples, mangosteens, and other delectable tropical fruit; bananas and rice fields thrived in the lowlands, and vast groves of coconut fronted the sea. Malay fisheries had already become renowned throughout the Orient, as had Malay ocean craft and ports.

Most of what Britain actually planted in Malaya was British capital, roughly a hundred million pounds of it. The ever-diverse people and the good, rich tropical earth did most of the rest. The original three Straits Settlements, including the mangrove swamp which eventually grew into the great island port of Singapore and the good and more or less age-old ports of Penang and Malacca, cover a combined land area somewhat smaller than the present city of Los Angeles. But as a group they were blessed with that tropical rarity, a deep-water harbor, plus protection from storms and exceptional freedom from local pirates.

Britain's founding of the Hong Kong Colony in 1842 robbed the Straits Settlements of much of their once decisive Chinese trade; French conquest of Indo-China had further reduced the tallies, as did the aggressive launching of Dutch shipping services between Holland, India, Sumatra, and Java. Even so, by 1900 Singapore had become one of the world's ten greatest ocean ports. As the British-boomed industries of rubber and tin gained world-wide leadership and great additional immigration poured into the archipelago, Singapore, in particular, became the clearing center for myriad cargoes of cotton, hardware, tobacco, and foodstuffs from Europe, India, and the United States, and the clearing center for weighty and valuable exports from all parts of the archipelago and lush, hot Siam as well.

By 1926 American and British demands for tin and rubber had boomed Malayan trade to well over one and a quarter billion dollars a year, which was more than that of all other British colonies combined. Even in the direly depressed 1930's, Malayan trade rivaled that of India and far exceeded the totals of all Africa. Notably, too, by the middle 1920's the United States had become Malaya's number-one customer, buying more than 40 per cent of all its rubber and more than 55 per cent of all its tin. Britain was a weak second, with about 19 per cent of the rubber and 7 per cent of the tin, while France,

Germany, the Netherlands, Italy, and Japan straggled along in that order. Singapore, meanwhile, lived and grew by the doctrine of comparatively free trade, a doctrine for which the British deserve some amount of credit, though Malayans deserve at least as much.

The Malay man in the white linen suit tailored in downtown New York enjoys recounting the eminent attainments in internationalism of this much-mixed tropical nation, on the grounds that tropical advantages, plus the seemingly inevitable admixture of tropical races, provide a particularly bright vista of the sort of internationalism that makes greater history and contributes to a better world.

In this connection he points out that in the instance of Malaya, at least, the intuitive judgment of the tropical man has excelled the profit-lustful speculations of the alien Western powers. For example, second only to opium, which by wicked promotion had become the British East India Company's most prosperous tropical enterprise, were the spices. Almost one and a half centuries ago, directors of the East India Company saw a chance for supplying British markets with cloves, nutmeg, and peppers from Penang. Accordingly, by 1847 at least half the island of Penang was covered with nutmeg and clove plantations. But a mysterious blight killed the trees. One after another, would-be profit crops, including sugar and coffee, failed. Rice and coconuts persisted, but at the time neither was a fortune builder. Then, in 1877, Malaya received the seed of Hevea rubber trees, stolen grandiloquently from Brazil and transferred with Her Majesty's sanction from Kew Gardens to the newly founded Botanic Gardens at Singapore.

By 1897 Malay's total of rubber plantings had risen to 345 acres, and seedling rubber trees had been transplanted to Ceylon, Java, Sumatra, Indo-China, and Siam, as well as to many parts of Malaya. Within forty years the first 345 Malayan acres of Hevea rubber trees has grown to 3,320,170 acres, to become the world stronghold of commercial rubber production. Almost two-thirds of the total were the property of alien rubber companies, about 70 per cent of them British, a few French, Belgian, and Danish firms, about 16 per cent Chinese, and 9 per cent Indians and other Asiatics. "Small-holders," some of them Malays, owned the tiny remainder.

Thus Britannia, for a momentously profitable era, ruled the rubber. But during that era, substantial areas of Malaya were reduced to cooliedom. The import of docile, perennially hungry rubber labor from India promptly passed the half-million mark. In this and other ways, the traditionally active tropical immigration into Malaya was both stimulated and deranged. Further, much of the best land of the archipelago was taken over by alien lease structures, which permitted no more than a remote drizzle of the rubber wealth to return to the land and people who so largely gave it birth and sustenance.

By 1925, in all the peninsula-archipelago the proportion of Malays had fallen to 42.4 per cent of the total population, or a mere 2,169,000, while the Chinese population had soared to 2,114,000 or 41.3 per cent. The starvelings from India, preponderantly rubber-plantation or mine laborers, comprised almost 15 per cent. And though Malaya had foaled an estimated twenty thousand millionaires in the greater London area alone, most Malayans stayed lean on their enforced diet of imported rice, much of it undergrade. Even so, in one way or the next, Malaya remained a nation.

"Amazing" is perhaps the best word for it. The life-sustaining native agriculture had been ruinously neglected and figuratively crucified by the lusty wealth grabbers from the distant and foggy West. What might have been life-sustaining palm plantations had become owned almost entirely by foreign capital. By 1925 native crops, including rice, coconuts, vegetables, fruits, cattle, hogs, and poultry, failed to feed as many as one-fourth of the people. The local industries were deplorably weak and, in major areas, completely nonexistent. Chinese interests controlled most of the banana and pineapple production. But nobody controlled the rampant practice of usury, which next to hunger and decimating poverty was the Malay's heaviest cross.

Somebody, preponderantly British somebodies, did control the tin, which, with the uproarious growth of the motor age and the canning age, had become a pre-eminent industrial metal. By 1924 Malayan production had climbed to 52,000 tons annually, and during the years between 1934–48 it exceeded the latter figure, with prices repeatedly soaring to one thousand dollars a ton or more. Accordingly, scores of the ancient mines in the Kinta Valley of Perak, where the shiny metal used to be washed from river sands by the modest panful, were replaced by batteries of power dredges and later by canals and giant pumps which feed "water cannons" that literally dissolve the ore-ladened earth. Rather promptly, too, British-owned Malayan tin smelters became the world's dominant refining centers for the great metal.

Importantly, too, other mineral wealth began to emerge from the Malayan wonderlands. In the unfederated states of Johore, Kelantan, and Trengganu, Japanese mining interests began taking out about two million tons of iron ore per year, a substantial part of which was presently used to overwhelm and temporarily conquer Malaya. Coal, gold, tungsten, and aluminum are among other notable Malayan resources.

The historian in the white suit paused to order still another drink, and to explain that he makes no pretense of being an industrial statistician or an international economist, that he is merely a Malay who loves both his country and its ever-remarkable story. Between 1915 and 1950, Malaya's population had more than doubled, with still more races and religions poured together. By 1950, Chinese were very nearly half the population and were becoming far and away the wealthier half. In addition there are perhaps twenty thousand recent Japanese immigrants, easily fifty thousand Singhalese Buddhists, twenty-five thousand or more Siamese; and numerous stray Koreans, Tibetans, Burmese, Filipinos, and Arabs, along with perhaps twenty thousand English, French, Swiss, Italians, Americans, and other white men, most of them residing in the ports. And still more impressively, about half, certainly no fewer than 45 per cent of all the people in Malaya today, are foreign born.

East, West, North, and South have met in Malaya. Each has endured, even though it has not attained what the sociologists term a "common standard." The Malay does not eat pork; the Hindu does not eat beef; the Buddhist does not eat any kind of flesh. For the most part, the Chinese guild worker will neither employ nor work with an Indian or a Malay. Virtually no Moslem Malay would permit his daughter to marry a Chinese, and in general these sentiments, or prejudices, are reciprocated.

Thus, in considerable part because of extreme religions and in some measure owing to extreme isolation, the intermixing of races in Malaya has actually remained far below tropical par. The small and ancient melting pot has not functioned as rapidly or as literally as many others.

Even so, during the past century Malaya has remained one of the more peaceful of nations. Contrasting races and creeds have founded a nation of preponderantly good will, and one that during the past third of a century has developed one of the most competent public school systems anywhere in the tropics. The colony school system now includes some two hundred and sixty English-speaking public schools, about one thousand vernacular schools for the Chinese, some three hundred rubber "estate" schools for the Tamils from India and other plantation workers, the Malay College of Perak, primarily for the sons of Malay chiefs, and, at Singapore, Raffles College for training teachers and colonial civil servants; there is also a colony medical school.

Thus, about one-third of the children of Malaya now have a chance to become literate in at least one language. This, of course, is sadly inadequate, but even so it is far above tropical averages, and the same can be said of public health services and, indeed, for the generality of local government works. For despite vast amounts of alien and frequently ingenious usurpation from afar, the citizen or colony government shows increasing competence in many fields. By 1940 it had sponsored a great deal of memorable medical research and had taken a noteworthy part in maintaining at Singapore the Far Eastern Medical Station of the League of Nations, which has now become the very important epidemic-reporting station of the World Health Organization.

By 1940, too, the home government had effected a colony labor code which, though extremely modest, had succeeded in obtaining specified wages for all plantation and minor laborers. These were coolie wages and in great part they still are, but the labor code put an end to enforced or shanghaied labor and the lingering enslavement of workers by means of indenture contracts. The code also established minimum safety and health standards for workers and joined with other enactments in reducing the damages committed by the usurers and the opium peddlers.

As of Pearl Harbor the life and times of Malaya were rather

clearly improving, though not rapidly enough and with many recoils or delayed injuries from earlier eras of British exploitation. Lack of facilities for self-defense was one notorious example. Severe and long-endured laws of non-Malayan origin had prohibited the ownership of any firearms by citizens, however reliable, except by strict licensing. Plantation workers had not even been permitted to carry pocket knives. In all Malaya the licensed firearms could not have armed a company of frontier skirmishers. As almost everyone remembers, Japan found Malaya one of the easiest pushovers in the history of conquest and potentially one of the most valuable prizes ever taken outright by any conqueror. Britain could not defend its richest colony, and the latter hadn't a Chinaman's or Tamil's or Malay's chance of defending itself. Accordingly, early in 1942 Japanese invaders swept through Malaya like a sharp hot knife through butter. Malaya fell, and to predict its restoration to complete prewar status is absolute lunacy. For the world is changing, and so is the most intermixed of tropical nations—changing most probably for the better.

The Malay man in the white linen suit brushed a large red ant from his right knee and clapped again for a drink. A dim fog-blurred moon had appeared from beyond the harbor and sea fog was entangled with the settling night. The Malay lit another cigarette and, on cross-questioning, began speaking more briefly about himself. He confirmed that he is one of the relatively few Malays who are born to wealth—a wealth acquired by his grandfather and father who, as native port "unofficials," pocketed sizable quantities of folding money, much of it, alas, bribe money and blood money derived from the opium trade.

But the young man in the white suit had no stomach for that kind of business. At his own request he enrolled in the trade school at Kuala Lumpur, intent on becoming a carpenter. But since he never before worked with his hands, he could not learn carpentry. His next urge was to become a schoolteacher, and since Raffles College had been reopened at Singapore to provide courses for "native" schoolteachers and civil servants, in the early 1930's the historian enrolled for the teaching course. But here his stomach failed him again, for he sensed a glum and odorous similarity between the starveling "practice students" and the one-time victims of an earlier era of prison cages.

He transferred to the other Singapore boarding school, which is the colony's medical college. Here the historian was obliged to resign at faculty request. As a medical student, or more accurately as a young man attending medical school, he could endure the diligent studies and plentiful cadavers, and he discovered poetry and true beauty in the study of human anatomy, but unfortunately in terms of a medical degree he seemed to find his interest gravitating toward the living anatomies of the young women medical students and the numerous student nurses.

Discharged from "Medical," the historian returned to Raffles College, enrolled in the civil servants' school, where he was graduated with honors and a somewhat mythical appointment to the Cambridge Examinations. But the historian entered colony civil service instead, becoming an itinerant tax auditor.

That was late in 1940. When local radios told of Pearl Harbor, the Malay historian predicted the immediate fall of the British Orient and booked air passage to Egypt. In Cairo he followed a lifelong desire to turn scholar and historian, submerged himself in Egyptian translations of Gaboriau's novels, of Balzac, Tolstoy, and Walt Whitman, delving meanwhile into Arabic tomes on astrology and the literature of the Kemals.

From Egypt he toured some of the North African cities after the fighting armies had withdrawn. Then for a delightful year he lived and studied in peaceful, corrupt Portugal, at Estoril, the shore-resort suburb of Lisbon. Then he returned to Singapore and got a job as "traffic expediter" for an American rubber company. At the war's end and since, Singapore traffic has needed lots of expediting. But during 1949 the rubber company discharged, or more politely "terminated," all native executive employees, in the light of, the alleged descent of the Iron Curtain of Sovietism over Southeast Asia. The historian could see no such descending curtain, though he could and did discern the usual Soviet-Communist infiltration techniques and the usual stentorious exaggerations of the latter as shouted or screamed by the still-prospering foreign investors.

Like many other able and reasonably objective observers, the historian points out that Malaya today is not only surviving but advancing, and thereby is gaining immense stature as bellwether to much of Southeast Asia. Though the white man's yoke is now considerably lifted, Malaya has not fallen apart nor degenerated into anarchy. The educational and other cultural resources of the land have not withered away. Freedom of speech, whether in Malay, Tamil, Chinese, or English, and freedom of religion, whether Moslem, Buddhist, or Christian, is more real in the dangling postwar times than in the tightly supervised prewar times. There are great and momentous problems and needs. But the latter are neither new nor invincible.

The Japanese conquerors destroyed many rubber factories, tin mines, bridges, railroads, storage centers, and other necessary facilities. As yet, not all of these have been rebuilt. Even so, Malaya is coming back. Its rubber exports are actually greater than ever before; its tin exports are about as great; its government has reverted very substantially to the diverse peoples of Malaya. There is still intense racial feeling. But the new colony government is showing remarkable vitality and is doing truly outstanding work in behalf of public health, public education, power developments, communications, and agriculture. At long last the ten provinces of Malaya are coming together in a workable federation. The most mixed of tropical nations keeps growing into a nation, nevertheless.

The Malay historian has noted that for several years the British and American press have been headlining and otherwise whooping up Malay violence toward outlying rubber planters as proof that the archipelago is becoming "Communist," Soviet style. The historian in white points out that, in terms of accredited records, 1948 was the most rugged year to date in Malaya's "reorganization." During that year a grand total of four British rubber planters were murdered by frontier Communist bandits. During the same year there were 8,704 recorded murders in the United States, and, as of this writing, about two-thirds of the latter remain unsolved and about four-fifths of them still unpunished. The colony government in Malaya has successfully convicted and punished most of the few Communist terrorists and in the interim has established "reorientation" centers for its people who have been misled into Communism.

Malaya, of course, is part of a changing world. Unquestionably, recent revolution in Siam and the liberation of India have influenced its thinking. But Marxian Communism, and its numerous Kremlin revisions, grows no closer to the tribal communism of an earlier Malaya.

In Malaya, as in most countries beyond Soviet Russia, postwar Communist strategy has centered its putsches on infiltration into the labor unions. In Malaya these labor unions were and still are inadequate. But the Communists (as supplied principally from the Indian Communist Party) have plainly failed to make them adequate or to win the friendship of the nation's workers as a whole. Early in 1948, the Singapore Harbor Board (by then Singapore was technically divorced from Greater Malaya as a whole) abolished the long-corrupt system of contract labor and instituted direct employment. The Malayan Communistic Party chose that occasion to call a strike. The strike failed.

Plantation strikes, such as those attempted on the rubber estates of Dunlop, have been generally unimpressive. The Communists keep trying, but at least as this page is written they have not proved or found Malaya a docile bailiwick of Sovietdom.

Malayan people, as a heterogeneous group, have never accepted Communism. This historian is supremely confident that Sovietism will not and cannot win in Malaya. He is no less confident that prewar colonialism cannot and will not win. He believes that Malaya, the most memorable conglomerate of peoples in all the tropics, is on its way not only to survival but to durable greatness both in self-realization and as a lasting stabilizer to the half-billion people of Southeast Asia.

The Malay man in white summarized with an intensity of conviction that not even his habitual pose of drowsiness could entirely subdue: "And so long as there are sun and stars and damp air and fertile earth, so long as there are full moons and harbor mists and flowering trees, that long Malaya will live as haven for all known kinds of tropical peoples. Malaya will live because Malaya herself is life, and she patterns the future of all the tropical earth. . . ."

## MAN OF AFRICA

SHADRACH Thursday looked toward the rock-littered coast of West Africa's graying Atlantic and the hibiscus-red sunset beyond. From the high rocky point where the Kru tribe used to bury their dead at sea, a rising wind put giant forest tops to waving until a murmur rose, like the song of a great ocean overhead.

"Throw yo' eyes yon!" Thursday said, mimicking any amateur speaker of pidgin, that peculiar hash of languages first assembled by bygone traders. In pidgin, "Throw yo' eyes yon!" means, "Look there!" As I looked, the deep red circle of the sun slipped down into the sea. Black night leaped down from the shoreline forests. Songs of the night wind became as one with those of the Atlantic and of Africa. Whitish lines of breakers continued sweeping shoreward in advance of the colossal African tide.

"Tide's in," I said.

Thursday pointed reverently toward a first dim rind of moon. "White man sees the tide, but African sees the moon." He continued slowly, "To you, a white man, the tide means many things. . . . To me, a black man, the moon counts much more. . . ." I pondered Thursday's magnificent profile, his thin and somewhat sensuous lips, his large eyes and his exceptionally high forehead. In his splendidly modeled features I felt that I saw Africa today and forever. As black night settled, I pondered the ways of the great sleeping giantess who is still called the dark continent, believing, as so many have believed, and as still more will believe, that Africa is the great provider and molder of the world tomorrow.

The latter reflection is not even remotely original. Hannibal believed it; so did the Persian conquerors and the Caesars. Centuries later, Napoleon, gambling both his empire and his personal future in a desperate thrust upon Egypt, as junction of East and West, declared that Africa would decide the destinies of Europe.

The French Empire today is Africa; the Congo Basin is Belgium; British Africa writes the future of the British Empire. The huge and shaky arch of the Middle East still rests on Africa.

Meanwhile Africa remains immense, both in size and in resources. Economically there are at least three different Africas; culturally, no fewer than ten. As with other huge land areas, talk about Africa inevitably builds itself into superlatives. Johannesburg is the gold-mining capital of the world today. The Rhodesias, great grazing and farming countries, are also world capitals for copper, chrome, and asbestos; the Congo is the world's uranium capital, and the Bomi Hills of Liberia are reportedly one of the decisive iron-mining centers remaining, and British Tanganyika has the world's largest mechanized farms.

But, inevitably, African peoples, ranging in color from ivory to ebony, speaking at least eight hundred different native languages, belonging to at least four thousand different tribes, are the best and surest measure of Africa's greatness. Actually there can be no "typical" African. But I reflected that Shadrach Thursday tends to typify, at least in some just part, the spirit and viewpoint of this magnificent continental scattering of peoples and races who, as an immune geographic group, have so miraculously survived wars, pillage, slavery, and rapine from abroad, and continue to live, serve, and aspire.

Like millions of other Africans, Thursday is the possessor of a distinctive quality of calm alertness which many African languages term "education." Like many other Africans, Shadrach Thursday regards "education" as a term of subtlety and distinction. As he understands it, education means a multitude of vital experiences: breathing African air; seeing, hearing and otherwise perceiving African places and peoples; feeling the hot breath of the harmattan winds; listening to the thunderous force of the tropical rains, to the endlessly varied drum songs of far villages; eating and relishing the hot, rich foods of Africa. Education, to the thinking African, is a word for life and all its vivid components: the mammies who harvest and winnow the life-sustaining rice; the Negro girl in a loose gay red cape who follows the tall man in white Moslem robes and red fez; the woman who carries a kerosene lantern on her head, in preparation for the black night which leaps down from the tall forests; the clean tribal villages with their lines of round mud huts with conical thatched roofs; the village families who gather at their once-a-day meals and become so happily busy shaping rice, peppers, cassavas, or doughy foo-foo into round balls which they eat directly out of well-washed hands.

Education means many other phases of Africa: loyalty to the tribe; love for children; the varied arts of tranquillity as evidenced, for example, by the African citizen who sits motionless before his hut, hands empty and unoccupied, not reading nor chewing nor doodling nor otherwise fidgeting but doing absolutely nothing, with eyes half closed and expression one of exquisite, durable peace.

African education also takes account of the magnificent variety of Africans—moderns and primitives: well-schooled physicians, lawyers, and engineers; native oarsmen who sing as they row, frequently in excellent harmony though in several different native languages; hammock bearers who still provide passenger traffic on bare black heads; the remote traders who still buy and sell with bush money made of twisted strips of iron (readily convertible to knives, hoes, or other tools in event of inflationary trends).

As Thursday knows particularly well, African education also means the talent for government, beginning with the agrarian commune of the tribe or clan. For Thursday happens to be a chief and the son of a chief who, as a tribal farmer, "worked his way up" to chiefdom.

Thursday is well aware that African chiefs have been, and in some instances still are, tyrants and despots. But he is also aware that tribal Africa as a whole, which still is most of Africa, has maintained democratic recourses for protecting the rights of tribe citizens, and one of the greatest of these is the tribe palaver, the perennial open forum wherein members are entitled to state their grievances, to discuss and argue claims and property rights, domestic and marital relations, and any other timely topics, however personal. The palaver is, indeed, a far-removed equivalent of the New England town meeting; it is a forum, court, and legislature in one. Chiefs and elders preside, but citizens speak. And this apparently was going on thousands of years before white men settled New England.

Thursday stresses the fact that, as the competence of tribal democracy grows, so does the discernible competence of the chiefs.

Throughout Equatorial Africa today, more and more chiefs are proving themselves competent leaders—frequently better leaders than were their predecessors. Interestingly, too, Africa still has women chiefs.

But Thursday was born a man. He believes and reiterates that woman's best place is in the home, provided there is or can be made a home for her, which plainly gets to be both a public and private obligation. He believes, at least as a figure of speech, that chiefdom today is more convincingly a man's job than ever before and that a competent chief nowadays must serve his tribe more ably and conscientiously than ever before. For the tribe remains the indispensable bulwark of African government, the premier instrument for keeping peace, and in many other ways the ultimate means of African survival and African advancement.

Thursday repeats that the challenge of African survival remains real and in many areas desperate, and this even though Africa has long been the most peaceful continent and in general the freest of violent crime.

But Thursday points out, too, that Africa remains an excessively tragic continent, particularly tropical Africa, which remains colony-ridden and still suffers some extremely incompetent colonies, such as those of Portugal and Spain, for example, and plenty more which, though improving, are not improving enough to keep pace with African needs. He notes, too, that much of South Africa is still afflicted with one of the most depraved strains of racial prejudice that remain anywhere, and as a tribal African he feels that such a blighting situation is as unnecessary as it is degrading.

But Thursday also insists that the most immediate and virulent of African enemies are pathogenic. Throughout practically all Equatorial Africa and much of the rest of the great continent, the death rates from epidemic diseases, infant mortality, neglected surgical needs, malnutrition, and from occupational accidents are so tragically high that many tribal lands, otherwise promising, are actually losing people.

Vital statistics of Africa are usually unreliable and frequently nonexistent. Frequently a chief is obliged to double as census taker or estimator. On the latter basis, Thursday concludes that the average

African lifespan today is at least a third of a century shorter than the United States average or, more simply, only about half as long. He grants that heart disease and cancer, the most relentless disease enemies of present-day Americans, seem comparatively rare in tropical Africa though both of them exist and destroy. But infant deaths, pneumonias, malaria, filarial diseases, sleeping sickness, leprosy, tuberculosis, and smallpox—vastly in excess of United States averages—keep on robbing Africa of unrecorded millions of lives every year.

Africa remains part of the sick man's world, but Thursday insists that it is pre-eminently part of a good man's world. He supports the latter declaration with about twenty years of conducting tribal courts and palavers, and from lengthy studies of local colonial courts. All these experiences and studies add to his certainty that Africans are pre-eminently good people and comparatively well educated in terms of the talent for peaceful lives.

Thursday thinks of tribal or tropical Africa primarily as a vast and sparsely peopled block of tropical earth, not as a nation of nations, for it has never had a chance to become a nation or nations. For dozens of centuries alien tyrants have swarmed over Central Africa to loot, enslave, and otherwise oppress the mighty homeland of the Negro. Yet Africa lives on, and in terms of education, Africa keeps gaining. Also, tropical Africa remains a vast frontier of physical resources of soils, mines, forests, and ranges. Accordingly, Shadrach Thursday is convinced that tropical Africa is arising to greatness, not as a nation or family of nations, but as a vast sphere of earth that has remained the homeland of tribes and agrarian communities, and of minds and spirits that are worthy attributes to all mankind.

Finished with these verbal reflections about tropical Africa, and also finished with viewing the incoming tide and the outgoing moon, Thursday led the way down a sandy path to his home, a modest tile-roofed ranch house that fronts the ocean. As we approached the elaborately screened entranceway, the door swung open and a subdued thumping of bare feet prefaced the first reddish glimmer of an oil lamp which in time revealed the squat, nightshirted form of Thursday's houseboy. The houseboy returned with a tray crowded with tall clay goblets. "Cane juice," Thursday explained. "Sweet but bubbling with power. . . . Cooled in a deep well. It's Africa's own drink," he continued. "Ripe for the spirit. . . . No harder on the belly than white man's whisky and much kinder to the purse. . . ." Thursday drank thirstily, emptied a goblet, and reached for another before I had finished bracing myself for a first cautious sip.

Then he began talking of the chief business in the African world today.

In his early forties, Shadrach Thursday is a clan or area chief of some sixteen thousand Krobo tribesmen of the Gold Coast colony on the great underbulge of West Africa, and there is an excellent chance that he may eventually become the paramount or all-tribe chief of all the approximately one hundred thousand Krobos. This is a possibility, not a certainty. The present paramount chief of the Krobos is one Mate Kole, who has established an exceptionally brilliant record in chiefdom and is beloved by the great majority of his people, including his schoolmate and lifelong friend, Shadrach Thursday.

In their earliest teens the two went through Poro or tribal cult school together; in their middle teens they attended the rickety and mildewed mission school where as dormitory mates they studied at night by the same oil-pot lamp. In their late teens, both qualified for admission to Achimoto College at Accra, the capital of the Gold Coast colony. Both finished the three-year course with honors, and, that done, both returned to their respective villages where each became a "messenger," or assistant, to his chief-father.

As son of the paramount chief and one of the richest men of the tribe, Mate Kole took advantage of superior opportunities to benefit the tribe as a whole. He began by changing an unwalled palaver house, formerly used as a public whipping post for unruly or lazy wives, into a model free school for children of the tribe. Kole appointed himself headmaster and chose his friend Thursday as the other teacher. Together they launched a primary school which supplemented the three R's with practical instruction in planting and growing gardens, developing grain fields, poultry flocks, and livestock—this in keeping with what the two had learned of practical agriculture at Achimoto.

After about three years spent as teachers, the two young "messengers" selected some of their more promising students for further training that would qualify them as primary teachers and farm demonstrators. The venture was laborious and teeming with lesser mistakes. Even so it became sufficiently successful to win the approval of several Krobo chiefs and still more tribal elders or counselors. Within five years both Kole and Thursday had been elected members of the Krobo council of elders or "chief's cabinet." Three years later Kole's father died and Kole succeeded him as chief of all the tribe. During the same year Thursday was "elevated" a clan chief to succeed his own father.

Kole began his chiefdom by setting up public grade schools in principal towns and villages of the tribe. From the beginning these schools have been supported entirely with tax or tithe money raised within the tribe, without financial help from the colony or from missionaries. All the teachers are tribe members, most of them are "home-educated," and most are under twenty-one. As a supplementary center, Kole, again with much help from Thursday, set up a central school farm and experiment station, doing this because more than nine-tenths of all adult Krobos are farmers or farm wives and are likely to remain so, and thus the tribe can prosper only with its agriculture.

As long as the oldest man can remember, the Krobos have suffered many sicknesses, and tribal health has continued to range from mediocre to desperately bad. Endemic diseases, malaria, filarial ailments, amoebas, tuberculosis, African sleeping sickness, and dozens more are pernicious runners. But like many others the young chiefs concluded that faults of diet were the more primary faults of health. Sick men cannot grow enough good foods, and lack of good foods is the perennial invitation to sickness.

Determined to meet health needs preventively and in terms of nutrition, Chief Kole made a lengthy pilgrimage to England and Scotland. At the medical school at Aberdeen he chose a young physician, appropriately named MacPherson, whom he employed to work ten years among the Krobos: to survey and attend sickness; to direct the training and work of native medicine men and midwives of the tribe; and most particularly to study the dietary needs of the children of the tribe.

The young Scot doctor proceeded to the Gold Coast where he has worked valiantly and well. Within five years the level of Krobo health was definitely upbound and Krobo agriculture has improved even more discernibly. For the first time milk herds are thriving on Krobo ranges, and lush gardens grow on lands which until recently were in fruitless bush. Tribe schoolchildren, in early English lessons, learn the old maxim that declares food is the staff of life.

The young chiefs agree that other staffs are required; like almost all of Africa, the Krobo country is badly in need of more hospitals and much greater surgical and clinical facilities. Ironically, Mate Kole, the paramount chief, contracted a severe filariasis while supervising the establishment of a clinic, and while under treatment for that malady, he contracted a virulent tropical tuberculosis. On physician's advice the tribe chief has begun "coaching an understudy" and a successor as required. Thursday is it.

But Thursday has no urgent desire to become a paramount chief. He is happy and completely absorbed in his present work as a mere clan chief and as the big chief's intermittent assistant and, as he admits, in "proving myself as good a man as my father was." It is traditional African reasoning that one cannot be as good a man as his father unless he is a better man; this is based on the premise that a good man inevitably transmits his goodness and wisdom to his sons, and that this munificence permits each new generation to maintain the wisdom and justice of the old.

Like most tribesmen, Thursday takes proverbs quite seriously. He takes the obligations of chiefdom all the more seriously because he learned from his father's career how a good and just man can stumble and tumble as a chief.

Thursday's father, Omoboe, had been a commoner, a superior farmer, and one of the most competent of hunters and meat suppliers. He was a big man, with courage to match his energy and shrewdness, and human warmth that made him immensely popular.

Omoboe was called the "Giver to the Poor" and the "Feeder of the Hungry," and after his election to chiefdom, he centered his great talents on farming and presently became one of the more successful grain and meat suppliers in all the Gold Coast.

As farming brought him still greater wealth and renown, Omoboe urged his followers to clear and plant more land, and repeatedly he assigned larger tracts of tribe-owned lands to members who showed the most talent as farmers.

The latter proved an excellent safeguard against the hazards of famine. Omoboe further committed the people of his clan to plant, grow, and attend several hundred acres of a then new and rather fanciful tree crop called cocoa, and to plant sugar cane as still another "trading crop."

With these crops, as with rice, cassava, and palm oils, the better farmers flourished, but for reasons baffling to Omoboe many of the poor farmers grew even poorer. But the clan chief encouraged the more successful farmers to buy and otherwise acquire additional wives to bear them children and serve as farm workers. Omoboe himself took the greatest number of wives of any and claimed the largest of the farms, assigning all additional wives to outlying huts that were convenient to the fields.

As years followed, the successful farmers of the tribe thereby became ever richer and more prolific. But the poor tribesmen kept getting poorer. When they became unable to pay their tithes, the chief took away more of the lands. When they became unable to feed their wives and children, the chief commanded them to sell or return their wives and let out their children as "pawns" or foundlings. Thus the proportion of wifeless men—"single boys" kept growing. Sickness and epidemics harassed the poor more than the rich. But Omoboe continued to frown on all debtors, whether sick or well, and to punish the more chronic debtors or those who appeared hopelessly lazy, though some of the latter were actually sick and others grew more and more discouraged.

Actually, the great farmer chief was breaking apart the indispensable human fiber of his once great community. As a child little Thursday, who was Omoboe's third son by his first wife, though the first of the three to live past babyhood, was well aware that in many ways, and from many sources, tribe morale kept sagging. Omoboe's sternness increased as his problems of chiefdom multiplied. He grew more and more annoyed by the quarrels within his own household, the bickerings of his "proper" or elder wives, and by the fierce and immensely feminine feuds that sprang up between the older wives and his newer ones. The latter dilemma caused little Thursday considerable concern, too, but he was fortunately a son of the first wife.

As age came upon him, Omoboe, increasingly irritable, sought to keep the friendship of his sons but urged them to grow harder and more commanding. "Women," the farmer chief declaimed, "were made to bear sons and work the fields. When they lag whip them."

It was impressive oratory, but Thursday knew very well that Omoboe rarely whipped his own wives. Thursday presently learned that as the number of his father's wives increased, so did the number of their transgressions. The dilemma reached its climax many years later, after Thursday had finished college and become a messenger, when one day in tremendous annoyance Omoboe granted permission to his two elder or "proper" wives to deal punishment to two of the younger wives. That proved to be the farmer chief's ultimate mistake.

Two of his youngest wives were plump, giggly, definitely insolent Fanti girls from a distant Nigerian valley. They were exceptionally pretty, and for that and other femininely understandable reasons, the elder wives detested them.

The older wives, who complained more or less chronically of what they believed to be the chief's favoritism toward the new wives, graphically and perhaps truthfully told of the laziness and insolence of the young and attractively curvaceous Fantis. "In all of a day the two together plant but one short row of cassava. And besides they steal our necklaces and girdle charms! We must flog them proper. . . ." Omoboe shouted in annoyance: "Then flog them! But no more than five lashes for the five, and stop humbugging (annoying) me."

The latter statement involved a lingual technicality, and Omoboe, the great farmer, was never a linguist. The Krobo, like many other languages of West Africa, is ambiguous in many respects; for one, its numerals are based on fives instead of tens, and all arithmetic is based on the fingers of one hand or the toes of one foot. (There is a Gold Coast legend of the richest of native traders who deliberately cut off three fingers of his right hand and four toes of his left foot.) In any case, by "five for the five" Omoboe meant no more than ten lashes.

But the wrathful elder wives chose to interpret the order differently. Discreetly, they waited until the clan chief had left on a tour of his more distant rice fields. Then they found the two pretty Fanti girls, dragged them into the central palaver house, and pulled them across the big whipping log. Taking turns at swinging the heaviest whip in the chief's possession, the "proper" wives dealt the newer wives with one hundred lashes apiece—five for each finger and five for each toe. Both of the Fantis died from the flogging.

Word travels fast in Africa. The clan chief returned to find his doorway blocked by two uniformed frontier guards. One of the latter pushed a bit of white paper into the chief's surprised hand. "Warrant for murder," he said.

"I have murdered nobody."

Omoboe's answer went unnoticed. The guard with chevrons on his sleeves slipped steel bands upon the chief's wrists. "Two of your women have whipped two of your women to death. You are the chief. As man of the house and chief of the clan you are liable."

They led Omoboe away along the dark forest trails to the commissioner's jail. There the chief suffered the supreme indignity of a common criminal's trial. The commissioner, a grim-featured, sun-reddened soldier from faraway England delivered sentence: "Your crime is serious. You have shown yourself to be a weakling chief. As commissioner I hold you liable for the death of two women who were your wives. I command you to deliver to the families of the dead women one-quarter of all your manor crops for this year; also half of your palm oils, your rice and cocoa, and pay all haulage to their homes. You will pay double tithe to my collector this year, and surrender to my office one-fifth part of all your chief's lands. My frontier guards will see that you obey this palaver. . . ."

Omoboe stood motionless, pondering the hard sunburned features of the alien commissioner. Then, after his wrists had been unbound, he turned about and trudged in the general direction of home. He knew his chiefdom was doomed. He had lost face and caste. His power and wealth were divided. His own wives had undone him. And as he trudged home, Omoboe resolved to relinquish his chiefdom to his most gifted son.

From Accra, where he had traveled to bargain for tribal school supplies, Thursday heard the news and, like a good son, set out to join his father. It was rainy season. Roads and trails were ripped and mired by floods. Thursday tramped for three days without rest. Arrived home, Thursday found his father sprawled in a filthy fly-festered hut, sleeping off an unprecedented cane-juice drunk. He found various of his father's wives quarreling loudly; also several fields of rice were waiting red-ripe and unharvested. He found single boys were lounging in the shade playing gambling games with shells and otherwise fascinating some of the chief's younger wives on the farther farms.

Though only a messenger, Thursday undertook to establish order in the midst of prevailing disorder. He commanded the vagrant wives to return to their homes or fields. The first to defy him received a resounding spanking which sent her whimpering back to work. The chief's son moved warily toward a rebelling group of single boys. His first urge had been to take along a whip and flog one or two of them soundly—as examples. But when he viewed the loungers more closely, he discreetly changed tactics. For he saw them not as willful loafers but rather as sick men, dejected and hopeless men who needed medicine and understanding far more than whipping.

So Thursday spoke to them as a friend, reminded them of the unharvested rice fields, coaxed them back to work by assuring an extra canister of rice and a handful of kola nuts for every full day of effective harvest labor. Most of the single boys returned to work. By the close of the following day most of the ripe rice had been harvested.

As a further reward Thursday called in the drummers, a literal term for the drum-pounding and traditional tribe musicians, appropriated all the cane juice left undrunk by his father, and proceeded to give a line dance for the delighted entertainment of all the people, using the cane juice as welcome refreshment, having first remembered to ask the two frontier guards to attend. Thursday spent the next day in palaver with his father. Then, at the latter's request, he returned to Accra and there finished his mission with the understanding that he would return as chief.

Thus Shadrach Thursday, eldest son of Omoboe, became a clan chief and began a lifelong service to his people. In this devotion, as already pointed out, he has worked loyally and usefully with and for his paramount chief, and he has proved himself as good a man as his father by making himself a better one. Thursday confides that his greatest reward from a lengthening career of chiefdom lies in his own maturing appreciation of Africa and Africans, in becoming one who reveres and loves Africa for what she is and will inevitably become.

He seeks to maintain his people as solvent African tribesmen, to keep their schools and farming and home life fitted to the patterns of

African thinking and needs and to what he believes the "true rhythm" of African living, since African life is so very essentially a matter of religion. This requires work, crowding, detailed, relentless, never-ending work—work to co-ordinate tribal schools and white men's schools, to co-ordinate the native arts of witch-doctoring with those of modern medicine, to co-ordinate ancient and traditional farming ways with selected portions of what is called "modern agriculture," to co-ordinate traditional African diet, "country chop," with beneficial rudiments of the white man's diet theories, particularly as regards protein foods which most Africans so desperately need. This means work, more and more work, palaver, persuasion, and always importantly, specific demonstration.

As Africans reckon time, Thursday is already past middle age. As years follow, he finds himself ever more African, and tending more and more strongly toward true African ways. As an African who leads and serves Africans, he makes no attempt to abolish polygamy in his tribe, though he seeks, principally by persuasion and partly by land apportionment, to keep the maximum number of wives down to three or four and thus to distribute more equitably the supply of marriageable women. Thursday himself has only one wife and only two children, both sons. He craves no more wives since he continues to enjoy the one he has. But he hopes for a daughter and at least another son on the rather general grounds that he likes children and, for that matter, all people.

He maintains tribal palavers. He rigorously fines or flogs parents who abandon their children. He has reinstated flogging as the standard punishment for more serious transgressions, believing it less degrading and knowing it to be less expensive than jail sentences. But all flogging is performed by a messenger, on verdict of the chief and his council, and with rigid limits.

Thursday has permitted about half the chief's lands, as inherited from his father, to revert to tribal commons—for growing community-owned palm trees, citrus groves, bananas, and other perennial crops for the benefit of the tribe as a whole. He has changed several worn-out rice fields to grazing lands for tribe-owned herds of sheep and cattle—this on the premise that common ownership is the best device for introducing what are to the Krobos new and important crops. He has carried on his work as friend and helper to the paramount chief.

Time and time again his labors become entangled, his work plans fail, and his projects and his people die.

But Shadrach Thursday works on. He has real and good people to serve. Many thousands of lives depend on him. He does not work for a nation, since there is no nation to work for. Tropical Africa, as a whole, has not yet arrived at the time or the place for nations, though Thursday hopes and believes that his sons will live to see the coming of such a time. But Africa today is tribe country. The tribe and clan are its vivid, living denominators. Thursday accepts this and works accordingly.

He summarizes in pidgin English, which he so delights in parodying: "We go softly-softly (slowly) but no leffit. . . ." (We do not stop.) Then he adds in classic English, "For though we die, great Africa lives."

## LAND-BUILDERS

TROPICAL peoples include those who sit and wait or vice versa, those who ponder and divulge or only ponder, those who stay or go forth and do, and an increasing variety of in-betweens.

Current census estimates indicate that tropical populations are increasing at the rate of about forty thousand people every day. The increase in specific tropical trades, though not strictly parallel, is notable and epochal.

A century ago, there were barely a dozen generally accredited trades in all the tropics. Those included the farmers, the native doctors or medicine men, the native political leaders, chiefs, Sultans, alcaldes, clan heads, and many other ranks and kinds of indigenous leaders or pretenders, the hunters and trappers, the housebuilders, who varied in skills from thatchers to mud daubers, the blacksmiths and metal workers, the spinners and weavers, the traders, peddlers, and native merchants, the priests, soothsayers, and other savants of religion, the rangers and foresters, the domestic and other servants, the fishermen and fish hucksters, and the water "witches" or water finders.

At present, no fewer than five hundred other professions, trades, and skills are being practiced commonly and tellingly throughout the tropics. This relatively immense roster includes location engineers, petroleum geologists, metallurgists, biochemists and industrial chemists, meteorologists, radio technicians, pathologists, surgeons and physicians, wheelwrights, hydraulic and pipelines engineers, electricians, dentists, plumbers and hundreds more.

The capacity of tropical citizens to master, apply, and frequently to excel at technical trades born of or in the temperate zone is one of the many bright hopes for the tropical future. Speaking as one onlooker, in Central America I have watched illiterate machete swingers change to competent tractor operators within a month. Some of the most capable truck drivers I ever watched in action are Liberian tribesmen who a year earlier had never even seen a truck or auto, much less ridden in one. In French West Africa I have seen native youths with less than a year of technical training excel as laboratory technicians for hospitals. Some of the most capable nurses I have ever known are tribe girls from the far spaces of Equatorial Africa. The best blacksmiths I have ever known are also tropical Africans, and some of the most capable pharmacists are Indians from upper South America.

Without crowding the facts or exceeding the experiences of one onlooker, this recitation could go on for many pages. In this particular book it will not. But at least some brief mention seems due Americans, specifically people of the United States, who give their lives and technical talents toward making the tropics better places for others thus benefiting the tropics, and inevitably all the world.

There are several thousands of these Americans gone tropical. The arbitrary selection of one or two as representative of the total is hard, all the more so because the great majority of our professionals and technicians who have gone to the tropics, there to serve all or most of their lives, continue to work hard, risk momentously, lose or win quietly, then to retire with minimum honors or fanfare into the nameless oblivion that is the usual American reward for devoted service to people and nations abroad. Meanwhile, as anyone can gather from reading the newspapers or listening to the radio, accounts of the white man's failures in the tropics are vastly better publicized than his successes. It is no less true that the relative chances for failure are greater, particularly when the newcomer dares to pit his talents and technical skill against the giant-size forces of tropical nature.

One good example is the stubborn and oftentimes ruinous issue of tropical rivers. Because of preponderantly steep terrains and heavy rainfalls, problems raised and devastation dealt by tropical rivers are far above world par. In general, water is the most damning enemy of tropical progress. In the tropics water rusts metals, rots woods, makes shambles of man's hopeful building more rapidly and relentlessly than elsewhere. Surface water, easily and frequently contaminated, deals ruinous diseases to people and to animals. Extravagant rains wash away lands, strip soils from new clearings, leach the life from the naked earth, amass into ruinous floods, keep people housebound or, too often, homeless and unproductive through long, wearying, and annually recurring months of the rainy seasons.

As a valid, century-old proposition, rivers are the most costly dealers of tropical water damages. This is all too obvious. The rivaling pity is that to date man has done so excessively little about it. Here, then, is a factual, terse account of two great and unhonored American engineers who have done a great deal about it.

They are Tom Barnett of Arkansas and Pat Meyers of South Carolina, two men who worked separately to reduce the destruction dealt by one of the hundreds of chronically ruinous tropical rivers and, by means of creative engineering, to beguile that river into building fertile soils instead of destroying them.

The river is the comparatively short but extremely wicked Ulua of Honduras where, as in most tropical countries, rivers remain watery ways to ruin. The dilemma just mentioned is, of course, more or less world-wide. Erosion experts contend, for example, that in the United States rivers carry away enough topsoil each year to feed at least ten million people. And rivers are but one factor in soil losses due to rains.

Experiments made by the United States Department of Agriculture, using a medium clay loam soil on a slight (3.6 degree) slope, located several miles from a major river channel, showed the following soil losses from annual water erosion, with a median annual rainfall of 38 inches or about half of the world-around tropical average. One acre of such land, plowed and left bare, loses about forty tons of topsoil per year. When planted in corn, the same land loses about twenty tons; to wheat, about ten tons; to a sequence of corn, alfalfa, and wheat, an average of about 2.7 tons yearly.

Thus, despite all the popular or classic songs and the nostalgic verses and the cozy books about rivers, people generally have excellent reason to resent and fear rivers and to view them as liabilities. Even in these United States, where rivers have served so valuably to open frontiers and to foal great industries, we keep right on spending billions of man-hours and dollars in curbing or otherwise working against rivers. For every dollar or work-hour we spend toward the end of causing rivers to produce electricity or other valuable commodities, we spend tens or hundreds in toilsome, frequently futile efforts to ward off destruction by rivers. We build thousands of costly miles of levees only to cause the bed levels of a given river to rise ever higher above the adjoining valley lands, thereby increasing the river's menace.

The case of man versus the river has no precise limits of latitude or longitude; it is a world-wide dilemma. Significantly, the Ulua of Honduras is broadly typical of the difficult and temperamental rivers of the tropics. Long before white men came, indigenous Indians named it the bad river. Hernando Cortes, the explorer, confirmed this by naming it Rio Malo. Interestingly, Cortes recognized the exceptional richness of the valley's land and founded a port settlement at its mouth. But the settlement died away, and not long thereafter the dismal malarial swamps returned.

The Comayagua River flows through a break in the *Montaña del Mico Quemada* (Burnt Monkey's Mountain) to join the low channel of the Ulua which winds corkscrew style through about eighty-five miles of sodden and swamp-strewn valley and so spreads to the Caribbean. The tributary Comayagua drops about thirty-five feet from the Santa Rita gap to its junction with the Ulua, which in turn drops about twenty-five feet more to the fertile area of Progreso; thence, by flattening grades, it drops about eighty feet down to open sea. The Chamelecon is another silt-carrying tributary of the Ulua.

The flood habits of the Ulua system are recurrent and generally typical. In Honduras, autumn and winter, from late September to

March, is the heavy-rain season. October usually finds the Ulua and its tributaries at flood stage. For an average of ninety days each year the river runs channel full, and as the heavy rains continue, the grim, brown waters spill over into the broad valleys, sweeping away or burying in mud any impeding fields, buildings, bridges, or railroads, and eventually spilling the floodwaters farther down into a huge crescent of pestilential swamp lands.

This had been going on for centuries. At flood stages the Ulua silt load climbs to 20 to 25 per cent of the water load. As with so many tropical rivers, as silt continues to settle in its channel, the Ulua's bed has been built higher and higher above the level of the adjoining valleys.

Accordingly, the prospects for effecting flood control for the Ulua were more than discouraging. As people toiled to build enbankments, or levees, the river bed became higher, and the best remaining hope of the valley inhabitants was that the next rainy season might "break the banks" further down the channel.

However, in the instance of the Ulua there was a very particular incentive for claiming and developing lands close by the ruthless stream. The nearby valleys provide the best banana lands in all the world. The climate, rainfall, and wind shelters are basically right for that particular and exacting crop, and the Ulua valley remains the most decisive production base for the international banana trade today and very probably tomorrow.

By 1919, two principal banana companies were clearing and planting costly and (they hoped) high-yielding, long-lived divisions of banana farms in the Ulua valley. On the east bank of the river were the men and farms of the powerful United Fruit Company. On the west bank or Cortes side were the farms and railroads of the Cuyamel Fruit Company, headed by Samuel Zemurray of Honduras, Mobile, and New Orleans, already destined to become helmsman of United Fruit.

For evident reasons banana companies rely heavily on the work of their engineering departments. More or less coincidentally, two then-young civil engineers, Patrick H. Meyers of South Carolina, for Cuyamel, and Tom J. Barnett of Arkansas, for United Fruit, began to diagnose the rambling, flood-tortured Ulua channel. Their initial work was customarily tough and sweaty jungle fighting—clearing parcels of the mighty forest trees and vine-tangled bush and palms, planting the bulbous roots or rhizomes of the bananas, building railroads, field hospitals, stores and workers' quarters, and otherwise making the wet, hot valley lands somewhat habitable.

The banana-growing pioneers, like earlier pioneers of the Ulua Basin, soon learned to respect the might and the moods of the Ulua. At first they built levees and opened channels to carry overflow waters away from the banana fields during the ruthless flood seasons.

This was hard, perilous, and expensive work which gave a clear impression of futility. Efforts to effect drainage were no more promising. Earlier valley plantings which depended for "natural" drainage on the river channel had been limited to extremely narrow strips, rarely more than thirty or forty yards wide, these being quite literally beside the river. Efforts to drain larger areas were usually blocked by floods and overflows.

The banana engineers had particular reasons to keep up their alert studies of the Ulua. Pat Meyers and Tom Barnett, working independently, identified, for example, that at high mark, or "banks full," the river carries approximately one-thirty-second of a cubic foot of silt per cubic foot of water, this at a current speed ranging from 2.5 to 5 feet per second. They approximated the Ulua's average annual discharge of water as about five hundred and fifty billion cubic feet. Of this volume about one-third passes through the channel during the maximum flood month, which is usually October. On a year-round basis, the Ulua carries about 137 parts of silt per one hundred thousand of water. This suggests that during the course of any year the Ulua carries in suspension enough highly fertile soil to cover about twenty-five thousand acres, or some forty square miles, with a one-foot layer of the rich, new soil—provided, of course, that the silt loads could be dropped at the right time and at the right place.

Therein lay the rub. Precedences were not very helpful. There is, for example, the ancient silt-recovery strategy as practiced along the Nile Basin. But the Nile is an extremely long river while the Ulua is short. The mouth and lower slopes of the Nile sluggish; the average grade is only one foot to 91,000, whereas the Ulua's is one foot to

4,500. The Nile's silt load is proportionately slight; it drops channel silt at the rate of about one-third of one inch per year and therefore is capable of depositing an average stratum of tillable soil, or about seven inches, in about twenty years. The Ulua, by contrast, is capable of building soil at the rate of a foot-deep stratum per year.

Along the lower Nile, soil-building by way of sedimentation is an aftermath of the essential irrigation there practiced. For dozens of centuries Egyptian farmers have drained the Nile's water into settling basins for later distribution to valley fields or gardens. As a rule the catch basins are built parallel to land contours, and in the natural course the river silt settles on the basin beds. When the latter become spread over with a considerable deposit of rich new soil, the soil builder makes a new impoundment, drains the older ones, then plants it to thriving crops. But this is practicable primarily because irrigation is indispensable.

By 1919, Pat Meyers, who was a lanky, deeply sunburned frontiersman from South Carolina, had acquired the hard way an expert knowledge of the Ulua, commonly described by the Gringos as the meanest-goddamn-river-anywhere. One autumn day in 1919, while in the throes of his perennial struggles to drain away the ruining brown overflows of the devil river, Pat was joined by his boss, the towering, determined Samuel Zemurray, of Warsaw, Bessarabia, Alabama, Louisiana, Honduras, and a somewhat breathtaking assortment of intermittent places. As president of the highly successful and rapidly growing Cuyamel Fruit Company (bananas), Zemurray was overlord of the west bank of the Ulua.

The boss beat a trail through sticky, knee-deep mud until he beheld a soggy, barren tableland newly raised by the most recent flood. There Zemurray pointed out the new creation of earth with such eloquence and emphasis that he sank at least a foot deeper into the muck. "Dat," he shouted "iss pruff of how good lands get builted up the nadure-al way!"

The great man had spoken. Deliberately and thoughtfully, the drawling engineer from lower Carolina set out to make more of what comes naturally. After ten days of intense thought and a case of Dewar's White Label Scotch, Pat Meyers began a first soil-building venture on the left or west bank of the Chamelecon, a short way above its confluence with the Ulua. As usual, the primary objective was to protect the low-lying banana farms from floods and to gain this end by recovering a small fraction of the silt loads that were available. Even so, within five years, a first five thousand acres of land, with silt deposits ranging from six inches to ten feet in depth, has been built up by this planned venture in silt recovery. For the purpose of banana-growing the river-built lands are worth at least two million dollars. Their actual cost was about twenty thousand dollars.

Even more valuable than the river-built lands were the practical lessons learned and the manuals outlined. In the beginning Pat Meyers had identified that a current velocity of 4.5 miles per hour is best for the purpose of land-building. Faster currents are almost certain to spread heavy gravel, stone, driftwoods, and other undesirable materials over the prospective fields. Slower currents are not sufficiently ladened with fertile silt.

Meyers and his helper had experimented with various kinds of collapsible check dams—designed to facilitate the spreading of silt by waters drawn directly from the river channel. They used draglines or steam shovels to dig small surface canals, *borquerones*. By means of these the river waters that poured over the spillways during rainy seasons were guided across the low stretches of valley at velocities which were decided by established grades. This permitted river-borne silt to settle and so to build up the swamp sinks that particularly needed building up.

The rudiments were simple: Minimize levee building. Cut into the river channel and take out the muddy waters before they reach flood stage. Direct the outtake into *boquerones* or small canals so arranged that the silt-bearing water can be distributed or "swish-swashed" in a manner to cause the silt loads to be dropped where most needed. Then provide exits for the silt-free water. This sounds basically simple. Like most other immensely valuable discoveries in the tropics, it is simple. Even so, and in great part because it is so simple, this finding is one of the most memorable engineering feats yet attained in the tropics. Granting there are room and need and incentives for hundreds more, this is one of the greatest to date.

Cuyamel's first successful silting projects involved the changing of a mere five thousand acres of miry valley swamps to tenable lands by the strategy of silt recovery. The feat was accomplished by means of nineteen *boquerones* or surface channels, each an average of two yards wide and from 2 to 2.3 miles long, spaced about 350 yards apart. To fill these canals, silt-bearing waters were taken out of the river channel by way of a broad, shallow-intake canal, about 240 feet across and eight feet deep. For discharging the spent waters from the *boquerones* Meyers directed the building of two drainage canals, both broad, shallow channels, one about ten miles long, the other about seven.

In time the silt deposits built up all the *boquerones* and the former swamp lands between them to more or less level tables of immensely fertile river silt which otherwise would have been carried into the sea. Within a decade these "made lands" were bearing the best grade of bananas ever received in the United States and Samuel Zemurray was a multimillionaire. Pat Meyers, still a mud-caked, sunburnt engineer with a four-digit salary paid in U.S. gold coin, could at least enjoy the fine inner glow of distinguished accomplishment.

The land-building continued. Along the last bank of the Ulua, Tom Barnett, of United Fruit, and earlier of Eureka Springs, Arkansas, where his father was superintendent of public schools, had centered his working hours on thousands of acres of valueless swamps which sedimentation by river water could in time change to valuable farming sites. In time the tall, thin, and sickly young civil engineer from the Arkansas Ozarks, a graduate of the University of Arkansas (a long-renowned engineering college), became convinced that in the Ulua valley alone at least one hundred thousand acres of then useless and troublesome swamp land could be built into superior farmlands by controlled sedimentation.

After 1929, when Cuyamel and United Fruit joined forces and properties, the two banana engineers joined forces and talents for land-building along the Ulua. By 1940 they had effected about sixteen thousand more acres of land-building on the east bank—in the Palomas and La Fragua sections, the whole of the Mezapa, Tolca, Melcher, and Meroa banana farms, and other banana farmsites including Guanacastal, Ticazma, Kele Kele, Tibombo, and Manacolito on former Cuyamel lands to the west. More recently privately owned banana properties, such as Finca Oro and the Birichiche Estate, have joined the venture.

The total of silt-built lands was more than thirty thousand acres as World War II began. War shortages of the needed heavy machinery and available ships impeded the work. After the war the soil-building venture began again, and at present the "built-lands" total about fifty thousand acres with somewhat more than thirty thousand acres planted to bananas or other crops.

Much more extensive "siltation" is possible. Engineers now agree that if the lower swamps along the Ulua were striated with discharge canals leading sixty or more miles to the Caribbean, one of the world's richest farming centers could quite literally be built from the brackish flood waters of one of the more anti-social of tropical rivers.

Building the discharge canals would require the removal of hundreds of millions of cubic yards of mud, and that, in turn, could be accomplished only by the use of enormously expensive floating hydraulic dredges. The cost for the total area so created would probably be somewhere between two hundred and five hundred dollars per built acre, depending on many factors, some of which are not readily predictable. In any case, it is highly probable that the value of the silt-made lands would be substantially more than their building costs, though the project just mentioned might very well cost a hundred million dollars.

Cost, of course, is relative, whether in the tropics or out. As a world-around average, land built from the recovery of silt loads in rivers is likely to be more expensive in money than land claimed by the homesteader's ax or cutlass or machete. But lands effectively recovered from rapacious river currents are certain to be rich lands which are a combination of valid recovery and worthwhile creation.

Still more notably, the Ulua venture indicates that soil recovery from tropical rivers, as already clearly proved in the low valleys of Honduras, is a bright possibility for hundreds or thousands of similar locales. The fact is also notable that the silt-built lands of the Ulua, as now planted to bananas, are yielding somewhere near twice the average banana harvest for the area as a whole: about twelve tons of the fruit per acre, as compared to five or six tons for excellent cultivations on other favorable valley lands in the same general area.

It is true that the soil requirements for commercial banana-growing are considerably higher than those of most other crops. But it is no less true that most of man's great crops thrive and bear abundantly on lands built of silt, and that the tropics as a whole suffer a superabundance of silt-bearing, soil-destroying rivers. The proposition grows that comparable work-patterns for soil recovery from rivers, duly developed and applied, might produce at justifiable costs tens of millions of acres of the richest soils on earth, thereby devising a new and better passport to farther-reaching abundance.

Here again, the goal cannot be attained cheaply nor easily nor overnight. No two rivers are precisely alike. Silt-recovery enterprises must be shaped and adapted to specific places and needs, after thorough and difficult research.

Also—and practically speaking, this is one of the more difficult hurdles—soil-building by sedimentation is best accomplished on or for large blocks of lands. This suggests or necessitates either government ownership of the areas chosen or a primary need for patient, long-time co-operation of many individual owners of farms. In the case of the Ulua Basin, one banana company (United Fruit) and nine citizen planters currently own all the lands so developed. For the most part it is necessary to remove or postpone all cultivations for building periods which range from one to five years. Along other river channels, twenty to thirty years of development time might very well be required.

But the Ulua experiment in recovering almost fabulously rich soils from river wastes seems particularly important to the river-harassed tropics today and tomorrow. As tropical spaces and tropical rivers go, the work accomplished thus far is a mere speck. In terms of cost, all the money spent to date on the soil-building venture would hardly build a "modern" hundred-room hotel or a fairly colossal corner movie theater. Yet the work as envisioned and very largely accomplished by two rather typical American engineers gone tropical strikes me as being exceptionally deserving of notice. The tropics, in general, are in the best position to make maximum use of superlatively fertile lands. There is evident and distinguished merit in recovering such lands from the age-old wrath and extravagance of the rivers.

Pat Meyers and Tom Barnett, toiling, splashing, sweating, and swearing along the grim, brown Ulua and its tributaries, have shown the way. It is up to other imaginative and more youthful engineers to follow along and better develop that way.

Neither of the engineering pioneers is young now. Pat Meyers, retired to the drowsy suburbs of an even drowsier cotton town way down in South Carolina, chain-smokes cigarettes, frequently day-dreams, and occasionally talks of the "old days" in frontier Honduras. As this page is written, Pat is an old, frail man, Honduras is still a memorable tropical frontier, and fabulously rich tropical earth deals tribute to his great work.

Yet neither this nor any other of his memorable tropical attainments have ever made Pat rich or even jauntily independent. He never asked for great wealth and never received it. Cigarettes, shelter, one good stiff drink, and one good meal a day, he avers, are all any aging tropical tramp really requires. "And whatever's left over," Pat adds, "providin' the rats won't eat it, nor drink it, you can give to the engineers. . . ."

Tom Barnett too, is getting along in years. Tom, meanwhile, reckons that the real dawn is only now beginning to break in the tropics. He used to tell me that more than a dozen years ago when we were together in the then wild thorn-bush frontiers of "south coast" Costa Rica.

Since then both of us have served time in many tropical places, several of which are honestly describable as hell-holes. When I returned from tropical Africa and Tom got back from the wilds of Ecuador, he was more than upset to find that his hair had turned from moderate gray to snowy white.

I sought to bolster him by pointing out that during a mere two years in tropical Africa my hair changed from jet black to complete gray. Also, that whereas he has remained as slender as a pipe-stem Paris model, I have grown abhorrently chunky—from a bare and fairly brawny 145 pounds to a calorie-watching 180.

"To hell with all that," Tom said, reaching for a cigarette and refill of Dewar's. "All I mean is . . . it ain't fair for a tropical engineer to get old. . . . We ain't got started yet—in the way of doing what we truly got to do."

## DEMOCRACY-BUILDER

TROPICS-ROAMING and tropics-benefiting engineers, such as Pat Meyers and Tom Barnett, have proved in their little-noticed and largely unrewarded ways how the many fields of tropical conservation continue to emerge and expand. Systematic recovery of rich soils which otherwise would be looted by rapacious tropical rivers is magnificent work in behalf of the most basic of natural resources.

And it is clearly symbolic of the well-planned conservation and anchorage of certain human resources, beginning with that of freedom for the human spirit. Democracy is still the best word for this latter and greatest of all fields of human conservation.

As a whole, the tropical earth still has far too little acquaintance with democracy. In the past, the tropics have been colonies. As such some have been more thoroughly looted by tyrannical colonial structures than by the most malicious of their rivers or storms. Deplorable colonial structures have been augmented by many other devices and growths which are no less lethal to the human spirit: by dictators and sawdust Caesars, usually raised and maintained in power by trite and cunning people who have been neither indigenous nor spontaneous nor noble. They have also been maintained by caste systems, too many of which are perpetuated synthetically and from afar, and by the old exploitation of human misery and degradation, as now practiced, sometimes deftly and frequently audaciously, by the cancerous cells of Communism and other regimented hirelings, slaves, or boot-lappers to the Kremlin.

As yet no tropical country has prospered in or because of Communism. The total tropical relations of Soviet Russia, like those of Czarist Russia, remain the least constructive and the lest competent of those of any major power on earth, which is saying a great deal.

Soviet Russia's "Point Four" substitutes propaganda for credit and intrigues and conspiracies for technical skills. In terms of current and bona fide trade with tropical nations, Soviet Russia still ranks below Belgium or Switzerland or Denmark, and this despite the fact that the U.S.S.R., since 1945, has actively sought such war matériel as natural rubber, uranium ores, tin, copper, and plating oils from many tropical sources; despite the fact, too, that recent Soviet attempts at penetrating the tropics have set new highs for diplomatic insolence, unsalved bribery, and unsweetened violence.

Yet very plainly Marxism, via Politburo expedience, is neither the meat nor the manna of the tropics. Speaking as one long-time reporter and worker in many tropical places, I am convinced that the great majority of tropical peoples prefer democracy or certainly would prefer it had they the opportunity to know and attain it.

This is much more than one man's opinion. In great part it is established history. For in the tropics-damaging courses of two world wars, and with a third world war in the evident offing, the tropics, in overwhelming majority and preponderantly at their own great and painful expense, have sided with the causes and the powers of democracy.

I shall never forget arriving in West Africa three months after the close of World War II and finding the greater spaces of French Africa still officially mourning the fall of Free France. As one reporter, I cannot forget how spontaneously and how generously tropical Africa, including the Belgian Congo, most of the British and French colonies and the former German colonies, opened their hands and resources to the Allies of World War II, raised volunteer armies, gave badly needed goods, and endured decimating losses of trade and shipping.

Unfortunately, all this is rather easily forgotten. So is the fact that 29 tropical nations were our allies in World War II, including Brazil, in area the largest of all. We also are likely to forget that our tropical allies supplied us with indispensable war matériel, such as rubber, copper, tin, palm oils, and specialized fibers, in the main at prices rigidly controlled and reduced by the United States and other major powers; that tropical allies granted us use of their seaports, air bases, riverways, and many other facilities; that in great part World War II was fought and won in friendly tropical spheres; and that tropical countries not only supplied indispensable goods and sites, but that they also supplied many men who fought and died that democracy might be.

These realities add to the great catalogue of reasons why one of the most decisive factors of human conservation in hot countries is the challenge of democratic government. Here, briefly, is the current and continuing saga of one man who works to shape and anchor what he and others regard as a new and durable basis for national democracy in the remote tropics. The man who is currently succeeding most notably in founding such a tropical democracy is an African Negro statesman named William V. S. Tubman (V. for Vacanarat, S. for Shadrach), who at least through 1952 is President of Liberia.

The striving and the outlook for democracy in Liberia gains pertinence from several background factors. It is supported by a nominal republic which has a constitution modeled closely on that of the United States'. Its territory has been strongly influenced and in considerable part pirated by the British and French colonies which surround it by land. Its people are preponderantly of long-established native tribes, comparable in many respects to the Gold Coast Krobos, whom able chieftains such as Shadrach Thursday and Mate Kole ably serve and seek to benefit. But the tribe remains an indigenous community, sometimes of excessive size but a community nevertheless. The tribes have not yet been converted to nations. Tribal democracy, though valuable and beneficial and oftentimes inspiring, is an attribute of a basically and conventionally segregated community, not of national government.

Liberia has the latter. Technically and literally it is a nation. And memorably for purposes of illustration and proof, it also has clearly established tribes and clans which are typical of indigenous tropical populations the world around.

Significantly, too, Liberia, the smallish (43,000 square miles) wedge-shaped gateway into the great western bulge of Africa, is the only republic in that huge, colony-ridden continent. In a rather vague ancestral sense, Liberia is American, since a handful of freed slaves from the United States, meagerly supported by the American Colonization Society and quasi-officially by President James Monroe, made settlements there beginning in 1822, and on July 26, 1847, proclaimed the founding of the Republic of Liberia. In a far more vivid and bona fide sense Liberia is African. And, as noted, Liberia is now exhibit A of a national tropical democracy in the process of development.

Haiti, the other Negro republic, is still far from being a democracy.

The majority of sovereign nations in the tropics remain in the varying shadows of dictatorship, though quite clearly more and more of them are tending toward democracy, including such impressive new and comparatively immense tropical republics as Indonesia, India, Pakistan, and the Philippine Republic. But Liberia is a century-old tropical republic that is being reborn as a real and advancing democracy, offering valid evidence that democracy in the tropics, even the more primitive and least-developed tropics, is attainable.

As in the United States of Jefferson's time, Liberian democracy is championed, theorized, and in considerable part effected by one outstanding individual. The latter, William V. S. Tubman, has been obliged to accept many situations which are intrinsically unreasonable.

One is that Liberia remains peopled principally by its 23 indigenous tribes who still make up, at fewest, some 98 per cent of its probable 1,600,000 people. In actual number, the English-speaking descendants of American Negroes, the freed slaves who first "settled" a fringe of the wet malarial coast, have never exceeded 15,000. Yet for somewhat more than a century this tiny minority has controlled and in actuality has been the Liberian government. Politics has been the chief trade and income source of the American group which on the whole has remained snobbish, greedy, self-seeking, and disdainful of the persons and rights of the tribesmen whom they smugly term, "the natives." Consequently, government of, by, and for the Negro immigrant has ranged from farcical incompetence to absolute Stygian corruption.

Tubman happens to be Liberia's first president of partially tribal or "native" blood. He is the great-grandson of a freed slave who came from Maryland but who, unlike his American fellow immigrants, disdained the parasitic life at Monrovia, moved down coast to the far and fertile Cavally Valley, there married a tribeswoman, and became both a tribe member and a farmer. Significantly and appropriately, the now President of Liberia shows many of the physical characteristics of the Grebo tribe: medium build, high forehead, oval face, medium lips, and rather large eyes; also a warm sympathy for the problems and the viewpoints of the tribespeople.

The Republic of Liberia was first proclaimed from Monrovia, the preponderantly thatch-roofed, seaport capital, during the early afternoon of July 26, 1847. Ninety-nine years and three months later Liberian democracy was also proclaimed from Monrovia during the early afternoon. By 2:00 P.M. the somewhat Victorian and termite-bothered legislative hall was groomed for action. Nine lanky Negro soldiers stood at attention beside the rain-cracked cement steps. The impoverished tongue-and-grove-lumber-sealed interior of the state house was freshly painted cream white and chocolate brown. The wooden columns were wrapped with alternating red and white strands of tissue paper, commemorative of the national colors. An immense flag of Liberia, with its broad upright red and white stripes halted by a blue triangle and a single white star within, covered about two hundred feet of the otherwise blank wall beyond the speaker's table.

Four minutes after 2:00 a shiny Lincoln sedan, with the left front fender considerably battered, drove to the entrance of the legislative hall. From its back seat emerged the rather handsome, deep walnut-brown President of Liberia. On that particular day he was wearing an almost blindingly red skull cap and an ankle-length, gold-striped toga, which comprise the dress-up garb for a paramount or head chief of practically any native tribe of West Africa.

Monrovia, by long-time tradition, is oppressed by what is probably the stuffiest and most sweat-provoking formal dress known to any capital of the present-day world. But on this particular day its tradition of official dress was tossed abruptly to the winds. The real-life appearance of the President of Liberia in the ceremonial robes of a tribal chief signalized the long-belated emergence of actual native representation in the Liberian government.

As President of Liberia, Tubman, like his 21 predecessors, is ex-officio chief of the 23 native tribes. His particular reason for appearing in chief's robes before his hatchet-coated, wing-collared legislature was to supervise the installation of the first tribal or provincial representatives in the national legislature. There were then three such representatives, all native chiefs from the far hinterlands: Botoe Barclay, representing the Central Province; Poo Derrick, the Eastern Province; and Flomo Fromoyan, the Western. All are tribesmen elected to represent the preponderantly tribal peoples. As a matter of African orthodoxy, all three wore the robes and caps of their chieftaincies.

Tubman strolled to the platform and read the oath of office to the three new legislators. The robed chiefs raised their right hands and in succession kissed the Bible, though none of the three is a Christian, and accepted membership in the legislature. Tubman commented in scholarly but easily spoken English that on that day his country had begun a new era of democracy. Chief Poo, speaking the somewhat singsong monosyllables of the Grebo tribe, proposed a toast to the birth of Liberian democracy.

A British chargé d'affaires whispered in one of those quarter-mile stage whispers which Colonial Office men do so well, "This Tubman is the first democrat in all Africa. . . !" A member of Tubman's cabinet smoothed the lapels of his richly bemedaled morning coat and nodded: "He is changing Liberia to a democracy at a time when so many other nations are changing to dictatorships, socialist states, or bureaucracies." A U.S. State Department man nodded. "Also, Tubman is the only Methodist preacher in the whole damned world who got a decoration from the Pope."

The latter comment was also factual. As a preface to the centennial of Liberia's statehood, the Vatican State awarded Tubman a papal decoration. And about thirty-five years earlier, on graduation from three terms of a Methodist Mission School at Cape Palmas, Tubman had been pledged or "consecrated" to the Methodist ministry.

He was never formally ordained. The night before the arrival (at Cape Palmas) of the visiting colored bishop from Alabama, Tubman and his roommates at the mission school had acquired an oversized bottle of French champagne from the steward of a Dutch boat then calling at the port. Convert Tubman, while striving to uncork the bottle, made a deep cut in his right thumb. (He finally opened the bottle by knocking off its crown with the mission's dinner gong.)

The bishop, noticing the hand wound, asked its cause. Like any good tribesman, Tubman answered truthfully: "I hurt it with a corkscrew, Excellency. I was trying to open a bottle of champagne."

The bishop stepped back in virtuous amazement. "Brother Tubman! *You* opening champagne on the eve of your ordination! Brother, I am shocked and disappointed. I had no idea you liked the stuff. . . ."

The next reply was also typically tribal African: "I like it, Excellency, I like it just fine. . . ."

Thus, William V. S. Tubman was not formally ordained in the Methodist ministry, though technically and by mission school attainments he was and is a Methodist preacher.

He returned to his tribal village, became a trader, and with exceptional effort saved enough money for two years at a white man's school, the University of Beirut. There he "read" white man's law, then returned to his tribe, to become a provincial commissioner, which in Liberia means a back-country or hinterland tax collector on behalf of the government at Monrovia, and a more or less honorary colonel of the frontier police, traditionally a sort of Captain Katzenjammer or Marx Brothers Army.

Next, as a member of the True Whig party, an American carry-over, he won a nominal though not particularly democratic election to the Liberian legislature.

As one of the more able Liberian lawyers, Tubman next served as an appointed member of the Supreme Court of Liberia. There, at least according to the opposition, he turned "liberal." Even so, in 1943 he won the Monrovia-decided nomination as the True Whig candidate for the Presidency, and he won an easy victory in the general election. The 1944 balloting was somewhat more forthright than usual. Both Tubman and his opponent waged American-style "speaking" campaigns, and it is reasonably certain that at least eighty thousand bona fide ballots were cast. Tubman "carried" the tin and thatch-roofed capital by a good margin, and his hinterland vote was outstanding even without benefit of the usual export and import of ballot boxes. "I'm deeply grateful," the tribe-descendant President-elect stated. "I will do my best for my people. This has been our best election so far. The next one is going to be better. . . ."

Tubman took office in 1944, one of the most difficult and dangerous years in all the difficult and dangerous history of Liberia. American and British bombers from Liberia's Roberts' Field roared over the scene of his inauguration, not in salute, but rather in furtherance of battle assignments to the north. Below, Tubman led a prayer for peace and democracy.

He had been pondering the latter philosophy for at least a quarter-century. Shortly before his inauguration he paid his first visit to the

United States. At the White House he was a guest of Franklin D. Roosevelt. From Washington, the Liberian President-elect proceeded to New York where he made a "friendly invasion" of Brooks Brothers, long-time men's clothiers. There he selected and purchased a completely informal wardrobe, American style, beginning with blazers, sport shirts, and sport slacks, proceeding to bathing shorts, linen suits, and lounging shorts and to double-breasted business suits, climaxed by a deep blue Tuxedo. He likewise invested in a sizable assortment of shoes of American build and styling. Experimentally he presented his "personal boy" (valet) with a pair of carefully fitted Brooks Brothers shoes.

African feet grow big, broad, thick, and almost elephantine with generations of barefootedness. His personal boy was utterly wretched in shoes; he clumped, he groaned and stumbled. The President-elect permitted him to take off the shoes and go barefoot during the remainder of his American stay. "I saw then," the President reflects, "that my people were not ready for shoes, and most likely will not be until a new generation replaces the present one. . . . Here in Africa there is great danger in overforcing the people. Here progress must come softly-softly or, as you say, slowly."

But the Tubman resolve to "informalize" the dress of Liberian officials in Monrovia was shrewdly planned. Back in Monrovia, the new President promptly aired his new American wardrobe. Repeatedly he appeared at traditionally morning-coat events in gray flannels topped with a gay blue collegiate blazer. In Monrovia this was generally comparable to a minister's mounting his pulpit in a bathing suit. But the social and official implications of informal dress seemed important to Tubman, and still do.

As already stated, Monrovia has long been one of the most dress-conscious capitals anywhere. For generations its formal dress has remained orthodox and productive of interminable itchings, profuse sweating, and extreme discomfort. Along with its extreme bodily discomforts, "official dress" usually deals a financial crisis on the modestly paid officials. An "official wardrobe" costs all of a year's salary or more, and too many electees have felt themselves obliged to pilfer public money or accept bribes in order to finance the excessive formality of dress.

Actually, and rather ironically, the prevailing garb of the country is scant shorts, sometimes supplemented by routine summer underwear "uppers," formerly and to some extent currently acquired from price-slashing Japanese cotton mills. Chiefs and petty chiefs and certain Moslem members still wear togas and sandals. But the nation as a whole is shoeless and about as nearly clothesless as any on earth. Tubman believes therefore that excessive formality of dress places very real barriers between the public servant and his people and otherwise molests the competence of government.

Even before his inauguration, Tubman had accomplished notable advances in circumventing or melting down some of the jagged ridges of snobbery which have long penalized Liberia. He selected his cabinet of eight with almost fanatical care to include Liberia's premier and long-experienced statesman, Gabriel Dennis, as Secretary of State, an intelligent, hard-working young lawyer named William Dennis as Secretary of the Treasury, and Liberia's wealthiest citizen, an American Negro immigrant named William Walker, as Secretary of Public Works. Shortly thereafter, when Tubman found Walker "shirking of official duties," he dealt him a scathing public reprimand and threw him out of the government.

Tubman broke precedences further by posting tersely worded notices that all officials and appointees of the Liberian government are required to work from 9 in the morning until 4 in the afternoon, with exactly one hour for lunch. In Africa such executive manifestoes are at least as rare as hen's teeth. But Tubman had learned that official laziness is the root of many governmental evils, and that the inevitable twin of official laziness is graft. He bluntly advised his colleagues: "With stealing permitted, we can never build a democracy!"

Firmly, the new and tribe-descended President "cleaned up" the post office system and employed several diligent auditors. Well aware that Liberia was not a democracy but merely a partial framework of a republic as built somewhat shakily and shabbily at Monrovia, Tubman saw even that framework in great peril. During 1943 Liberia had formally entered the war on the side of the United States, a repetition of its course in World War I. Like most other African countries, Liberia stood to lose by taking either side. Its action in joining the United States had been distinctly gallant and more than casually hazardous.

Almost instantly, able packs of German submarines had taken advantage of the strategically favorable African shore to blast British, French, and Dutch shipping to rubble. Bereft of shipping excises, long the principal income of Liberia, public revenues fell distressingly. In particular, the chronically underpar school system, bereft of its principal support, was at the point of collapse. The ivory trade was virtually dead. Big-game hunting, ordinarily productive of considerable license revenue, had ceased. Mining operations and scattered ventures in lumbering were halted.

Firestone rubber was the only continuing export and excise source, since the normal trade in tropical fibers, coffee, palm oils, and other lesser crops was paralyzed by the lack of ships. (Rubber was being carried out by plane and U.S.-chartered ships.) For the then desperate war needs, Liberian rubber was important. In 1944 the country's rubber production totaled a mere 19,000 tons (though at present it approaches 30,000 tons per year). Even the 19,000 tons gave Liberia second place to Ceylon as the most important source of natural rubber for the Allied fighting forces. The catch or, as the Liberian says, the trap, was the then foreboding fear that all natural rubber might presently be made obsolete by the new and heavily subsidized industry of synthetic rubber. More recent history has disproved this fear.

Tubman found his country at crisis. In the normally verdant interior, serious droughts had occurred. These had been followed by grievous rice famines. Since rice is the sustaining food of the interior, hungry tribespeople were moving desperately and ominously. As Tubman knew, the tribes had long been growing apart from the politicians' mecca at Monrovia. Inland chiefs had complained bitterly, and with reason, of greed, graft, and incompetence on the part of politically appointed district commissioners. Tubman, who had pondered and probed into all these dark situations before his inauguration, waited restlessly to go into action.

At his inaugural reception he proposed one brief and amiable toast: "... To democracy, and to the many eyes that are watching us." The toast was as African as it was spontaneous. The jungle man, as a rule, is ever conscious of being watched—by keen and not always friendly eyes which he can rarely see. A son of the Cavally swamps and the Ivory Coast elephant pastures beyond, Tubman knows the jungle. He knows the shrewdness of its eyes and the fierceness of its claws. He knew, further, that Liberia was being watched by the great warring powers, both friends and foes. He also knew that a great part of the official world was and is peering and peeping to see whether or not an all-Negro government can be honorable and competent. Tubman knew then, as he knows now, that he and his government were being viewed as prime exhibits of the political and social competency of a race.

During the exhaustive formalities of inauguration, while the Liberian Army band blared a loud salvo of Jerome Kern dance music, a roving correspondent for a New York morning newspaper edged to the President's side:

"What do you prefer to be called, Mr. President?"

William Tubman grinned impishly, "Call me the convivial cannibal from Cape Palmas!" Still grinning he proceeded downstairs in the somewhat rococo and still uncompleted five-storied executive mansion to preside at the first cabinet meeting. The French Ambassador proposed a toast to William V. S. Tubman, "Africa's outstanding statesman." The band played again. Even above its slightly harmonic uproar the celebrants could hear the President's laughter. The Tubman laugh is the quintessence of gaiety, an ultimate boiling over of sheer African joy. "Tell us another story, Mister Secretary!" After a brief pause the laughter again sounded and reverberated. Then the conference room door banged shut, and the laughter was done.

Tubman's instructions to his new cabinet were amazingly terse: "Cabinet members will work all this week end at your respective desks. Early Monday we leave officially for the interior. We will there spend the next ten or twelve weeks—without holidays and without limit to work hours! . . ."

The following week marked an upset in all government precedences. From Monrovia the new President led a lightly luggaged entourage of cabinet members, secretaries, and two auditors, plus a native cook and a retinue of native burden carriers. There are no passenger railroads in Liberia, and at that time most of the hinterlands were completely lacking in roads and bridges, though this is not the case at present.

During most of its way the official procession tramped the steep and bush-grown foot trail. African country-style, they had one meal daily, that in the late afternoon. Tubman called his group the overage Cub Scouts, and the diligent patrol spent the nights where darkness found them, whether in guest huts in far back tribal villages or pup tents pitched in the open. The first itinerary included the principal village chief's homes of fourteen of the twenty-three tribes of Liberia and included several communities so remote that they can be reached only by way of dugout canoes.

It was far and away the most diligent political workout in Liberian history. But there were no fatalities, and the trek set the pattern for recurrent "hinterland palavers," which repeatedly have taken four or five months of the President's year. By now Tubman's hinterland palavers have gained orthodoxy. The President, followed by his official party, proceeds to the chief's hut or house or the village palaver center. There the President seats himself on a log, or a council robe or a folding chair, and proceeds to the business at hand, while the local chiefs, petty chiefs, and the tribespeople circle about him.

The local or nearest district commissioner is on hand to "speak for the government." The President's role is somewhat like that of the moderator at a New England town meeting. However, as a preliminary step, Tubman inspects the commissioner's records and tax books. The latter have to be correct and legible; otherwise a new commissioner.

Then the President lights a cigar, tilts it at an angle of about seventy degrees, and for hours and hours listens, with methodical replacements of the cigar.

Tubman revels in the traditional tribal palavers which he defines as the world's oldest and best "rootbed of democracy." Usually he seeks to direct or lead the talks along lines of real and long-proved needs, which are plentiful. Chiefs, elders, and commoners alike rise to state urgent problems: Wild elephant herds are ruining the rice crops. Leopards are killing the sheep and goats. "President" should therefore send soldiers to shoot down the elephants and leopards. Sometimes the President agrees. Frequently he attaches his consent to counterproposals in the common good: If "tribe" will build a schoolhouse, "government" will supply teacher; if Buzzies will build and keep five leagues of trail, Bassas will build and keep five more, and government will build and keep another five.

Many talk. The combined wordage is colossal, and though Tubman speaks at least seven of the tribal languages, frequently he is obliged to use interpreters, since at least sixteen tribal languages or dialects are still used in rural Liberia, even though English is the official language. As a rule the President suggests while the chiefs, elders, and tribe members decide or agree. Tubman believes that this, too, is requisite for developing the primitive community as a workable democracy. He is entirely convinced, too, that what the visiting sophisticates call "primitive" man has a vivid and valid interest in the work and uses of government.

Accordingly, William V. S. Tubman, the only tribesman ever to be President of Africa's only republic, resolved to take national government to the people so that the people in time will come to national government. Rather promptly his arduous hinterland jaunts began to pay off. During his first official palaver trip he had urged the tribe chiefs, elders, and principal farmers to double their rice plantings as a safeguard against recurrent famines and as a protective device whereby he saved the ruinous expense of importing costly and oftentimes inferior rice from foreign places, particularly since Siam, Ceylon, or other rice-exporting countries seemed rather permanently shut off by wars, civil strife, and collapsed currencies.

For the most part the Liberian tribes "played ball," as Tubman puts it. Within a year the rice plantings were almost doubled, and there have been no more famines or hunger migrations since Tubman took office.

The interior shows other notable improvements. Peace and order are far more uniform than before. Records of thefts, assaults, manslaughter, and other major crimes are at a long-time low. The era of intertribal wars has passed. Tubman points out several rather convincing reasons for this, among them the fact that, for a long-needed change, the government commissioners who deal with the tribes are more competent and honest than before. Another reason is that a cycle of bountiful crop years has largely erased the threat of literal starvation, and public education is on the upgrade with more tribal schools at work than ever before, though still not nearly enough.

Yet Tubman returns from his successive palaver trips with many worries and painful recollections. Most Liberians are tribal farmers, and though hinterland agriculture is improving, it is still far from adequate. Also, disease problems remain serious. The tribespeople still suffer most known diseases, and, alas, many unknown diseases. In many rural centers population is falling off. Substantially avoidable diseases, such as smallpox, still ravage and torment the tribes. For example, among the Kpelles, Tubman witnessed at first-hand a smallpox epidemic in which hundreds of the tribespeople, from babies to the oldest patriarchs, languished, stank, and suffered in the direly inadequate "sick bushes" or primitive isolation camps, and almost a tenth part of the tribe perished.

Like any other traveler in back-country Liberia, Tubman sees the hundreds of fields, farms, and villages that are now unproductive and abandoned. These and other mortal adversities seem almost as permanent and invincible as the lush dark-green hills of Liberia. The nation remains chronically lacking in medical facilities and revenues for supporting them. Except for two good but incessantly crowded hospitals on the Firestone plantations, four overcrowded and impoverished mission clinics, and one smallish government hospital at Monrovia, Liberia had no hospitals at the time Tubman became President. The nation has never had a medical school, and, as of 1944, it had only one mission school for nurses. In 1944, except for the Firestone medical staff, all Liberia had only three licensed physicians, two of them Haitians and the third a refugee from Nazi-land.

The United States Army, which had moved into Liberia somewhat like a bumbling and undecided tornado, brought along a routine detachment of medical officers, who centered their respective attention on building latrines, chlorinating water for the troops, setting up "stations" for venereal prophylaxis, and mimeographing the usual and sordid warnings against syphilis and the dire seductiveness of the native women.

The latter action annoyed Tubman. Like any experienced tropico, he knows that syphilis is never a major problem in places where malaria is endemic, as it has long been throughout Liberia. He knows, too, that the wiles of the native women are distinctly within global patterns and averages.

Thus, even while U.S. Army jeeps speeded like crazy over the almost roadless countrysides, and bomber fleets roared to the north, even while wining and dining American officers and enlisted men, Tubman calmly insisted that he was not President of a nation of syphilitics or of streetless street-walkers. He accepted willingly and thankfully the service of a medical mission as provided by the United States by way of the U.S. Public Health Service. The mission proved helpful to Liberia. Particularly in the area of Monrovia it effected an important anti-malarial "crusade," refurbished the enfeebled national hospital, set up a nurses' training school, a medical laboratory, a prenatal aid center and a dental clinic in the capital, a training center for native midwives, a first visiting-nurse service, and a valuable campaign of smallpox vaccination.

Tubman hurriedly earmarked Liberian revenue with which to supplement the good work. He appointed a capable Liberian health commissioner and effected a plan for providing primer lessons in hygiene to all pupils enrolled in the eighty-four grade schools maintained by the Liberian government and the seventeen rural grade schools kept by the tribes. Responses were excellent, but the uncomfortable truth persisted that the total school enrollment of all Liberia was barely 22,000 in 1944, and is only about 36,000 at present; the literacy rate in all written languages combined, whether English, French, Arabic, or Nilotic, though perhaps slightly above current tropical averages, remains below 20 per cent of the known population.

Tubman has toiled to meet that situation. By the end of 1950 Liberia, in terms of proportion of total income, was spending more on public health and more on public education than any other sovereign nation: about one-third of the entire national revenue for public education and about one-fourth for public health.

Even so, the most is still not nearly enough. The expansion and improvement of government services must have the support of an expanding economy. During Tubman's first year in office the total revenue receipts of Liberia averaged barely one dollar per capita (the U.S. dollar is now the official currency of Liberia). By 1947 the national revenue approached two dollars per capita: a memorable increase yet one that leaves Liberia one of the poorer nations in terms of public revenues. Even so, the little nation's foreign trade has almost doubled since 1944 (about 27,000,000 dollars in 1950 as compared with about 14,200,000 seven year earlier), and during Tubman's administration, the public debt has waned to a bare 40 cents per capita, which is currently the least among all the sovereign nations. Further, Tubman has dutifully maintained the long-remarkable Liberian tradition for never failing to meet punctually every commitment for public debt retirement. Liberia, not Finland, has remained in truth the "little country that always pays."

Tubman has evidenced no desire to change or interrupt the latter tradition. In fact he is rather grimly determined that Africa's only republic, and the only real semblance of a Negro democracy on earth, must maintain, at all costs, its immaculate record as a debtor. There is an understandable issue of pride and race obligation involved, and there is also an urgent, well-motivated desire to keep the nation out of hock to other powers, not excepting the United States.

Even so, the toils, needs, and expenses of government keep climbing, in "darkest Africa" even as at home. Agricultural services, debt services, basic government costs, more or less requisite public schools, roads, bridges, airports, pensions, and health facilities require several revenue dollars for every revenue dollar as yet forthcoming.

Tubman believes that more and better schools are the first necessary step for "evangelizing" the needs and practices of public health, better agriculture, and durable national democracy. His administration has begun granting government fellowships whereby about fifty talented young Liberians are enabled to study medicine and other "useful arts" in a wide selection of American colleges and universities.

Also, the President set out to attain at least a piecemeal solution to some of the basic farming needs of his country. He managed to employ a distinguished rice agronomist from Ceylon who now roams the interior to demonstrate and tactfully advise the tribespeople on ways of expanding and bettering their greatest subsistence crop. He has succeeded in "borrowing" from the U.S. Department of Agriculture an able young agronomist who is out to teach Liberians how to grow garden crops.

At its inland town of Kakata, Liberia has one noteworthy technical school, the Booker T. Washington Institute, where sons of chiefs and petty chiefs are taught the trades of farming, animal husbandry, and basic engineering along with manual crafts such as lumber-making, carpentry, blacksmithing, an automotive mechanics. All the graduates, most of them in their late twenties, who leave the school with a speaking knowledge of English and several worthwhile trades, are returned to their villages and tribes. The President and his administration bank heavily on the Booker Washington Institute, which is one of the most effective tribal schools in all Africa.

These and many other of Tubman's moves and reliances are well definable as democratic moves. The tribesman President states with forthrightness that his most decisive and most personal task is to comprehend what democracy really is in the confused and blatant world of today. In this quest he feels that he has gained most from his very personal studies of the letters of Thomas Jefferson. It is no coincidence that the accredited yearbook of Liberia has come to be the President's state-of-the-nation address which this reporter regards as the most distinctive Jeffersonian documents in the present-day world.

In this attainment Tubman remains one of the few living heads of state who invariably and completely writes his own addresses. He explains, "Jefferson did so, and I am also a Jefferson man."

Accordingly, several weeks before the annual convening of the legislature, the Liberian President retreats to "the cottage," a squat, chocolate-pie-brown bungalow which waits at the ocean's edge in Monrovia, well hidden by boungainevillea and flowering trees, where with ample liquid fortification he writes his painstaking and highly philosophic reports in longhand and with a hard-lead pencil.

The reports follow a determined orthodoxy. They begin with a careful review of the current work of the various departments, swing briskly into such perennial Presidential recommendations as suffrage for all Liberian women, most of whom are still multiple wives, an equitable income tax for all Liberians, a drastic expansion in facilities for public education and for public health, then an eloquent appeal for more and better public roads (mileages of public roads in Liberia are now about seven times the total when Tubman became President, while several dozen of the narrow, swaying stick bridges of an earlier tribal era have been replaced by durable bridges of steel and cement). Finally there is a Jeffersonian-Lincolnian appeal, sometimes in near Ciceronian rhetoric, for a government of, by, and for the people.

Finished with his once-a-year formal speech, the President retreats to the ocean-side "cottage" where he is usually agreeable to talking further, renewing Scotch highballs, and listening to the current crop of real or would-be funny stories. Later, the chances are overwhelming that Tubman will slip into his gay blue blazer, bought at Brooks Brothers, look out the high window at the tranquil, black-blue Atlantic, and launch into a soliloquy more or less as follows: "Once democracy is built, it will, for its own perpetration, build schools, hospitals, roads, bridges, experiment farms, clinics, churches, and the many other good things that Liberia needs and must have. Here in the African tropics it is more than averagely hard to build such goodnesses as churches, schools, and hospitals; and it's hard to keep them going after they are built.

"It is even harder to build a democracy, in the manner of modern government and needs. Here it took about ninety-nine years to get the first three tribe representatives into our legislature. More recently we have succeeded in getting a few more of the actual tribesmen, who have always been the overwhelming majority of Liberians, into our government at Monrovia. They have made good and useful legislators, and at long last, after a century of rule by the few, and rule by the immigrants, these hinterlanders are helping us qualify as a democracy. . . . It is good and right that we mix the Foos, Twes, Flomos, Botos, and Sobos with the Thompsons, Kings, Barclays, Hubbards, and Tubmans. It is good and right because it is democracy . . . which, I believe, is the great fine hope of Africa and the world . . . the right spirit and the ultimate grace of government now and tomorrow."

The President scoots his highball glass to a convenient table and reaches for an oversized cigar. "So far as national government goes, democracy is young here in Liberia, though, of course, in terms of the tribes it is old as the hills. But national democracy is being born here, too. I am convinced that it will be born in other tropical places. The sperm is made. The wombs are waiting. The tropics are half of mankind, and half of mankind will not be left ungoverned. Democracy remains as the salvation of the ungoverned."

Tubman blows a police whistle to indicate that his glass requires a refill: "I have had the job and the honor of serving first as midwife, then as wet nurse to democracy here in this capital. Liberian democracy today is getting somewhere near the babyhood of American democracy during Jefferson's last term of Presidency. By the time my term is up—Liberian Presidents get only one term apiece—I am hopeful that this baby democracy will be as far along as American democracy was during Monroe's time. Nursing a baby democracy is no easy job. But it's a hell of a lot easier and simpler than carrying a colony or propelling a dictatorship. . . ."

The President relights his cigar and clamps it between his well-tended white teeth. "The only real choice today is between democracy and dictatorship. The colony is dead everywhere. Actually the colony has been dead and smelling for a long time. But the day that Jap bombs fell on Pearl Harbor signed its formal death warrant. Actually, since Pearl Harbor most of the tropical earth has been in anarchy. That is what my tribe forefathers called the Hades of being nowhere."

Tubman strolls to the open veranda where giant African moonflowers sway in the night wind. "Socialism is not really government. . . . It's an affliction—a parasitic disease of government, like the leper's sore, like the cancerous throat, like the stinking breath of a man dying of tuberculosis. . . . Socialism is a sickness of government . . . just as is what some Americans call statism. . . .

"Here in Liberia, as throughout the tropics and elsewhere, man's choice is between democracy and dictatorship. I am certain that men who are even partly free prefer democracy. Where this is not already born, it can be begotten. The wombs are waiting. God and men will see them filled. . . ."

As a long-time champion of democracy, and one of its most effective builders, Tubman keeps finding that the life of a democracy-builder is a hard and busy one. For like the weather, democracy is easy to talk about and difficult to do about. Accordingly, his eight-year marathon of democacy-nursing has required interminable work, hard, exacting, oftentime nettlesome and painful work. It has called for abandoning personal ease and leisure, the tossing out of affable, career government men and replacing the gay and witty companions with tough and mirthless auditors.

Also it has required the handing out of slaps and heaves to the long-entrenched, vocal, and long anti-democratic American Negro minority in and around Monrovia. In his laborious "wet-nursing" of a tropical democracy, Tubman has worked and built in the face of momentous odds. He has been obliged to endure many annoyances and other liabilities from abroad, such as brazen advances by Soviet agents, the leather-lunged, though generally well-meant improprieties of U.S. military missions in Liberia, and the international publicizing of ill-planned and miserably failing industrial promotions. In reality none of these have built up Liberia in any conceivable way. All have hurt Liberia and impeded the progress of its democracy.

Yet in Liberia, as elsewhere, great work transcends annoyances. The great work there currently is that of changing Africa's only republic to one of the first tropical democracies. An inspiring if grim and sweaty beginning has already been made grimly and sweatily, yet more or less inevitably and decidedly inspiring because the new embryo of Liberian democracy grows out of a typical tropical womb of democracy. If it can gain strength and stature in Liberia, it can find strength and stature throughout much or most of the tropical earth today and tomorrow. Actually and provably, democracy is gaining strength and stature in Liberia.

Tropical land-builders are important. Builders of tropical democracy are even more important.

Like all other spheres of earth, the tropics are changing. By the hundreds of millions, tropical peoples and their governments are in mutation. The tropical colony no longer makes convincing sense. Tropical tyrant states continue to be born and continue to fade into foul-smelling mists. Particularly, in Southeast Asia, and by intermittent probes and pushes in many other tropical lands, Communism, via the U.S.S.R., keeps seeking to infiltrate and to seize power.

Yet tropical leaders like Tubman of Liberia, and many other leaders and men and women of good will in the tropics, are well aware that

Communism, like the Victorian and pre-Victorian concept of subservient colonies, does not actually belong in the tropics. Meanwhile the tropics remain people, lands, sun, rain, and growth, and these together remain in mutation. But the mutation is forward, not backward—to Victoria or the U.S.S.R.

# Tropics Are Tomorrow

~ * ~

THE tropics are made up of people and sunlight, of earth, air, and water, of rapid growth and great fertility, of great history featuring pasts which overlap futures, of memorable trends and causes.

Inevitably some of the latter are tied in with or grow out of trends and causes in other spheres of earth. Many are literal steppings back to temperate-zone histories of a century or longer ago; many are literal steppings back toward or into U.S. history.

For one example, memorable industrial eras or "industrial revolutions" are pressing ahead in many tropical countries—great parts of Brazil, India, Rhodesia, the Belgian Congo, Puerto Rico, and Malaya, to name only a few. An actual majority of all tropical countries are either entering industrial eras or are headed toward the thresholds thereof.

All this is plainly important. Even more important are the social evolutions. What is eloquently termed the century of the common man is steadily penetrating the tropical earth. The penetration is perhaps late, but it is real. At last the Lexington-Concord shot, as fired by the duly renowned Minute Man of the American Revolution, has been heard more or less completely around the equator. In temperate-zone terms, the hearing has been late, and many tropical terrains have been hard for liberty, equality, and fraternity to move over, even as for people to move over.

Nevertheless, the inevitable era of human liberation is going tropical. It is a laborious, hard-plodding transit. It is raising higher and higher the required levels of work, skills, and health in the tropics. The subservient tropical colony is at least as out of date as the celluloid collar and removable shirt front.

For the most part, tropical caste systems are yielding ground. There are no more Eli Yales getting piously and culturally rich from the slave trade. At best or worst, slavery in the tropics is abating. There are no more Cecil Rhodes, and, on the whole, the tropics are being treated better by the principal world powers than ever before, though there is still plenty of room for improvement and for more capable self-realization.

Quite inevitably, the United States has a part to play therein; the tropics are very close to us, and they are getting closer. Unavoidably we are part of their world and they of ours. As in the past, we continue splashing the tropics with broadsides of noble sentiments which, however eloquent, are about as nutritious and durably satisfying as a splendid banquet eaten in a dream.

But the tropics as a whole are entering a rather well-determined age of self-realization, and for that reason and many others, we can help them, and they can help us far more than ever before. Both publicly and privately, officially and unofficially, we can help them help themselves, and it is heartening to see and report that far more than ever before we are beginning to do so.

For example, at present, the United States government is carrying on in miniature a number of co-operative public works in the nearby American tropics through the agency of a federal corporation called the Institute of Inter-American Affairs.

This work is distinctly midget in terms of present-day international enterprises: the non-profit government corporation is currently receiving about seven million dollars per year from Congress. That is slightly less than the postage expenses of the U.S. Congress and less than half the annual cost of garbage collection in New York City.

Even so, dollar for dollar the latter-named seven million dollars, which is being matched at a present rate of four-to-one by about a dozen governments of the American tropics, may very well be the most highly beneficial international spending now in progress. It is particularly noteworthy because it demonstrates the growing tropical mood for self-help and self-realization.

# HELPING OTHERS HELP THEMSELVES

THE embryo of this noteworthy but all-too-little-noticed work story began taking form back in 1930 when, by a grudging Congressional permission, the U.S. Department of Agriculture warily undertook to establish a first tropical agricultural experiment station at Mayagüez, in Puerto Rico. The station's work was necessarily modest in scope, but from the beginning it had excellent direction.

The move gained momentum during the early 1940's, when the Co-ordinator of Inter-American Affairs, then enjoying a $55,000,000-a-year appropriation—"almost as much as it costs to shell a very small Pacific atoll"—set up a government corporation called the Institute of Inter-American Affairs, which after the demise of the Co-ordinator's Office in 1946 was continued as a federal corporation with directors appointed by the Secretary of State.

The Institute continues to represent the United States in several co-operative enterprises concerned with serving agriculture, health, and education in the American tropics.

The latter work actually began during 1942, with first undertaking, in co-operation with sixteen other American governments, including Brazil, Peru, Venezuela, Paraguay, Haiti, Costa Rica, Panama and Nicaragua, to increase food production in those countries as required for the latter's "war efforts" in connection with supplying us such strategic war materials as wild rubber, palm oils, and cinchona bark for quinine, and provisioning the U.S. Armed Forces stationed in the American tropics.

A considerable part of the work failed—in part because it was poorly planned and poorly directed or both; in part because, for one reason or another, good work was abandoned prematurely. Much more important, some of the work was good, and a great part of it has endured.

There is not room here to tell of all the far-flung and varying enterprises of the Institute. But a few typify the many. For example, there was and there still is STICA (*Servicio Tecnico Interamericano de Co-*

*operacion Agricola*) of Paraguay, as launched in 1942 by the Institute of Inter-American Affairs and the Paraguayan government. Paraguay is typical in many ways of the borderline tropics. Though distinctly tropical, its climate is friendly toward numerous temperate-zone crops, yet most of its forests, prairies, native ranges, and its many hydroelectric resources remain scantily developed—so much so that, until recently, Paraguay's domestic farm production was never sufficient to meet home needs, even though its sparse million people are overwhelmingly agrarian.

The *Servicio,* alias Paraguay and the United States, began by establishing near Asunción, the capital, a 500-acre experiment farm as a center for seed-testing, crop introduction, and distribution of planting materials to citizen farmers. On the nearer outskirts of Ascunción, the *Servicio* has established a model dairy farm to demonstrate ways of overcoming the prevalent tropical dilemma of no milk. In 1946, at the end of its third operating year, the "demonstration" milk farm had become self-supporting, as had the Paraguayan government's new 27,000-acre beef cattle ranch.

To help its citizen farmers benefit from these and other enterprises, the Paraguayan government, using its own funds (the total United States contribution is barely a third of a million dollars), next organized a rural credit pool to assist interested farmers in growing some of the crops and using some of the farming techniques previously "demonstrated." In return for a small one-year loan, the farmer agrees to plant the seeds that are supplied him and to cultivate the crops and improve his pastures. To date about 99 per cent of the one-year loans have been recovered.

Also, the *Servicio* has developed a small corps of itinerant farming advisers (corresponding to county agricultural agents and home demonstration agents in the United States) and a demonstration farm colony where tenant farmers are permitted to take over small plots of good land, improve and plant the land, harvest crops, and in time buy the farms with their own earnings. STICA also provides short-term loans to enable cattle ranchers to buy pure-bred bulls for their herds and grass seed for improving the ranges. In Paraguay, as in other countries, such ventures have been condemned as government meddling in farming. Perhaps, in a sense, it is that. But there is a case to be made, too, that any government worth its salt and gold braid has very real obligations to serve the most basic trade of its people, particularly, as in Paraguay, where agriculture has remained so poorly developed and so evidently in need of help.

Thus far the Paraguayan venture has stressed the development of crops already established rather than the introduction of new crops.

## BRILLIANCE IN COSTA RICA

IN OTHERS of the warmer American nations the co-operative *servicios* have made memorable advances in introducing new crops as well as refurbishing the old ones. One rather typical example has been the Costa Rican vegetable-growing venture as begun in 1942 by about two hundred citizen-farmers with help from the Institute of Inter-American Affairs, to the end of proving that many of the common garden vegetables much needed in tropical diets can be grown effectively in many or most tropics.

By 1942 food shortages were more than ordinarily acute throughout most Caribbean countries, which for generations have been importing meats, dried fish, lard and fats, grains, beans, rice, and other staples and paying for them with exports of sugar, coffee, and, more recently, bananas. During the early dark months of World War II, Caribbean shipping was all too literally blasted to pieces by Nazi submarines. The resulting food shortages were intensified as U.S. Armed Forces were poured broadside over the Panama Canal area and its various outposts. Costa Rica, with fertile soils and many competent farmers, is nearby the Canal Zone and otherwise promising as a land of gardens.

The Institute of Inter-American Affairs undertook to encourage the growing of vegetable crops by guaranteeing minimum prices for the urgently needed harvests, setting up receiving warehouses, and supplying interested local farmers with suitable seeds, soil testing, and technical advice as requested.

Promptly, unprecedented truck farms began to appear in many areas of Costa Rica. By 1944 these were supplying about fourteen million pounds of fresh vegetables yearly for the use of Canal Zone garrisons and Pan American highway workers, and about half again as much for local markets.

Among the temperate-zone vegetables successfully grown were beets, cabbage, carrots, lettuce, green peas, bunch beans, broccoli, cucumbers, onions, peppers, squashes, sweet corn, sweet potatoes, and tomatoes. For the most part, tomatoes and pineapples proved the most profitable of the list. Pineapples, of course, are a tropical or subtropical crop to which many Costa Rican lands are particularly well suited. But tomatoes, though indigenous to the American tropics, long ago lost their place on the roster of tropical crops.

Costa Rica's new ventures in vegetable-growing have been impeded by fungus and insect enemies and even more so by the lack of adequate refrigeration. But all considered, the venture has been an impressive exhibit of the fact that many of the great vegetable crops of the temperate zone can be adapted both to tropical growing conditions and to the unhappily limited diets common to most tropical peoples.

## PERUVIAN EXPERIMENT

IN PERU, at a cost to the United States of $176,165 per year for five years (and to Peru of about seven times that amount), the Institute of Inter-American Affairs has helped introduce still another tropical farming enterprise called SCIAPA (*Servicio Cooperativo Inter-Americano de la Producion de Alimentos*). Here, as in Paraguay and Costa Rica, most of the program is self-sustaining. *Servicio Cooperativo* has developed an agricultural extension service variously adapted to Peru, its hot, coastal valleys, its cool, tillable highlands, and its foggy wonderlands of forests.

The undertaking includes the establishment of co-operative pools of farm machinery for the benefit of the majority of small and preponderantly poor farmers who may now rent power machinery which SCIAPA employees operate and maintain. Field offices distribute seeds of forage, field, and garden crops at cost to the mainly Indian farmers, and they make sprays and insecticides available at or near cost. In an effort to combat the many ruinous livestock diseases, SCIAPA has set up quarantine stations and has also imported breeding stock—for the most part registered cattle—for resale to Peruvian farmers.

Here again the work undertaken is noteworthy, not because it is sufficient—it is nowhere near so—but because it seeks to show the way toward a more competent agriculture which is of life-or-death importance to Peru, as it is to most other tropical countries. For here, as in so many other countries, improved agriculture is superior internationalism and ever-necessary human conservation.

The Institute of Inter-American Affairs, with its varied successes and failures, keeps demonstrating that tropical agriculture can be benefited on a government-to-government basis, and that such work does not necessarily impede or challenge the respective sovereignties of nations.

There is need for such works. It is part of tropical development, indeed, of tropical survival. For now, as in the past, the lack of variety in crops and the lack of valid and needed subsistence crops remain among the most grievous shortcomings of tropical agriculture, which is the great and age-old fulcrum on which the lever of any rising tropical economy must rest.

## BIG BUSINESS FARMING

FOR the most convincing of reasons, better agriculture for the tropics is vivid, living internationalism. It need not be attained solely by governments; indeed, it cannot be so attained. Everyday, workaday farmers and other citizens are its indispensable standard-bearers.

But the fact is memorable that business, big business and little business, in the past principally big business—"Crown companies," "special privilege companies," and other "big business,"—have also had much to do with the ups and downs of tropical agriculture. A half-century ago more than five hundred major companies in the British Isles, France, Germany, Holland, and Belgium alone were powerfully active in various phases of tropical agriculture.

The latter number has fallen to a bare thirty. Most of the one-time mighty Chinese firms in the tropics have also lost ground there. The United States today has only one major corporation (capitalized in excess of a quarter-billion dollars) engaged principally in tropical agriculture. This is the big and still-growing Boston-born United Fruit Company, which now operates seventeen principal tropical divisions scattered from Cuba and the Dominican Republic throughout Central America, in Colombia, Ecuador, and, by way of Elders and Fyffes, a British affiliate, in the Cameroons and Nigeria in West Africa.

On the whole, the larger tropical farming companies have done appallingly little to diversify and otherwise improve tropical agriculture. Admittedly there have been exceptions, among which Dutch companies have been the most numerous. But the majority have tended to intensify the crippling shortages of subsistence crops and to reduce the variety of useful crops generally in the tropics. Rubber companies have raised rubber groves to the exclusion of most or all other crops. Spice companies have grown only spices; tea companies, only tea; palm oil companies, little or nothing except palms; sugar companies, only sugar; and banana companies, only bananas. One-crop agriculture, bad anywhere, is particularly bad in the tropics.

But fortunately, as noted, there are exceptions to the list of one-crop companies in the tropics. In terms of size, strength, and prevailing work in crop introduction and diversification, United Fruit is the most notable of these exceptions. It is likewise a particularly noteworthy proving ground of the abilities or inabilities of big and profit-making business to benefit tropical agriculture substantially while helping itself. Here, again, the story is one of ups and downs, of a few immensely important successes and some highly significant failures.

Back in 1942, United Fruit began the most ambitious and the most varied crop introduction program ever attempted by any one organization in the American tropics. The undertaking was formally announced in July, 1942, as United Fruit's "Middle American Charter" . . . "a new fundamental policy":

That of extension of production in Middle America, and the Caribbean Nations, of certain essential tropical crops needed by the United States to make us less dependent on the Far East. Countries in which these crops will first be introduced include Guatemala, Honduras, Nicaragua, Costa Rica, and Panama. . . . It is and will continue to be a fundamental policy of this Company to utilize its organization and its tropical resources to assist the native population in growing such products without expectation of profit to the Company other than good will from friendly neighbors.

It happens that this reporter, then an executive employee of United Fruit, wrote the original draft of the "Middle America Charter" and prepared its "interpretation."

Since 1942 and before, I have followed the Company's crop-introduction ventures closely, watching some of them succeed and others fail and pondering the multitudinous details, the problems of tropical crop introduction, and the changing ethics of international business generally.

United Fruit's ventures in introducing or otherwise developing new crops for the American tropics include plantings that cover about two hundred square miles of tropical earth at total costs approaching twenty-five million dollars. Two of its experimental crops, abacá and African oil palms, have already assumed important places in terms of U.S. supplies. Abacá, the banana-like perennial from which Manila fiber is taken, was planted and brought to production at the expense of the United States. The rest of the experimental crops, numbering in all about fifty, have been introduced at the United Fruit Company's expense and principally by the work and talents of its employees in the tropics, somewhat more than nine-tenths of whom are citizens of the countries where they are employed.

The "experimental list," as originally selected, included vetiver grass (which supplies a root oil used in making fine perfumes, and was formerly grown in Java and Ceylon); oil palms from West Africa; castor beans; several tropical varieties of tung nut trees from the Philippines; soybeans; several different species of bamboo (mainly from the Pacific tropics); a fiber plant called roselle (from India);

also the kindred tropical fibers, jute and mammee; luffa, or vegetable sponge; Malayan derris (now the most common source of rotenone insecticides); lemon grass and citronella, and other grasses that supply volatile oils; also a number of tropical and subtropical fruits, including oranges, avocadoes, mangosteens; and a particularly promising list of tropical timbers, including Australian pine, Burmese and Indian cassia wood, Central American cedars, East Indies harpullia, Honduras mahogany, West Indian mahogany, Burmese and Malay rosewoods and teak, Central American rosewood, eucalyptus, and others.

The mixing of failures with successes was anticipated by the planners. On the failure list are such immigrant crops as vetiver grass. Brought into Central America, the bizarre grass from Java proved uneconomical because of unreliable markets, proportionately high company wages in Central America, and certain chemical inconsistencies of the product. The records of the "essential" or grass oils particularly, lemon grass and citronella, were fairly promising in terms of routine agriculture, but the crops can be grown quite competently by citizen farmers with small acreages available. Accordingly, after the grass oils had been introduced and after citizen farmers had adopted them, United Fruit reduced its introduction work to an experimental basis.

Castor beans were another failing experiment. This rather horrible medical standby also has important industrial uses which give it particular promise as a world crop. Theoretically it is grown best in the tropics where the handsome red-stalked plants frequently produce two or even three crops in a single year. But the lowland soils of Central America seem to be too rich for the castor plants, which are further penalized by a great variety of blights and root rots. In Honduras, Costa Rica, and Panama the experimental plantings failed after a capable try-out.

United Fruit's experimental plantings of tropical types of tung trees, which produce the valuable nut oil used for making fine paints and varnishes, proved a comparable failure, at least to the extent that the Philippines varieties of tung, transplanted into the American tropics, thus far have been unable to compete with the Chinese types of tung that are being grown with considerable success in the U.S.

South. The Company has succeeded notably in expanding plantings of citrus fruits, pineapples, and various tropical fruits, principally mangosteens, as purely local crops for the use of employees.

Introductions of Malayan derris, already mentioned as the principal cultivated source of the insecticide rotenone, though handsomely proved in Malaya, Java, and other eastern tropics, have not thrived promisingly in Central America. Trial plantings of the tropical fibers, jute, roselle, and mammee prospered, but United Fruit has thus far been unable to develop adequate markets for the fibers. As I see it the principal fault here is with the Company, not the fiber crops, though there is some consolation in the common knowledge that the hardy fiber crops just named can be grown by everyday farmers and require no very costly routines of introduction.

The two most costly and lamentable failures in the United Fruit's experimental program deal with two of the most needed of tropical crops, namely tropical types of hybrid corn and soybeans, both of which crops require patient and skillful introduction and trial propagations far beyond the ready facilities of most citizen farmers.

Long recognized as the greatest of the leguminous crops, the soy is now one of the most versatile and widespread of utility crops. There are numerous species or subspecies adaptable to hot countries; the high protein content of the bean makes it particularly valuable in tropical diets, which remain so expensively lacking in proteins. The fact that it is leguminous, or nitrogen-restoring, is of exceptional benefit to tropical soils, and the soys provide excellent feed for livestock, so badly needed throughout the tropics.

The crop-introduction venture of United Fruit included eight varieties of soybeans, supposedly adaptable to tropical use. Five of the eight failed to prosper—a fairly normal "risk." The other three, one from Puerto Rico and two from the Dominican Republic, showed decided promise in various areas of lowland Central America. The experiment proceeded for seven years. Notably in lowland Honduras, the soybean crop flourished during the wet seasons but wilted and parched during a succession of freakishly dry seasons. The results in Guatemala and Costa Rica were better, though inconsistent. But total results were sufficiently promising to justify expansion of the experiment which, of course, called for expert and patient work in plant-breeding, painstaking extension of field tests, and the subsidizing of five to ten more years of experimental plantings on many thousands of acres of varying lands.

As I see it, United Fruit relinquished the work prematurely, though in some small part it is being resumed. Precisely that applies to the Company's all too pipsqueak ventures in introducing hybrid corn into the several corn-importing Caribbean countries where "Maya Maize" is so urgently important for people and livestock alike, and where prevailing corn yields are so naggingly and expensively inadequate. The advantages of hybrid corns, which alone have increased U.S. corn yields by more than a fourth, are common knowledge.

So are the difficulties incident to developing and adapting suitable hybrid strains of corn to the many and varying tropical places where it is so stubbornly needed. The task is big, nagging, demanding of much time, expense, and detailed, next to interminable work. But big companies, like men, mules, and other creations, were made for work, and there is certainly no point to keeping a robust elephant just to pick up toothpicks.

Hybrid corn suited to the tropics, and tropical types of soybeans, are particularly noteworthy examples of great excellence attainable only by great effort and expense. For the most part, ten or more generations of plantings must be made, tended, recorded, compared, discarded, and selected. All that accomplished, the finally selected seeds must be distributed widely and preferably gratis to individual farmers, particularly small farmers, local "elders," and *milpa* lenders.

Research and demonstration are necessary, since the everyday farmer rarely has facilities for accomplishing them alone. It follows that a new crop is born only when real workaday farmers, several hundreds of them or, better still, several thousands of them, are enabled to see the new crop in planting, growth, and harvest and thus can make their own decisions as to whether or not they choose to risk their time, toil, sweat, and lands in growing the crop.

More than most corporate organizations, United Fruit has had opportunity to learn all this from vivid, first-hand experience. In some instances the crop-introduction work has proved both the understanding and the ability to place the new crops into the hands and lands of all manner of local farmers. This United Fruit has done freely in at least eight countries. Thus far, abacá and African oil palm, both mentioned previously, are supplying the best examples of a world crop from the Philippines and a world crop from West Africa, both of them succeeding in far-spread areas of the Caribbean lands.

In tropical work, even a few successes outbalance many failures. United Fruit has accomplished other notable crop-introduction work as regards tropical timbers. One of these is Australian pine, a splendid, rugged, and fast-growing tree which is proving brilliantly successful in Central America. Honduran mahogany, of which United Fruit has planted about two thousand acres, is proving itself an excellent lumber crop, a superior timber for house-building, and housing shortages in the tropics are hardly less than incessant.

Burmese rosewood, a soft wood somewhat similar in texture to fir, is another excellent tree crop; hardy, fast-growing, and valuable for house-building and furniture-making. The tree appears to thrive better in the valleys of Central America and other American tropics than in Burma. Teak, formerly from the Far East tropics, is another of the more promising tree crops for the American tropics. Teak trees are fast-growing, exceptionally hardy, and the wood is particularly valuable. Eucalyptus, similar to North American red gum, is another exceptionally promising forest crop for the American tropics.

United Fruit's experiments in growing bamboo, one of the more decisive crops of the tropical East, are also impressive. Test plantings have totaled about one thousand acres, principally of the common yellow or Chinese bamboo, which is fast-growing and easily propagated from culms (or stalk sections) and in this instance highly usable for propping harvest-heavy banana plants.

Unfortunately, there are still no adequate experiments in the American tropics with bamboo as a source of pulp wood and newsprint, which entirely too many tropical countries are still obliged to import, or with the giant bamboos which, as any Orient traveler knows, are superior and inexpensive materials for building homes in the tropics. In many Far East places entire houses, including sills, rafters, beams, floors, wall coverings, and roofs and furniture are built of locally grown hard bamboos—remarkably inexpensive houses which are termite and borer-free and strongly resistant to the wear and wrath of tropical weather. The structural types of bamboo remain virtually unknown in both the American and African tropics, which is quite really a pity.

The bamboos, as any botany text will confirm, are a rather immense family of giant grasses, most of them tropical. Some, as noted, are excellent for house-building. Some are almost as strong as structural steel. Others can be used very effectively for water pipes and drainage tile. Still others are superior sources of newsprint and other paper, while others provide the nearest ideal tropical furniture and, contrastingly, the best of tropical fencing. The story of the superbly important, too-little-developed and too-little-used bamboo crops is just one more brief entry in the still vast catalogue of underdeveloped or undeveloped tropical crops.

From the beginning, United Fruit has defined its motivation for introducing new crops in the American tropics as "enlightened selfishness" on the very plausible grounds that whatever durably benefits the American tropics inevitably benefits United Fruit, and on the grounds, too, that highly technical "high finance" crops such as bananas can no longer be grown effectively by either a majority or near majority of citizen farmers (in some part because nowhere near enough technically suitable land is available for this most exacting of tropical crops) and that many tropical crops can be introduced only by great and costly quantities of co-ordinated effort and risk.

More clearly and more competently than any other American business firm, United Fruit has demonstrated that business can add greatness and beneficial variety to tropical agriculture. In general the weakness shown by the demonstration is that, like the boarding house pie, there just isn't enough of it.

## CROPS TAKE WINGS

THE story tends to transcend routine business enterprises and to reiterate the fact that the trails of Johnny Appleseeds, present and future, are leading south. That became clearly apparent during the dark and generally confused years of World War II, after Japan had overwhelmed the more productive million square miles of the South Pacific and Southeast Asia.

Demanding war shortages and aggressive leaders in war hastened to prove in fact what the slower-paced agronomist had known in theory for a long time, namely, that most great tropical crops are readily transferable along lines of latitude, and that the exact lines of latitude, are usually not absolute, so long as the seed or other planting materials can be transported rapidly. (The seed of most tropical crops have a way of dying when they are moved slowly.)

A great new air age is providing the necessary rapid haulage. Seed flying became one of the memorable stories of World War II, and it is still possessed of particular moment to the tropics. During the last global war British and U.S. military aircraft flew selected seed of Hevea rubber trees from Japanese-seized lands of Sumatra, to India, West Africa, and to Central and South America. To Madagascar, South China, Burma, and Egypt, planes delivered the seeds of long-staple cottons and disease-resistant wheats and ryes. Live ewes and rams were carried by plane into wool-short Africa to replenish African wool and meat supplies. The work of these flyers and those who now succeed them demonstrates that the world-wide migration of great crops can be carried on as a two-way traffic—not simply an export of crop seed and planting stock from one specific nation, but rather as a commonly beneficial exchange of crops between locales, nations, continents, and distant islands.

The air age proceeds as a particular benefactor to tropical agriculture, including the valid migration of not only such crops as seeds, bulbs, cuttings, and nursery stock, but of livestock as well. Plane transport of breeding animals is being implemented by the techniques of artificial insemination by means of which the semen of highly valuable bulls or stallions or rams or other animal sires can be packed, insulated, flown thousands of miles by plane, and used to impregnate dams in another country or another continent.

## VIRTUE OF BALANCE

REPEATEDLY in the past, and even without benefit of rapid transport, world-influencing tropical crops have moved much or all the way around the equator from their places of beginning—rubber, spices, bananas, coconut and other oil palms, to name only a few.

The migration of worthwhile tropical crops is now gaining much greater effectiveness. The advantages are impressive. The process is demanding of work—in some instances, public or corporate work, at least as regards preliminary research and experiment; in almost all instances, private enterprise and work.

Granting this, many great tropical crops are clearly on their way toward worldwide importance and immensely expanded tropical benefit. This is because so many hundreds of millions of tropical peoples so urgently require a greater variety of crops—industrial crops and nutritious, health-defending subsistence crops as well.

Tropical agriculture can be brilliantly productive and an almost infinitely expansible science as well. Every day, farmers, government, and companies alike are proving this, and the scope and crescendo of the proofs continue to increase.

Even so, there are still far too many one-crop spheres in the tropics; the more decisive tropical crops are still numbered in fives or tens instead of hundreds, as they might be and should be to contribute the maximum good to maximum numbers.

For a long time the decisive centers of tropical production have remained direly out of balance. More or less unwittingly, the United States has done a great deal to keep them out of balance. But the God of growing things inclines towards impartiality. It follows that principal tropical lands remain in perpetual competition with other tropical lands. Competition, admittedly, is the blood and guts of capitalism; it is also the working sinews of democracy, and, as the United States has led in proving to all the world, competition is the best key to abundance.

The tropics as a whole have competition—naturally supplied. Memorably, and for inescapable reasons, the United States has inherited the task of refereeing at least in some part the globe-circling competition among the great tropics.

In part this competition is one of producing soils and how best to use them. In part it is an urgent, laborious race to reduce the ruinous loss from erosion and past abuses of soils, forests, and other great natural resources. Inevitably, too, the contest is one of the citizen farmer and the citizen community against the foreign company, the cartel or supply-and price-control groups, or the government confiscator.

The United States, in some part deservedly, in greater part by luck, has acquired a dynamic floor position for viewing the game and drama of tropical production. From this vantage we can view clearly and we can push aside many false credos, such as the one that contends that coolie wages are indispensable in tropical competition.

People still say, for example, that the American tropics simply cannot compete with the seventeen-cents-per-day Dutch-approved ceiling wage of rubber labor in Sumatra, or the seven-cents-per-day wage of southern China, or the Dutch-sanctioned Javanese sugar wage of eleven cents per day for men and six to eight cents a day for women and children. It is common knowledge that shockingly bad wages persist in much of the American tropics: in coffee lands, where peon wages remained substantially frozen while raw coffee prices climbed from eight cents a pound to sixty cents or more; in great areas such as Ecuador where farm workers can still be hired for as little as twenty cents a day; in many Central American highlands where farm wages still lag at lows of twenty-five cents per day; in parts of Haiti and Mexico, as little as thirty cents; in the inflation-cursed British West Indies, two shillings—optimistically forty cents per day.

But it is more than equally common knowledge that these and similar starvation wages do not lead to favorable commodity prices, and that in the tropics, as elsewhere, coolie wages are usually the most damnable of all extravangances.

They are unnecessary extravagances as well. Many of us have had good chances to see and to benefit from the remarkable ease and speed with which most tropical peoples, given the chance, change to highly skilled workers; how quickly a bull-cart people can rise into the aeronautical age; how swingers of machetes or cutlasses can change to expert tractor operators within a few weeks. Indeed, throughout recent warfares, "primitive" tropicals actually built air strips, unloaded cargoes, laid pipelines, built railroads, fueled and serviced tanks and bombers, and otherwise proved adaptability to technical and crucial needs.

Recent and current tropical history keeps proving that millions on millions of tropical workers, adjudged in terms of potential competence, are deserving of the greatest avalanche of pay rises ever deserved at vast wholesale.

In general, the competence of tropical labor remains grotesquely underrated and inadequately realized. The same is true of tropical soils. In the tropics as in the temperate zones the best soils have a way of recurring, not in huge concentrations, but rather in scattered zones or "pockets": in favorable locales, such as river valleys, prairies, or plateaus, at the base of ancient volcanoes, among newly formed deltas, or in the debris of great forests.

Quite evidently, the more fertile soils of the earth have not bypassed the tropics. Whatever the eloquent and by now well-healed bemoaners of our plundered planets or the easy-chair pointers out of our roads to survival may say (and it is a safe bet that they will continue repeating what their more scholarly predecessors have said better many times before), we know in a general way that somewhat more than half of the principal concentrations of rich soils remaining are in the tropics, and we know that while some of these areas are being depleted, many others are being increased by natural or, in a few instances, man-made procedures.

But, as noted, the actual proportion of good tropical soils currently in use is appallingly slight. Africa, for one example, which probably has somewhere near one-third of the more fertile soil remaining on earth, produces no more than 5 per cent of the food crops now grown. This admittedly is an approximation, but based on current surveys which will shortly be mentioned, it is a rather valid approximation.

For the tropical earth as a whole, the proportion of usable lands actually in use must be estimated, not in substantial fractions of the whole, but in infinitesimal fractions, and frequently in fractions of a single per cent.

Even India, which is the most populous of all tropical countries, now finds within its boundaries millions of acres of good lands waiting development—so many acres, in fact, that the present Indian government's campaign to raise domestic grain production from a current average of 40,000,000 tons yearly, somewhat below the famine line, to 50,000,000 tons, somewhat above the famine line, is succeeding.

Billions of acres of usable tropical lands remain unused, and as a very broad generality, the tropics of lower Asia and Middle Africa appear to hold the largest concentration of highly fertile soils remaining on earth. Importantly, the billions of acres of still unused tropical soils include all three of the productive levels of tropic altitudes: low wet-lands, best suited for growing palms, cocoa, rice, sugar cane, and other heavy harvests; the midlands and savannas or plateaus for more general agriculture, including grasses and grains, citrus fruits, pineapples, garden crops, and livestock; and the higher shelf lands and mountainsides for traditional highland crops such as pasture grasses, coffee, wool sheep, many valuable timbers, and many temperate-zone crops.

As yet, few of even the most densely populated tropics have reached or even neared the maximum productivity of their soils. Java, for example, the island headquarters of Indonesia, is only a little larger than Pennsylvania, yet it has about fifty million people. It somehow manages to feed that number, who are mainly farmers; its tonnages of crop exports have grown threefold during the past half-century, and there are numerous prospects for future improvement and increase in Javanese agriculture.

The United States today has about fifty people to the square mile. Tropical Africa as a whole has fewer than ten. The average for all the American tropics is below twelve people per square mile, probably somewhere near the population of frontier Kentucky during the times of Dan'l Boone. About 1,200,000 square miles of the lower Amazon Basin has no more than two million people, and there is excellent reason to believe that aboriginal Indian populations of the United States, even before Columbus was born, far exceeded two per square mile.

The point of this and all similar recitations is simply that the tropics have abundant room for growth of populations and growth in good uses of soils, all the more so because tropical agriculture is the most versatile productive institution now even vaguely known to man. Its world-influencing importance grows even more momentous with the now proved facts that most temperate-zone crops can be adapted to the tropics and that the man-bettering tropical crops, with no really important exceptions, can be moved from land to land and hemisphere to hemisphere, as man's needs require.

This means, of course, that the otherwise destructive competition between one producing area and the next can be alleviated by the studied diversification of crops. In the big cartel days, the United States used to draw some 88 per cent of all our tropical imports from what were then British Malaya, the Netherlands Indies, and a few smallish but intensely exploited areas in the far Pacific; a bare 7 per cent from all the American tropics; and less than 2 per cent from all Africa.

Such fantasies in favoritism are now highly avoidable. They never helped the United States as a whole, and they have proved detrimental or deadly to the causes and needs of internationalism. We can do better. Even more importantly, so can the tropics.

## NEW ERA OF TROPICAL PLANNING

THE most decisive pioneering trails of today and tomorrow lead south. The very feat of seeking out such trails, or otherwise following untried paths, usually leads to various aches and pains and immense rashes of conversations. By the best traditions, American and otherwise, pioneers are a talkative lot, much given to charters, plans, programs, orations, and talk and more talk.

Words by the thousands and millions persist in accompanying every new or notable pioneering development and great numbers of developments which are neither new nor notable. In the United States the latter began with the first haphazard colonies, carried on through the era of the covered wagon, pony express, and grazing longhorns, and so to the present. Trail blazers simply must talk.

There are many paralleling issues between the old trails west and the new trails south. It can be said, I believe, though possibly my objectivity is somewhat blunted, that the current crop of pronouncements and appraisals of present-day tropical affairs are somewhat more accurate and somewhat less silly than the still-echoing chronicles of the ways west, and love among the buckskins and buffalo chips, with just a salting of quaint old, droll, bearded humor with or without feathered headdress but with clearly proved box-office appeal.

In political terms, too, the tropics are still rather essentially new, not quite as new as television, but the color is much better. As already mentioned, the United States has developed such noteworthy and official, even if undersized tropical conning towers as the Institute of Inter-American Affairs. We have developed a generally admirable precedence for reciprocal trade. We have greatly improved the status and stature of U.S. corporate business in the tropics, though in all these advances we still have substantial distances yet to go. We have at least tended toward moderation in terms of what is rather loosely termed dollar diplomacy, and there is not even a dim shadow of doubt the U.S. diplomatic competence in and toward the tropics has improved memorably during the past twenty years.

And as every reader or listener knows, we have been given a pocketful of dreams known as Point Four. The latter, which seems to apply preponderantly to the tropics as the main arena of "underdeveloped nations" outside the Soviet barricades, breaks long-time precedences by actually saying remarkably little while encouraging commentators, editorial writers, businessmen, and others to talk themselves almost to death.

Rather grandiloquently dubbed the Bold New Program, Point Four actually is much less than bold, since its total commitments remain considerably less than 1 per cent of Marshall Plan aid to Europe for any one of the five years following 1945. It is hardly new, since its apparent point of view was stated far better, as noted, more than a century ago, as well as in specific British legislation dating back to 1929. And by lack of statutory or other official definition, Point Four is not yet a "program." Even so, it has inspiring qualities, and it has important counterparts.

The largely factual background for Point Four includes these generalities: In the world today about 70 per cent of all peoples, at least 1,565,000,000, live in the "underdeveloped areas"; about 389,000,000, or 16.6 per cent, live in "transitional areas"; and about 384,000,000, or 16.4 per cent, in "developed" areas. The present "underdeveloped areas" include slightly more than seven-eighths of all land surfaces in the tropics or subtropics: most of Latin America north of Argentina, all of tropical Africa, most of the Middle East, most of lower Asia, and some fringes of eastern Europe. The "transitional areas" cover a few subtropical places such as Mexico, South Africa, Tunisia, and Algeria, and many temperate-zone lands—the U.S.S.R., Finland, Iceland, Turkey, Austria, Greece, Italy, Spain, Chile, Czechoslovakia, Hungary, Rumania, and Bulgaria; while the "developed" areas include the United States, Canada, Argentina, Western Europe, Norway, Sweden, Denmark, New Zealand, and Australia.

Estimated life expectancy in the underdeveloped areas is about thirty years; in the transitional areas, fifty-two; in the developed areas, about sixty-three. Average illiteracy in the underdeveloped areas is about 78 per cent; in transitional areas 20 per cent; in developed areas, 5 per cent. Average annual income per capita (estimated for the years between 1936-40) is $1 for the underdeveloped countries; $154 for the transitional areas; and $398 for the developed areas.

Point Four remains an idea and, in some measure, a philosophy of internationalism in what remains of or arises as a free world. It is not yet supported by competent legislation or even a competently detailed plan of action. But it is a sort of primer of neighborliness and internationalism for a world which can countenance democracy. Any sincere devotee of the tropics is for it as inevitably as a devoted preacher is against sin.

## THE BRITISH TRY A WAY

PEOPLE, of course, are infinitely more important than plans, even the noblest of plans. But the self-realization of tropical peoples requires plans.

Today, the biggest and most impressive panorama of such plans is the British Colonial Development Acts, as currently active in about twenty of Britain's tropical colonies and territories. These plans and works, as devised and financed in substantial part by the colony or colonies or territory or territories concerned, cover an immense variety of enterprises, ranging from building local roads, phone lines, public markets, and power dams to the education of native teachers, doctors, and engineers.

In principal part the enterprises feature local people working together. The exceptionally memorable venture began in 1929 with an act of Parliament which granted a first million pounds for "advancing economic development of underdeveloped colonies." From the beginning the legislation has been exceptionally, indeed amazingly, nonpartisan. All political parties have supported it, with the recent exception of the British Communists, and Conservatives, Liberals, and Labourites alike have worked and voted to expand and extend the work.

During 1940, Britain's then "darkest hour," Parliament renewed the nonpartisan measure for a ten-year period and raised the stakes to five and a half million pounds annually, for five years. The Colonial Development and Welfare Act of 1945 appropriated £120,000,000, currently about $336,000,000, for a ten-year period ending March 31, 1956.

Part of the money is being allocated for widely spread work in research, education, and scientific surveys. In most of the colonies the money is being used on a share-the-cost basis, British taxpayers paying one-third, the local colony or territory an average of two-thirds. Each plan is approved and presented by the colony or territory or other group participating. During 1947 the Colonial Development and Welfare Act was supplemented with the Overseas Development

Act, which set up the Colonial Development Corporation with credit resources of about $308,000,000 and the Overseas Food Corporation with about $154,000,000 for promoting food production in the colonies. Both corporations are quasi-governmental, responsible to the Secretary of State for the Colonies.

Spokesmen for both the Labour and Conservative parties pointed out that these measures are neither charities nor devices to increase colonial dependence on the United Kingdom, but rather to "help the colonies help themselves."

In a typical report on recent administration of the Acts, Creech Jones, speaking as Britain's Secretary of State for the Colonies, pointed out that of all "new monies" currently expended, at least half are going into "directly productive economic activities," about one-third into the maintenance and expansion of public utilites essential to development, about 16 per cent into social services, the rest into research. Further, that

> . . . Alongside the problem of population is the increasing demand by the Africans and other tropical peoples that they should enjoy social services . . . which are expensive to maintain. . . . We must therefore try to do everything we can to improve the standards of cultivation of the peasant, and to make him realize that he cannot reach and enjoy the social standards he demands while his methods of production are as primitive as they are. . . .
>
> At the same time there must be very big schemes for transport development and power development, and of those essential works and utilities on which the good economic life of a territory depends. Therefore . . . the development must be over the whole field—large-scale production where we can get it . . . and, at the same time, every encouragement for the small producer, in order that he may not only feed himself but have a surplus to help feed the population generally, and so help to keep it healthy. . . . They [the colonies] are according to their means putting an enormous amount of their own natural resources into the development of their territories. . . .

## PROGRESS IN PITH HELMETS

BY 1950 the number of research projects with partial support from "Colonial Welfare" had reached 195; "development" projects totaled 284; medical public health and sanitation projects, 140; social service projects, 64; nutrition studies, 14; housing and land-settlement "programs," 48; education projects, 88; water supplies, 70; telegraph and telephone systems, 12.

In research, which is so crucially needed throughout all the tropics, about 40 per cent of the Welfare and Development Act's work is concerned with tropical agriculture, veterinary and forestry projects; about 13 per cent with fisheries, which are also immensely important in terms of tropical food supplies; about 19 per cent with medical, public health, and sanitation needs; about 5 per cent for research in insect and fungus control; and about the same percentage to products development research. At present about 30 per cent of the research is being carried on in East Africa, about 20 per cent in West Africa, about 15 per cent in the West Indies, 15 per cent in the South Pacific, most of the rest in lower Asia and the Mediterranean islands.

Typical entries include a field research station in West Africa's Gambia Basin, a soil research center at Trinidad's Imperial College of Tropical Agriculture, and agricultural research and experiment station in East Africa's Nyasaland, soil surveys of about a quarter-million miles of tropical Africa, grants of about ten million dollars yearly for fellowships and special training for talented colonial students, and also a public school research and support program for Central Africa.

The ventures in "development" are still more varied: a soil-conservation program for Kenya in East Africa; handicraft and cotton-growing projects for the West Indies; a telephone system for Africa's Tanganyika; first public libraries for Rhodesia; English lessons for the Sarawak police cadets; a major road system for East and Central Africa; various other works in North Borneo, Aden, Cyprus, the West Indies and most of Britain's tropical Africa.

Quite evidently the importance of these works is not measurable wholly in terms of size. Actually some of the humbler ventures are the more memorable.

A good and timely example is that of the introduction of pure-bred chickens as a subsistence and export crop for Gambia, one of the poorest and most painfully underdeveloped colonies in all tropical Africa.

For time unmeasured the people of Gambia have been hungry. The climate is generally obnoxious, for the country is one in which the jungle meets the desert frontier head on. Livestock is almost non-existent, and until recently no attempt had been made at competent poultry-growing.

During 1949, in co-operation with about a dozen local tribes, the Colonial Development Corporation undertook to introduce a native-run poultry establishment for the colony, capable of supplying eggs and fowl for the quarter-million people of Gambia and to supplement the development by exporting eggs and dressed poultry. The Corporation leased a first 10,000 acres of unused forest lands back of the seaport called Bathurst, which the Royal Air Force had developed as a transport base but had abandoned. Dimming roads and abandoned power lines were restored, and an American poultry man named M. J. Phillips was employed to launch the venture. Phillips began by employing local tribesmen to clear the forest lands, plow them with tractors, and plant them to barley, sorghum, and other suitable feed grains.

Early in 1949 Phillips supervised the purchase from several New England hatcheries of a first lot of 10,000 setting eggs, which he carried to Gambia by plane and three days later placed in electrically operated incubators at Yundum. In the tropics, as a rule, no more than one setting egg in five hatches. But in this instance the first incubator setting of 10,000 eggs produced more than 7,000 healthy chicks, a workable average. By 1950, for the first time Gambia had more chickens than people, first exports of dressed fowl and eggs were being made, the tribes were taking part in the work, and a great new crop was beginning to succeed.

This is a success story, modest but typical. And plainly, too, it is one more addendum to the important task of establishing new tropical crops. There are dozens more. In Africa's remote Nyasaland colony a new tung nut center is in the making. In famine-troubled Nigeria, the only overpopulated territory in tropical Africa, the new Nigerian Department of Commerce and Industries is succeeding in such notable public-good ventures as building and operating seven co-operative palm-oil mills, which are urgently important to Nigeria's greatest crop, and a succession of about twenty co-operative milk sheds, which are substantially helping the expanding cattle industries of the great Fulani tribe and others by converting the raw milk to cheese and butter.

The territorial government is setting up textile centers where spinning and weaving are taught gratis to interested citizens. In Nigeria, as most of tropical Africa, textiles are in severe shortage. On completion of the free training, graduate spinners and weavers who want to set up business for themselves are permitted to purchase reliable looms at cost and on loans made by native authorities. The results are entirely evident. Nigerian cotton and wool production are growing rapidly. The output of much-needed broadloom cloth is being doubled by the year and is becoming basic to a beneficial era of barter trade among the tribes.

As part of its participation in "colonial development" and in greater part at the expense of the more than twenty million tribespeople of the great territory, Nigeria's Industries Board also sponsors local fiber mills for manufacturing rope, burlap, bags, twine, mats, and cheap rugs, and gives instructions for growing and harvesting these and other tropical fibers. It is also helping citizens to develop orange groves and to begin a fruit-juice and other canning industries and a much-needed native sugar industry.

Another Nigerian undertaking in self-development is the first widespread and competent geological survey (which is currently being extended into other areas of tropical Africa). Still another is a pioneering venture in treating cattle herds long harassed by the ruinous disease, trypanosomiasis, or animal sleeping sickness, which is carried by the tsetse fly. The treatment features the use of an important new drug called Antrycide, both as a preventive and cure. As this page is written, about half a million Nigerian cattle have been treated with the drug, and though much remains to be proved, Nigerian experiments indicate that a single injection of the specific can cure cattle of two of the worst forms of the disease and also clearly benefits other animal victims including horses, camels, and swine.

As yet the drug called Antrycide has not been produced in the quantities needed, though its production shows a marked advance. This is important, because the drug as thus far used in Nigeria, when duly improved, could very well be a decisive factor in changing Africa from a continent still preponderantly undeveloped to the greatest range land in the world. The present cattle population of the entire continent is estimated as fewer than twenty million. Meanwhile experts believe that if cattle diseases, of which animal sleeping sickness is far the most destructive, could be controlled, the mighty ranges of the continent could be made capable of "carrying" as many as a quarter-billion cattle, enough to supply beef, milk, and leather for at least three times that many people.

The Colony Welfare Acts are helping to introduce many valuable crops: sugar cane, oil palms, and food dates for the Anglo-Egyptian Sudan, currently "co-dominion" of Britain and Egypt; date palms for Somaliland; a renovated coffee industry for Kenya; a great new cotton center for the Middle Nile Basin; and a promising list of vegetable crops in Borneo.

Paralleling these, and in important part supplementing them, are many memorable undertakings which can be described as educational. Among the latter is a new school to study and teach nutrition in the tropics: this is part of the new Makere College in Africa's distant Uganda. The world has much to learn about the vital fundamentals of tropical nutrition. As a long-time Cuban doctor friend states the case, we just don't know *frijoles*—beans about it. However, we are beginning to assemble some likelihoods and a few certainties; one of the latter is that tropical diets remain tragically lacking in proteins. Another is that prevailing starch diets vary immensely in competence. Still inexplainably, some of the more ruthless tropical diseases continue to harass areas where one particular root or grain food is pre-eminent and to shy away from others where diets feature other starchy foods with approximately the same caloric and "vitamin" contents.

Very evidently, much depends on how the various food crops are harvested and prepared for the table. For example, the red rice of Equatorial Africa appears to provide a more disease-resistant diet than does the common swamp or white rice of Southwest Asia. I do not know why this is the case; it just is, or at least seems to be. Specific sources of foods and the manner in which they are cooked, seasoned, and served seem to do much to decide ultimate nutriment values and health sustenance. Speaking as one tropical roamer, I can recite hundreds of specific examples, and I should like to if your time and my space permitted. As a compromise, here is a smallish handful of remembered experiences.

In the Congo Basin I once visited an area where the tribespeople lived principally on raw fish and raw crabs. They suffer tragically from filarial diseases, dysenteries, and leprosy. Apparently, they do not have cancer and little malaria. About eight hundred miles farther up the "Big River," a closely similar tribe lives principally on cooked fish and cooked crabs. The latter tribe has little leprosy and almost no filarial diseases, but the people suffer tragically from cancer, malaria, and tuberculosis.

Some years ago, in Liberia, a Firestone rubber plantations manager discovered to his head-jolting amazement that Liberian tribesmen, like most other Africans, eat only one meal daily and that in the late afternoon, after which they sleep. Rubber-tapping is early-morning work, since the latex flows are halted by the heat of midday. The manager from Akron decided, therefore, that it would be a good and humane idea to serve all the rubber tappers a hearty early-morning breakfast to help them in their work. He did. Promptly all the tappers picked soft, shady spots and went to sleep. That day no rubber "bled."

In the now-abandoned Ford Motor rubber colony in Fordlandia and later at Bel Terra on the Tapajós in the great and ever-wonderful Amazon Basin, the original and opinionated Henry Ford resolved to "modernize" native workers. He paid the Brazilian labor what were then startlingly high wages, but the latter found excessively little to do with their wages. As a first step they bought silk stockings (from company commissaries) for their women. But most of the *mujeres* had never worn shoes, and silk stockings do not go far in deep mud. Señor Ford instituted dances on the village green. In the Amazon country, where there are few villages and far fewer village greens, the antipathies toward folk dancing are next to overwhelming. Señor Ford also instituted a company cafeteria, featuring good old-fashioned Michigan home-cooking. In Portuguese and various Indian dialects the Amazonians said nuts to that. Rather bafflingly, most of those who patronized the honest homey Michigan cooking became violently ill of diarrheas, dysenteries, other extreme digestive upsets, and intense allergies.

Ford's Amazon rubber project failed, and eventually he gave it back to Brazil and the Indians. But along with supplying some of the heartiest laughs ever enjoyed by the besoaked fraternity of earth-prowling tropical developers (all right, go ahead and call us tropical tramps), the sage of Dearborn gave a particularly pertinent demonstration of the fact that Michigan home-cooking served cafeteria style somehow does not fit in the deep and generally damp tropics, and, indeed, that the entire field of tropical nutrition remains wide open to more study and better understanding.

The Welfare and Development Acts have heeded this reality along with several other areas of essential study and most-needed understanding.

Some 9,000 miles west of Uganda the Welfare and Development Acts have helped found a sociological research center for the British West Indies as well as a Micro-Biology Institute, the latter already usefully busy at isolating antibiotic drugs from tropical soils. Tropical West Africa's newer research centers include a marine fisheries institute, a forestry research center, a veterinary research station, a building and housing research organization, and a rice research station—each with a corresponding institute in East Africa.

The list continues to lengthen. There is, for example, a new $20,000,000 development in North Borneo which includes road-building, town-planning, and home-building, plus harbor, railroad, and airport construction. Still more closely in keeping with that wonderful word, "education," Borneo, so long synonymous with the remote, backward, and savage, now features a revival of diversified farming, a renovated public health service, including field clinics, mobile dressing stations, and a base hospital at Jesselton (which doubles as a training center for native medical workers); it also has a first teacher's college and an admirable new inter-island school system.

In the hot west frontiers of British Guiana of upper South America, rice experts from Britain and the United States are meeting with some degree of success in refurbishing the long-dormant rice industry of that badly lost colony. In the distant Fijis, a newly reorganized, colony-run Copra Board is seeking to restore the coconut palm to its losing place as a great and beneficial tropical crop. Fiji coconut groves are among the best remaining, and newly built co-operative plants are processing yearly about twenty-two thousand tons of copra or dried coconut "meat," about ten thousand tons of coconut oil and five thousand tons of coconut meal for export.

Late in 1949 the considerably revised Federation of Malaya succeeded in opening the new University of Malaya. During 1948, the University College of the West Indies, the University College of Nigeria, and the University College of the Gold Coast made almost simultaneous appearances as colony-supported centers of learning. During 1950 Makere College of Uganda made its official bow, and Achimota College, of the African Gold Coast, founded by a great international educator named Kewegyir Aggrey, expanded its many works and instituted its seal which shows both the black and white keys of a piano, "so that all may play as one." All the new tropical colleges have able departments for social and economic studies. They join in pointing out that since 1920 the number of colleges and universities in all the tropics has risen from forty-three to ninety-six, with total student enrollment now somewhere near ten times that of 1920. During the same years the circulation of tropical newspapers has increased almost twenty-fold, while literacy throughout the tropical earth as a whole very probably has doubled; as a reasonable guess it has risen from fewer than 10 per cent to somewhere near 20 per cent.

## MORE LIGHT

THOUGH there is hope and great heroism in many of the current ventures in better self-realization in and by the tropics, most evidently there are still nowhere near enough schools, colleges, research centers, or public health facilities, and nowhere near a sufficient diversity of crops, or nearly enough accurate surveys of the great forests, mines, and other decisive natural resources. There is nowhere near the needed total of momentum and co-ordination in developmental work within the tropics. There is nowhere near enough literacy within the tropics.

Yet in all these lacks, partial fulfillments are being made, many of them gallant and inspiring. There are heroic advances to report in many aspects of literacy, including more light, literal as well as figurative. Here again the appetizers are so enticing that one drools for the real meal.

One who travels the tropics, even if he merely looks down from the air, can hardly miss seeing the immensities of undeveloped hydroelectric resources, the rain-perpetuated eternities of water power, which, if developed, could operate great industries, supply refrigeration, change deserts to rich green fields, and certainly, no less importantly, yield light for tropical homes.

The relationship of light and understanding is remarkably literal. In the tropics one simply cannot overlook the nagging impediments that go with the appallingly widespread lack of light by which to read. It is a more than averagely safe bet that of the quarter-billion tropical homes of the present, no fewer than an eighth of a billion, or half, still do not have household lighting of any kind. It is an equally safe bet that this lack of home lighting has much to do with the continuing preponderance of illiteracy in the tropics. It would be very nice indeed if one could state factually that one tropical home in every hundred now has electricity. But personally, and without absolute statistics, I am afraid that such a statement would be gross exaggeration.

For the most part, tropical youth has no chance to read by the light of open fireplaces, like the youthful Abraham Lincoln, because there are extremely few fireplaces in the tropics. There are, of course, many millions of kerosene and gasoline lamps or lanterns, but throughout most of the tropics the excessive costs of petroleum fuels makes them an extreme luxury for the great majority of the people. Palm oil is a fair lamp fuel, but here again the costs are excessive, the more so because so many tropical peoples desperately need the palm oil as food.

Apropos of all this, during the latter years of World War II and thereafter, the British Isles, hungering for oils and fats, in the habitual manner of hundreds of millions of tropical peoples, sought to increase palm-oil imports from West Africa by the rather logical expedience of making kerosene cheap and available to the "natives" and thereby obtaining as food some part of the palm oil which would otherwise be burned in household lamps or "fire pots."

Having placed a rather severe price ceiling on palm oils, the Colonial Office and Ministry of Supply arranged to deliver cargoes of kerosene to several West African ports. American oil companies shaved shipside prices of kerosene to six or seven cents per gallon, or about one-tenth of the prices then obtainable for palm oils. Yet by the time the kerosene had filtered into the near interior—by launch or dugout canoe or more frequently on the heads or backs of native carriers, and via the usual succession of traders—its price had climbed to a dollar a gallon or more, certainly more than the established "trader prices" for palm oils. Thus the tribespeople who are sufficiently "rich" to afford any kind of a hut lamp were obliged to keep on burning palm oil, even as the British nation grew lankier and hungrier.

This instance is neither remarkable nor extreme. Anybody who knows tropical Africa has noted that, in the run of tribal villages, the coming of night is heralded by an outdoor fire, partly as a safeguard against evil spirits, but more actually against leopards and other predators. By nightfall, however, the interior of the huts or other homes are usually pitch black. When householders return home after dark, which they usually try to avoid doing, it is traditional for them to enter a dark hut stealthily and with much handclapping. Usually the first one inside claps his or her hands loudly, and after a deliberate wait the other member or members enter. Meanwhile, if the handclapping within fails to materialize or ceases too abruptly, the member who waits outside calls or runs for help, on the premise that the handclapper has been bitten by a lurking snake or attacked by a leopard or overwhelmed by an unfriendly spirit.

Lack of home lighting throughout most of the tropical earth remains appallingly commonplace, and the lack or scarcity of reading light remains one of the more remorseless barriers to public education throughout the greater part of the tropical earth.

Rather evidently, the U.S. public does most of its general reading at night, partly from habit, partly from superior facilities, but most largely because, as an extremely busy people, we can rarely do general reading in daytime. In some part the same holds in the tropics; more so, because of such national factors as heat, sun glare, sweat, insects, and scarcity of suitable places, which make it particularly difficult to read in the daytime in hot countries.

For a long time schools in the tropics have demonstrated and otherwise learned that their pupils study far better at night than in the day, provided there are lighted and otherwise suitable study rooms.

By the dozens, schoolteachers in the tropics have told me of their many promising students who learned to read and write, then returned to unlighted homes where they ceased to read or write and, after a due number of years, practically speaking, forgot how. The same dilemma can happen here, of course, but not for the same or any similarly commanding reason. For, as noted, there are stubborn, functional, specific reasons for the nagging preponderance of tropical illiteracy.

This emphasizes, with pertinence, the immense and human importance of the many hydroelectric projects now functioning or in the building in the tropics and the much greater number that await building and development. Britain's Colonial "works" are taking account of several of the latter, but other particularly noteworthy hydroelectric developments have materialized independently, and previously.

In all the tropics today, the most impressive venture in providing light for the remaining unlighted spaces of earth is centered in the determinedly historic Nile Valley. Practical internationalism is truly at work there; the governments of Britain, Egypt, the Sudan, Uganda, Ethiopia, the Belgian Congo, and others are working as one. This particular internationalism affects more than five thousand miles of the destiny-shaping Nile Channel, and it involves at least a third of a century of correlated construction. The first "stage" features a principal hydroelectric dam now being built across the "White Nile" at Owens Falls in Uganda, to regulate the discharge of Lake Victoria (which is about as big as Ireland) and thereby influence the waterflow the entire course of the great river. The Belgian government has agreed to build a similar dam at Lake Albert, on the Congo-Uganda frontier. Together, the two dams will make possible important new irrigation areas for both the Sudan and Egypt.

The dam at Owens Falls, which will include the largest hydroelectric station in Africa, is being built co-operatively by the Egyptian government and the Uganda Colony government, the latter having paid about two-thirds of its cost to date, under the direction of the Uganda Electricity Board. Though costs of the great new hydroelectric center are great in terms of local ability to pay (they have already exceeded fifty million dollars), Uganda has important cotton gins, sugar factories, phosphate mines, and other new industries ready-built and waiting cheap power from the White Nile.

The Nile projects include the building of a series of canals which permit the river's channel to by-pass the "Sudd," a huge swamp area of the southern Sudan, and thereby restore great quantities of water to the central channel in the dry-lands below. Another great hydroelectric dam is being built at Lake Tana, in Ethiopia, to control the water levels of that lake, to store water for irrigating dry-lands, and to generate electricity.

In the Zambezi valley, about two hundred miles below the great Victoria Falls, is a giant natural bottleneck called the Kariba Gorge. A 300-foot dam now in the building will provide water to operate a 750,000-kilowatt generating plant which will supply electricity for most of Rhodesia, including the colony's great iron mines. The cost of the electricity here developed will be less than one-half cent per kilowatt-hour, one of the lowest power rates anywhere on earth. In addition, the Zambezi "station" will provide water for irrigating tens of thousands of acres of heretofore desert veldt. The total cost, including the construction of 125 miles of necessary railroad, will be between sixty and seventy-five million dollars.

Already the various Nile "schemes" have merged into the most ambitious and far-influencing river authority as yet conceived. Several of the earlier phases are already successfully at work, and the concept as a whole long predates the African enterprises of the Colonial Welfare and Development Acts.

In the Gezira area of the upper Sudan, west of Khartoum, and between the White Nile and the Blue Nile, the Sennar Dam, now completed, supplies waterpower for irrigating about a million acres of flatland fields which previously were deserts. The long-time desert now blossoms. It produces cotton which supports an immensely promising and much-needed fabrics industry, and it grows numerous food crops which are now life to more than a quarter-million people.

The Sennar Dam now produces about one-fourth of the entire revenue of the Sudanese government, and still more notably, the Gezira facility blazes a particularly interesting trail for forthcoming tropical developments.

It was built by a triple partnership consisting of the Sudan government, which still owns 40 per cent of the stock, the Sudan Plantations Syndicate, which owned 28 per cent, and the native landholders and farmers who buy the irrigation service and own the remaining 32 per cent of the stock.

During 1950 the Syndicate withdrew from the partnership, leaving the Sudan government, which financed the long-term investment by loan, and the landowners and tenants as co-operative owners. All landowners receive rents for their land, with owners' rights permanently guaranteed. The tenants hold contracts which define and make durable their rights of tenure. They pay their rents and water fees with approximately one-third of the cotton harvest, but grow food and forage crops free of rentals and water tolls.

When completed, the Nile projects will bring electricity within reach of a probable six million African homes now without electricity and many or most of them still without home lighting. It will supply irrigation for at least twenty million acres of otherwise fertile lands which are now desert, and drainage for about ten million acres of present-day swamps; it will make possible electric refrigeration and the development of mines, factories, and many other beneficial industries.

At present, the Nile Basin is the greatest proving ground for hydroelectric development in all the tropics. Moreover, it is a relevant example of the working partnership both of neighboring nations and private investors, landowners and public funds—all for the common good.

There are many other memorable instances of hydroelectric development in the tropics. For example, in Malaya, without help from abroad, the Federation government is striving magnificently to restore and increase its badly needed hydroelectric sources. Also, in the green-gold picture book of the Gold Coast of West Africa, the electrical age is likewise being born, with a great new hydroelectric center at Ajena, on the Volta River.

Fortunately, the prevailing list of hydroelectric developments is long, far too long for individual listing here. Even so, passing mention, however brief, is deserved by Ceylon's new Gal Oya Dam for flood control, irrigation, the opening of new lands capable of supporting at least half a million people, and a 20 per cent expansion of Ceylon's present total of electric power. Also India's progressive list of impoundment and power dams in about twenty different river valleys combinedly will provide an additional 26,000,000,000 kilowatts of electric power per year, open at least five million dry acres to useful crops, and increase India's grain production by at least ten million bushels per year, a margin for life for at least one hundred million of India's people.

## ALONE AND AFAR

BRITAIN'S great pioneering program of tropical works goes ahead, supplemented by many new projects shaped by the Colonial Development Corporation, which thus far has helped to sponsor nine industrial operations in the West Indies, seven in the eastern tropics, and eleven in Africa, with both the number and the need steadily growing. Here as elsewhere the facts stand that the tropical territories continue giving and gambling much more than the homeland and that many of the colonial development enterprises are entirely independent. Back of these actualities is the basic working philosophy and knowledge that man cannot stand alone in the tropics, that human resources, public utilities, and private industries must be developed and advanced in co-ordination, for together all can stand, whereas separately all may fall.

This philosophy is definitely not one of socialism or totalitarianism. In several basic respects it is impressively American and a studied logic of business and enterprise which seeks to tie the past, present, and future into a continuing and beneficial whole. Some of the enterprises as sponsored or encouraged by Britain's various Colonial Development Acts have failed. But of the somewhat more than six hundred specific undertakings, at least two-thirds already have succeeded or show strong indications of success.

This proportion of success is the more significant because the total of British colonial enterprise is certainly no more than a fourth part of the development projects currently in progress in the tropical earth as a whole. The British remain the world's most able publicists.

In the case of the British tropics, the accompanying publicity efforts are diligent and expert. But fortunately they are supported by admirable, tangible works and accomplishment. The British Commonwealth is seeking to checkmate Soviet-led Communism in the tropics, and they are grappling a hard and costly job. For the British are talking and doing, and thus far in the tropics, the U.S.S.R. is only talking—in terms of constructive work.

Also encouraging is the fact that Britain's many tropical colonies have no semblance of monopoly on self-development or self-realization. Many tropical countries are making memorable developments, some in discernible stages of accomplishment, more in the inevitable planning or borning stages. Here again there are hundreds of examples, preponderantly good, and again the normal temptation is to mention only the biggest and most successful. If it kills me I will squelch the temptation and hold up only one small handful of the smaller peaches.

In the low hot wet-lands of Santa Elena, the Ecuadorian government is helping its farmers establish what is now one of the more promising rice-growing centers in all the western tropics. In the dryish shelf lands of Peru about three hundred Indian farmers are carrying on a program of selective improvement of native corn or maize, in that particular homeland of what is now the most valuable of all crops. Meanwhile other Peruvian farmers are pioneering the potentially great Pachitea River lands which, without benefit or liability of cheesecake or press agents, they term the improved Florida of South America.

On the significant conception list is the current work by the Brazilian government in seeking to determine factually what the stupendous Amazon Basin is and what it actually has. Brazil's and all other reading publics have been pelted and assailed by grossly imaginative or completely phony accounts of the vast dark Amazon, by babblings about missions to Manáos, and by fanciful and impossible claims of abundance in the Amazon lands.

At long last the Brazilian government is learning the facts about such vast Amazon states as Amazona and Para and the immense frontier of the Matto Grosso. Some of these facts are powerfully discouraging. It has been established, for example, that an evident majority of the lands of the great Basin are poor and acid, that hardly more than one-twentieth of the land is dependably above the water line, and that hardly more than one-tenth of the *varzeas*—land regularly covered by water during the flood seasons only—is usable. But this land is frequently replenished with river silt and because of recurrent floods acquires considerable immunity from fungi and insect pests. Even so, the amount of Amazon land usable at present seems considerably less than formerly guessed. Brazilian government explorers estimate the total as about a quarter-million square miles of widely scattered lands which, if brought together, would be about the area of Texas.

But even for the usable lands, the limitations remain severe. As a rule the *caboclo,* or Amazon farmer, still lives in a palm-thatched hut propped discreetly on stilts on the high grounds or along the river banks. As a rule he tends one or two garden-sized fields with his hoe, machete, and hand ax. His usual crops are *mandioca,* the tropical starchy root equivalent of potatoes, "beans," similar to cowpeas, and such "greens" as *couve* or collards. Usually he hunts and fishes, and sometimes he keeps a few chickens which live dangerously in a homemade cage conventionally swung aboveground for protection from the snakes and other predators.

In many Amazon areas it is possible to grow bananas, mangos, papaya, oranges, jaci, bacury, and other fruits and a number of vegetables including edible greens, such as caruru and bertalha, okra, or *quiabo,* which most Brazilians like immensely, a sort of cucumber called *maxixi,* and, as noted, *couve* or collards. It is possible to grow them, but not many do.

Nevertheless, the Brazilian Ministry of Agriculture is proving that many edible crops can be grown rewardingly throughout much of the Amazon Basin; these include such badly needed vegetables as carrots, cucumbers, eggplants, green beans, lettuce, squash, tomatoes, and turnips, as well as watermelons and muskmelons and many types of edible peppers. Sweet corn does not thrive, and the future of field corn is doubtful. But there are possibilities, nevertheless, for a reasonably satisfactory subsistence agriculture.

Similar findings are emerging from great areas of the American tropics. In Peru, which remains one of the hungrier nations of the New World, the aboriginal potato agriculture in the Huayao Valley (apparently the home of what has become the greatest of all vegetable crops) is being impressively restored. Meanwhile, as a result of both public and private efforts, more and more new or newly restored crops keep appearing in many arenas of the nearer tropics: mint oils in Brazil, lime oil in Mexico and the West Indies, valuable insecticides from the Sierras of Peru and upland Brazil, in Colombia fique fiber (for making coffee bags), impressive silk farms in lower Brazil, tea orchards in various Andes areas of Peru, Bolivia, and Ecuador, and olive orchards in Uruguay and northwestern Argentina.

Though food crops remain far forward among the critical needs of the tropical earth, there is varied and heartening progress in meeting these needs. Many instances have been cited already. But perhaps one more could stand brief mention. This one is the gradual, belated, private-enterprise restoration of open-range cattle.

One of the best instances can be seen on the most bountiful natural ranges remaining, the llanos of Venezuela. On the llanos the Criollo cattle, the tropical and present-day counterparts of the early Texas Longhorns, have lived and multiplied for more than four centuries. Earliest Spanish settlers brought the cattle from the now-faded ranges of upland Spain and the sturdy Criollo has survived—strong enough to fight for its life against the puma, the bobcat, or other ruthless predators, to leave the grassy lowlands during the rainy season, and to follow the best of the seemingly eternal grass higher and higher into the hills.

The llañero, or native range rider, fits the cattle. He is an exceptional instance of the *tropico* on horseback. Usually he is a smallish Indian or mixed-blood who rides a correspondingly smallish Arab Spanish-type horse and works ably with his standard working tools which are a machete and a rawhide lariat.

His usual garb is a shirt without sleeves, breeches whacked off at the knees, flimsy homemade sandals, called *alpargatas,* as a substitute for shoes, a broad-brimmed hat, usually made of straw, and an almost incredibly wide leather belt which he uses to carry money, if he has any, and small knives and luck charms, and, by way of double usefulness and at the slightest quick-tempered whim, to whip his wife.

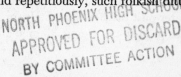

But primarily the llañero lives by cattle; milk cows are his durable anchorage. Unlike his *norteamericano* counterpart of the faded era of Longhorns, the Criollo man on horseback also milks cows, as many as a hundred, and that once a day, usually in the morning. As a rule he sings while milking, nasally and repetitiously, such folkish ditties as *Vaca vieja, Vaca vieja dame la leche!*—"Old cow, old cow, give me your milk!" When the cows have heeded, he "sets" the milk for cheese-making. Cheese and beef are what he has to sell.

Spaces are far on the open ranges, and, as in the glamorized Longhorn days, the big and yearly drive to market becomes the payoff. Drives are companion to the dry seasons, and they usually find the ranging cattle in quest of fresh green grass in the faraway hills. The trek to market is traditionally rough and rocky and usually requires a month or longer. At the river crossings alligator and electric eels take their toll of the calves. *Cimarrónes,* or stray cattle, break away from the herd and vanish in the bush.

Arrived at the foothills and borderlands, the llañeros slow down the big drive to take advantage of the lush valley grass—"fattening pastures"—and, as in Longhorn days, the final stop is the market town or "killing plants." There is no grain feeding and extremely little refrigeration. The cattle trails still wind through hundreds of miles through lands that are unfenced and substantially untenanted, west to the open spaces above Valle de la Pascua, south and east through the lost world that is boundaried by the Orinoco and the sprawling Guiana highlands.

The survival of the Criollo on open range and for scores of cattle generations, and the modest and unending saga of the llanos, pastures that wait green and unfenced through the centuries, and the llañeros, who through succeeding generations keep on riding the ranges and tending the cattle, shapes a forthright parable of a time when great and beneficial herds may again roam and thrive over much of the tropical earth.

## OPEN SEASON FOR DISEASES

But the most hopeful parable that rises from the tropical earth today is the rapidly unfolding odyssey of disease hunting. This odyssey is also an intensely human document, in great part public, in greater part private. Separately, or in groups or teams, tens of thousands of men and women in medicine and related arts, sciences, and enterprises lead ways and blaze new trails toward better health in the tropics and the world at large.

Already noted but worth repeating is the truth that tropical medicine is essentially global medicine. Like tigers, leopards, lions, and other man-killing beasts, most of the ruinous diseases of man long ago took refuge in the tropics. They remain the pre-eminent killers. Sudden and painful deaths from leopards, tigers, lions, and other natural predators number in the bare hundreds per year. But those from the predator micro-organisms of disease still number in the millions—far too high, though not as high as formerly.

For one example, until very recently malaria, still the most widespread of man's communicable diseases, has afflicted at least one hundred million people and brought death to an estimated four million every year. The chances are that in all history, man-killing animals, serpents, and other visible predators have not destroyed anywhere near that many people. According to World Health Organization estimates, newly developed anti-malarial drugs, including atabrine, plasmochin, pamaquine, pentaquine, and paludrine, as tested and proved in the tropics, are already preventing at least a million malaria deaths yearly, and this despite the fact that no "perfect" cure for malaria has been found as yet.

Typhus is a much better example of a once ruinous disease that has taken refuge in the tropics and is there being conquered. In 1939, according to the All-India Health Institute, about two hundred people of India were killed by wild animals, principally by tigers. During the same year more than four million people of India died of typhus. But today anti-typhus vaccines are making this one-time ruiner obsolete and comparatively unimportant. The story of cholera is similar. Recently in southern India Dr. C. G. Pandit, of the King Institute of Preventive Medicine, directed the anti-cholera inoculation of about a million people. In this group cholera occurrences promptly dropped 96 per cent. Similar onslaughts against bubonic plague, another ruthless killer that lurks in the tropics, are brillantly successful. There is every reason to believe that "the plague," once man's most terrible enemy, can be virtually erased by the use of anti-plague vaccines, sulfanilamides, and various anti-biotics.

Another major hunting ground in the new and current global quest of disease is tuberculosis, which remains a principal enemy and killer in many tropical countries, mainly because tropical tuberculosis is usually fiercer and kills more quickly than do the temperate-zone "strains." Dr. A. C. Ukil, director of the All-India Institute of Public Health at Calcutta, reports that tuberculin tests show that from 21 to 34 per cent of the rural peoples of India are afflicted with tuberculosis, as are 35 to 70 per cent of those living in the smaller towns and 70 to 90 per cent of those in industrial cities.

India fights back with renewed studies of basic pathologies, mass surveys that feature the use of X-rays and photo-fluoroscopic equipment, treatment with such impressive drugs as streptomycin, and wholesale vaccination. "Chest trucks" are rolling over the narrow streets of hundreds of India's towns and villages. Tens of thousands of tubercular children of India are receiving competent care in hospitals and sick shelters. The struggle is still intense, but medicine has begun to win.

For the first time in several centuries, the health of India is upward bound. But one still sees and smells death in the most overcrowded of the principal tropical countries. Hunger not only lurks, but it attacks aggressively. Starving children still hold out emaciated hands to beg. Pilgrims continue to crowd the *molas* for holy bathing and thereby renew epidemics. And one continues to thank God for the cleansing sun. For the sun still shines and India still lives. As spring returns, the mustard fields again turn green and yellow. By the tens of thousands, India's women, wearing green and yellow saris, kneel to listen to the prophets. Despite its direly troubled future, there is renewed springtime in the heart of India today.

The tropics have become the forward bastion in the current world-wide struggle against infantile paralysis. In the past this poliomyelitis had not been generally associated with the tropics. But during World War II Allied fighting forces in the Middle East, India, the South Pacific, and several Indian Ocean areas encountered virulent outbreaks of polio. Epidemics were officially reported in such far-flung tropical places as Malta, Singapore, and New Guinea.

Polio appears to have distinctive developmental characteristics in the tropics. In the first American epidemic (1916), about 85 per cent of all cases were children under five years of age. At present only about half are under that age. In tropical climates polio is still primarily a disease of infants or the very young. In recent outbreaks in Malta, Mauritius, and Singapore more than three-fourths of all cases have been under five years of age. It is further noteworthy that tropical polio occurs without apparent relation to season. These, or scores more facts or appearances, could be clues to understanding what remains as one of the more baffling of mankind's maladies.

Many polio clues are emerging from the tropics. A distinguished Cuban doctor, Filiberto Ramirez Corriea, of the Carlos Finlay Institute of Havana, is working research-wise to confirm his theory that the polio virus is carried by birds, either native or migratory.

In South Africa, Dr. J. H. S. Gear of the Johannesburg Institute, notes that in Africa as a whole Europeans are about ten times as liable to paralytic polio as the natives, and he concludes that the latter have somehow developed a natural immunity to endemic strains of the virus. He and his fellow workers are seeking to determine dietary, climatic, and other factors in this apparent immunity. Across the continent, in Tanganyika, a Lutheran medical missionary, Dr. J. B. Friberg, is directing the building of a hospital and health-study center at Kiamboi, where he is making a first-hand investigation of native remedies and drugs used in combatting infantile paralysis.

Polio is a question-mark disease which remains unconquered. A king-size example of another murderous question-mark disease is human trypanosomiasis, or African sleeping sickness. Men have not yet conquered it. But they are fighting it with growing effectiveness. The tsetse fly, of a species somewhat different from those that carry animal sleeping sickness, spreads human sleeping sickness and therefore earns the grim title of "ruler of Africa." The Nigerian Medical Department is challenging that title, though still in a limited and only partially successful way. In the Anchao district of northern Nigeria was an old tribal town, which was disease-ridden and filthy, and about a third of all its people had sleeping sickness.

Tsetse flies roost and breed in river bush. Under supervision of the Nigerian Medical Department, the tribespeople of Anchao chopped all the bush along all streams and rivers and in all jungles and swamps throughout a corridor seventy miles long and about ten miles wide.

That done, about a mile from the old town the tribespeople built a new town which they named Takalfiga (Walk in Health). They opened wide and clean roads, a new and sanitary open market, made many miles of drainage ditches, and dug wells that supplied good water. About half of the people of the old town voluntarily moved to the new; then in turn the old town was "cleaned up."

They built a newer model village of mud-walled, palm-thatched huts and permitted tribe members from other stricken areas to move into them. The facts about sleeping sickness are still a long way from really being known, but the fact is noteworthy that, after centuries of suffering and premature death, the Anchao country has begun to rid itself of the ruinous disease.

Quietly, determinedly, the great globe-circling quest for health in the tropics goes on. The odds and problems are still formidable. The tropics, as a whole, are still the sickest part of the earth, with the apparent exception of several populated areas of the subarctics. But the hunting improves as devoted doctors and nurses work with the help of such beneficial weapons as compact portable X-rays, antibiotics, electronic microscopes, radioactive cobalt needles, radioisotopes, and other able accouterments.

The technical competence of tropical disease hunters is almost on a parallel with the rapidly increasing appreciation of health needs on the part of most tropical peoples. There is not one tropical government of any kind or size in the world today which does not have a public health service. And their proportionate spending of public money for health needs ranges from three to more than fifty times that current in the United States.

But the great struggle for health in the tropics remains immensely specific. It is a globe-circling crusade which can be appraised only in terms of typical examples. A few of the latter have been noted. Many more deserve notice—many more again than the pages of this one book can possibly accommodate.

I should like, however, to list a few, and this quite briefly. I should like to point out that at Sungei Bulch, in Malaya, more than ten thousand linear miles from where most of us now sit or stand, history's most relevant fight against leprosy goes forward. Leprosy, a scourge of mankind for thousands of years, remains a serious enemy to many tropics. The disease is not one which a person acquires by being touched by the slinking, horrendous form of the leper—Hollywood-style. Rather, it is the bitter harvest of years of association with lepers—usually from being raised in a leper family in a poor and squalid house or hut.

Today the hope rises that leprosy can be conquered. At least the unmerciful disease is being arrested. More convincingly than anywhere else, this is being proved in Malaya's "model" leper settlement at Sungei Bulch where about six hundred Malayan lepers are being observably benefited by the studious use of new sulphone drugs. Of the latter, one specific called "sulphetrene" when suspended in oil has recently shown markedly favorable results in 145 of 194 cases treated. The course of treatment now takes about two years—a short and merciful time compared with what used to be a life-and-death sentence.

Around the globe from Malaya, Mexico's admirable Ministry of Public Health and Welfare is devoting itself to the furtherance of four nation-wide and basic programs: mother-and-child health services, tuberculosis control, venereal disease control, and public sanitation. The latter stresses the common, life-saving tropical need for adequate and sanitary water supplies. Mexico's medical statistics show that about 22 per cent of all Mexican deaths still are caused by water-borne diseases, owing principally to the use of contaminated water in homes. Of Mexico's 115,000 towns and cities, barely 700 have water services, and few of these are either adequate or safe. The fact that 24 Mexican cities or large towns are currently installing adequate water and sewage-disposal plants therefore takes on noteworthy importance.

South of Mexico is another great and primitive Indian country, Bolivia. Here one meets the high tropics—figuratively on top of the world, literally on top of the Andes, which is pretty much the same. In Bolivia the sunlight is blindingly bright; the people are Indians, an almost incredibly colorful people who feel warmly at home in canary yellow breeches and blood-red shirts or in purple skirts with lavender stockings and green shawls climaxed with brightly colored blankets and hilariously bright derby-styled hats.

But Bolivia is also a land of tragic sicknesses. Its infant death rate is one of the highest in the world; at least a third of all children die before they reach fifteen. Therefore the fact that the Bolivian government has already established in operation ten successful public health centers is also important news from the tropics.

The doctors in charge of these health centers include Bolivians, Peruvians, Brazilians, Argentinians, and at least one Irishman—Dr. Percy Boland who came down in 1906 and now directs the prenatal clinic at Santa Cruz. Between patients and deliveries, this doctor sometimes ponders the possibilities of staying on permanently. Three of the ten Bolivian health centers are located in three of the world's hottest and most inaccessible tropical towns, Cobija, Trinidad, and Magdalena, in the much lost and very steamy jungles of Bolivia. *Conquistadores* reached these outposts afoot. Today white men cannot; they are obliged to fly in. Once arrived, the struggle to exist is next to overwhelming. As a La Paz doctor explained: "All you can do for entertainment is read and you can't do that. One night I tried to read. But the light of my one little candle couldn't break through the indispensable mosquito netting." For entertainment, the clinic staff, lacking movies, radios, books, electricity, or for that matter mattresses, are obliged to rely on one undersized, crank-wind phonograph with four aged, heat-warped records.

The far-isolated, jungle-edge public have never had medical care before, and for the most part they are sick people. The new health center in Trinidad, the capital of the Bolivian state of El Beni and a town of less than ten thousand is already treating about twenty-one thousand sick people. Magdalena, which has about two thousand people and never before had a doctor, has become a mecca for about ten thousand sufferers from approximately all diseases of the land, most particularly hookworm, intestinal parasites, malaria, tuberculosis, and, understandably, tetanus in the newborn. Here, as in tens of thousands of other tropical places, the struggle for health blazes trails to survival and self-realization. It is heroic life-saving work which is tracing patterns for the tropical future.

## SELF-HELP FAR SOUTH

TODAY'S handwriting on tropical walls and the far greater scrolls of tropical fields is certain to become a memorable part of world history tomorrow.

The tropics have all the ingredients of great history: people with time and reason to ponder; superior sunpower, rain, and fertile soils; the most versatile and expansible agriculture the world has ever known, a perennial agriculture now entering a great new era of migratory crops. The tropics hold foremost vantages in tenable frontiers and inexpensive lands; in recoverable forests, waterpower, irrigation sites, minerals, and petroleum; in improving health, rising literacy, expanding trade totals, and a highly contagious, even if intuitive, urge for self-realization.

At present the more momentous and definitive logic of the tropics is most vividly concerned with better living, with the production and acquisition of goods needed to make life longer and more enjoyable. This means trade, honorable and mutually beneficial. And here is where we, the United States, came in. And here is where we cannot afford to go out.

For the world as a whole, tropical trade is essentially good and upward bound. League of Nations statistics, still among the most accurate and intelligent, name 1910 as the approximate birth year of sovereign tropical trade. Prior to that time, though tens of billions of dollars in goods had been drained out of the tropics, the trade as a whole was colonial and subservient. Between 1910 and 1929, the totals of U.S. trade with tropical countries increased more than fivefold. With only brief lapses, they have been upward bound since. Even during the strangling years of world-wide depression—between 1929 and 1934—tropical trade remained exceptionally strong. And as noted, almost magically it kept rising during the dark and bloody years of World War II, while intervening years have seen an even more spectacular continuation of this increase, despite all obstacles.

Tropical trade keeps gaining. It is the major part of bonafide U.S. foreign trade; it still is the literal life's blood of the British Commonwealth, which remains, believe it or not, the world's largest trading unit.

The latter is persistently true despite the appalling lack of equilibrium in balances of payments between sterling and dollar areas. Most of the British Commonwealth, excepting Canada, remains in the sterling areas, along with such nations as Eire, Burma, Iceland, and Iraq; and the current populations of the sterling areas exceed half a billion people.

At present, all members of the British Commonwealth, as "sterling countries" and as chronic debtors, are obliged to economize drastically in terms of "hard" currencies and gold. Trade restrictions of the sterling areas remain serious impediments to trade with the tropics.

Yet in Britain, as in the United States, much of Europe, and in many tropical countries, the volume and variety of tropical trade keeps growing. The United States remains the foremost exporting nation. But the United Kingdom, since 1945, has more than regained its prewar trade volume, and it has more than doubled its prewar tropical trade. Principal exports from the United Kingdom to the tropics remain textiles, autos, machinery, and industrial chemicals. But patterns of tropical imports are changing impressively. For example, India now supplies the United Kingdom with about six times as much jute and five times as much tea as it did in 1938; Ceylon supplies about nine times as much tea and three times as much rubber as in 1938; Burma now supplies the United Kingdom about three times as much of both tea and rubber as before the war; West Africa supplies about eight times as much cocoa as in 1938.

Though the greater part of the tropical earth remains "underdeveloped," its capacities to produce valid goods are today impressively greater than they were a mere ten years ago. Tariff barriers remain. Trade agreements and treaties are still feeble. Official policies toward the tropics, though improving, are still jumbled and inconsistent. Yet the levels of tropical trade keep rising.

For example, until the present century, U.S. trade with the tropics kept within a distinctly narrow range: cotton and cotton cloth, shoes, oils and fats, salt meats, dried or salted fish, wheat and flour, tobacco and dried fruits, with the bulk of the trade centered in three tropical areas—the Caribbean, Brazil, and Southeast Asia, the latter largely by way of Singapore.

At present U.S. tropical trade includes more than two thousand commodities. At present, the leading twenty-five of these are grains and grain products, industrial machinery, autos and their parts and accessories, petroleum and petroleum products, steel-mill products, electrical machinery and equipment, cotton manufactures, raw cotton, agricultural machinery and implements, tobaccos, synthetic fibers, iron and steel manufactures such as engines, turbines, and parts, dairy products, canned and dried vegetables, industrial chemicals, medical and pharmaceutical goods, rubber manufactures, chemical specialties, paper and paper products, copper and copper manufactures, animal products, including meats and lard, fruits and fruit preparations, coal tar products, and office equipment.

Our three tropical trading centers of earlier times have become five. The nearest and most dynamic of these are Mexico and Cuba (both of which are perennially among our six best tropical customers), the six republics of Central America, Haiti and the Dominican Republic, the Canal Zone, and about half a hundred of the Caribbean Islands including the French West Indies, Curaçao, Jamaica, Trinidad, the Bahamas, the Barbados, and Bermuda.

Next closest and at present next largest is the South American area which includes ten republics of that continent (all tropical except Argentina and Chile), also the three Guianas. The third trade center, conveniently tagged the "Lower Asias," takes in such immense tropical markets as India and its dependencies, Malaya, the new republics of Indonesia and the Philippines, as well as subtropical or near-tropical Palestine, East Syria, Lebanon, Arabia.

The fourth center, which is Africa, includes most of that great continent. The fifth, "Oceania," includes the subtropical portion of Australia and several hundred tropical islands of the South Pacific which in all comprise the least developed, though not necessarily the least important, of our tropical trade areas.

In all five of these tropical arenas, U.S. trade gains. In the Caribbean we have attained what is far and away our best position in international trade. With only minor exceptions we absorb more than three-fourths of the exports of these countries and we supply almost four-fifths of their total imports. In "Lower Asia" our expanding trade with India more than compensates for the political enfeeblement of

Indo-China and Siam. Our African trade keeps leaping ahead, and to Africa as a whole we continue to sell from two to three times as much as we buy. In every one of the five prevailing centers, tropical trade is generally advantageous to the United States.

In terms of geography as well as variety and sums, the range of U.S. tropical trade continues to expand. As this page is written, the twenty foremost tropical customers of the United States are as follows: Brazil, with exports to and imports from the United States totaling $1,011-409,000 yearly; Cuba, $815,136,000; Venezuela, $789,501,000; Mexico, $766,811,000; Philippine Republic, $695,301,000; Union of South Africa, $627,375,000; India, $563,589,000; Colombia, $433,268,000; Central America, $351,792,000; Malaya, $351,701,000; and thereafter (in order) Curaçao (Netherlands West Indies), the Indonesian Republic, British West Africa, Peru, Saudi-Arabia, Belgian Congo, African Gold Coast, Egypt, and Ceylon.

Totals and proportions keep changing, and for the most part they keep increasing. From a limited list of tropical countries including Brazil, Colombia, Malaya, Uruguay, Curaçao, and West Africa the United States usually buys more goods than we sell, in considerable part because of our particular dependence on these countries for strategic materials. But the total story stresses and proves tropical needs for U.S. goods. To Cuba, India, Indonesia, the Belgium Congo, Egypt, Saudi-Arabia, Venezuela, Mexico, Peru, the Philippine Republic, and Central America and to the Union of South Africa the United States usually sells substantially more than we buy.

As a whole the tropics are not inclined to begrudge or argue these preponderant trading "advantages" of the United States. As a whole the tropics desire and need more of our goods, as much as they can pay for, and much more than they can afford at the present time. "Nationalism" emerges like summer colds, but it is at least as curable as the latter, and like the latter, it may even become preventable, when and as we arrive at a valid and distinctly possible standard of multilateral trade supported by competent credit. For credit, after all, is both a premise and a sustaining need of the capitalist system. It is not "charity"; on the contrary, for many centuries past it has been the premier way in which rich people and rich nations have become rich and so remained. Fully accepted as both a first need and premise of "capitalism," credit, so far as the present-day tropical world is concerned, is also a first need and a first premise of democracy.

## CONSIDER OURSELVES

DESPITE every known type, size, and shade of impediment, ranging from monsoons and hurricanes, revered opium peddlers, and tyrannical dictators to absurdly high "protective tariffs" for "infant" industries long since grown to giant size, to profoundly vicious lobbies in scores of world capitals, to outright high-seas piracy, tropical trade has survived and increased. Since 1945 it has more or less plunged into a great and self-perpetuating era of growth. Plainly this growth is the business of the free world; it is one with the tropics tomorrow, and one with the survival of democracy.

In his memorable inaugural address of 1949, President Truman proposed abstractly but with a somewhat rare and evident sincerity a course and a goal of U.S. policy which would ". . . help the free peoples of the world, through their own efforts, to produce more food, more clothing, more material for houses, and more mechanical power to lighten their burdens. . . ."

Such a course and such a goal take for granted that a more generous and more stable world economy is the backbone of peace; that more than two-thirds of the world's peoples live in countries which need outside help to assist them in finding and attaining "a decent and productive standard of living"; further, that the United States cannot continue to flourish in a world that remains preponderantly a slum, pesthole, or poorhouse.

This so-called Point Four doctrine is far from being original and even farther from being "radical." For more than a century past, U.S. businesses have been carrying out developmental programs in underdeveloped countries, for the most part in the tropics. As of 1900 there were about ninety more or less reputable U.S. business firms operating in tropical countries. Now there are about two thousand. With admitted exceptions, these business enterprises have tended to benefit both the people and the countries where they have worked—chiefly without financial or diplomatic support and frequently without even the moral support of the United States government. The long-term record of U.S. business in the tropics averages fairly good—what there is of it. There still is not nearly enough of it.

Since 1944 the United States has been "exporting" more than 60 per cent of all international credits. These have been supplemented by direct grants of somewhat more than thirty billion dollars of U.S. taxpayers' money for "recovery" efforts, the great majority of which have been directed into Western Europe and the British Isles which, by way of comparison with the tropics and excepting only the United States, Canada, and perhaps Venezuela, Brazil, and Argentina or parts thereof, remain the silk-stocking rows of the present-day world.

This book makes no argument with the Marshall Plan or its tenets of "recovery." We are fighting for our lives and for a free world against Communism, alias the U.S.S.R. No other course remains. But many salient realities do. And one of the latter is that with the Marshall Plan and supporting works the United States, in seeking to oppose the world march of Sovietism and pleading for the capitalist or free-enterprise system, has contradicted its own words by too much by-passing of private business while pouring avalanches of taxpayers' money into the not too naïve or helpless hands of post-Atlantic politicians. This paradox is being reduced somewhat, but the statement as just made still has a strong fabric of truth and not so much as a frazzle of poetry.

For the most part the tropical earth has neither asked nor received gifts from us or any other nation. As noted, practically all development grants thus far made to tropical countries are comparatively small, specifically designated, and matched or far exceeded by funds provided by recipient nations or colonies. It can be argued convincingly that the latter types of grants are more likely to build up productiveness and otherwise facilitate self-realization than the oversize handouts of public funds from in-power politicians in one national capital to in-power politicians in another.

This reporter is last to deny such a premise and sides strongly with the former alternative. But the persistent inadequacy of credit and investment capital for and in most tropical nations cannot be denied either. Most tropics, in the manner of all frontiers and most agrarian nations, require credit and investment capital, much as the United States did a century ago. The needs are both bona fide and urgent. More production is the best and apparently the only cure for dollar shortages and "soft monies" which continue to afflict the greater part of the tropical earth.

The United States, meanwhile, has nearly 70 per cent of the total industrial capacity of the present-day world. We can produce—and except in direst crises we are producing—more goods than we can possibly consume at home over any long interval. U.S. industry requires great and expanding production since the latter seems as basic to our economy as the very air and sunlight. Expansion, indeed, is implicit in free enterprise, and expansion means that we must export.

The tropics require goods far beyond any measure yet allotted or provided. They also require partnership capital and, quite bluntly, partnership capitalism. And not at all incidentally, the latter is a weapon which the U.S.S.R. and all its heelers and lappers cannot duplicate or ably oppose. This reporter is one who believes that Britain and Europe are worth saving from the Kremlin, and that the tropics, as the potentially decisive free world of tomorrow, are doubly worth saving from the Kremlin.

The United States has immense, well-proved talents for forming productive partnerships. U.S. industry and U.S. business are the best proof of workable, ever-growing partnerships between people and capital. It is an extremely safe bet that there is not one tropical country on earth which does not or, if adequately informed, would not hope and pray that it could also create such partnerships. Fortunately, some tropical countries can create and, indeed, are creating such partnerships. But the tropics as a whole are acquiring people much more rapidly than capital. The tropics as a whole need more people. But they also need much more capital and credit, and most crucially they need the two in workable proportions.

We ourselves have faced such needs, and with the help of capital abroad we succeeded in fulfilling them and in repaying handsomely the foreign venture-capital which made possible most of our earlier railroads, turnpikes, canals, many of our basic industries, and other enterprises which became decisive.

This is not an exclusive pattern. It happened here; it can happen elsewhere. For the economic parallels between many tropics today and the United States of a century ago are as evident as an old-fashioned washday, and this goes for the long-proved facilities of tropical trade to benefit both the sellers and the buyers.

Now, as in the past, foreign trade involves hard and knotty work. Already many of us have learned this by rugged, bone-jolting experience and excessive work-hours. But fortunately U.S. business still thrives on a diet of hard jolts and hard work, and in terms of winning friends and stopping Soviet Russia in the tropics, fair and well-managed business is our best possible wand and weapon. It is, indeed, the basic stuff of Truth Bombs. Ways to markets remain ways to peace—probably the only remaining ways to peace.

Following President Truman's inaugural speech of 1949, the U.S. Secretary of State studiously worded an appeal for a "climate" of tolerance and friendliness toward U.S. investment capital beyond U.S. boundaries. The appeal was lucid and pertinent, and quite appropriately it was "beamed" toward points south, where in the main it was received cordially.

Shortly before, representative businessmen from about forty countries, including thirty-three tropical countries, had found no insurmountable difficulty in agreeing on a master code of fair treatment for foreign investments. The International Chamber of Commerce had accepted the code promptly in its entirety. The ease and directness with which the traders' agreement was put together was more satisfying than surprising. A Brazilian steel maker explained forthrightly: "We are all business people. There is no real difference between us. We seek the same goals. . . ."

## WE SEEK THE SAME GOALS

BRAZILIANS have a particular talent for sharpening proverbs and otherwise accepting the inevitable. They, like the great majority of tropical peoples and like the great majority of free or partially free peoples everywhere, have long taken for granted the correctness and necessity of profits as a motive for trade.

In Africa, Central America, South America, and elsewhere in warm countries, I have dealt with a great many native or local citizen traders. I have never met one who objected to or challenged the essential correctness of a profit motive. The same goes for the many other outspoken tropical people whom I have known. In the tropics as out, "shop talk" remains the nearest thing to a universal language, and business friendships have a way of outlasting most others.

Aside from this, and in some part because of it, U.S. business has accomplished memorable good in many tropical countries, and this fact is likewise the bone and blood of oncoming history. In many tropical places, U.S. business has served to raise wages and living standards and to benefit otherwise the pursuit of happiness by contributing such outstanding American facilities as the use of machines, the techniques of mass production (which date back to the time when Thomas Jefferson helped Eli Whitney gain a contract to manufacture a first "standard-parts" rifle for the U.S. Army), and the good worker's right to promotion.

There is exceptional relevance in the fact that the southward flow of U.S. capital is growing. At present it totals somewhere near half a billion dollars per year. Members of the Truman administration have predicted or publicly hoped that by 1952 U.S. venture-capital for all "undeveloped" countries might reach two billion dollars yearly. Though this hope is by no means groundless, timetables for venture or, better-named, partnership capital abroad are meeting numerous delays, no few of which stem from official preoccupation, doldrums, and dogfights in Washington, D.C., from comparable dilemmas in several tropical capitals, from civil strife or tense uncertainties in otherwise promising tropical areas, or from the fast-rising capital costs of tropical developments.

Business history keeps proving, however, that such delays, though more or less inevitable, are not insurmountable. Despite all impediments, U.S. business, like tropical trade in general, keeps rising to the far south. And it keeps on incubating its own broods of proverbs and generalities. One of these is that major tropical enterprises cannot be started on financial shoestrings or merely by audacious publicity campaigns.

This latter simplification is recently proved by the wretched failure of the Liberia Company of the late Stettinius Associates, which has provided one of the better manuals of what not to do in the tropics. Most regrettably, U.S. business lost face throughout tropical Africa.

There is example value here, but it is negative. In the same little tropical republic, Liberia, Firestone has provided a positive demonstration of how to build and perpetuate a valid, mutually beneficial tropical property. By developing two highly productive rubber plantation centers, with all needed accouterments including up-to-date hospitals, research farms, low-profit commissaries, recreation centers, churches, excellent housing, and the systematic training and upgrading of some thirty thousand native workers, Firestone has developed one of the "model" rubber properties in the present-day world. It is now a paying proposition. But it has required the well-planned and experienced investment of more than fifty million real dollars.

There are no absolute rules of bigness or littleness for tropical developments beyond the entirely evident proposition that the investments need to be sufficiently big and durable to stave off the forces of rust, wear, and natural mishap; they must also be sufficiently strong and well-enough directed to enable man and his works to stand against the might and power of tropical vegetation and weather. On the other hand, the amounts of investment capital must not be overwhelmingly great. They must be absorbable into the local economy within a reasonable time, say five years, or at most ten years. However trite and grumpy they may sound, such semi-proverbs as the foregoing are based on recorded fact and long-time experience, and they are applicable. They gain great pertinence from the many recorded examples of unfortunate extremes in tropical investments: too-littles and too-lates versus too-muches and too-soons. Examples of the latter are as conspicuous as swollen jaws or black eyes.

Those of us who spent some or all of World War II in the tropics saw one or many more examples of hurricane-style economic upsets brought about by the varied, oftentimes frantic succession of war expediencies. Time after time, we were more or less obliged to recruit tropical workers overnight or during the very early morning hours to build airports or landing strips, to lighter cargos, drain swamps, or "sanitate" morose and sickly jungles for the benefit or the minimum survival of our fighting forces.

Some of these ventures caused severe upsets in the local economies, bad precedences, and unfortunate wastes of public money. But unhappily for efficient people, war is war; it is neither nice nor invariably logical nor entirely controllable, and we can at least hope that war will not be the habitual American way of life. In any case and despite all mistakes committed in haste or grim expedience and without sufficient prior experience or planning, tropical countries and peoples alike responded and in the main functioned almost amazingly well. There were no really irreparable or completely ruinous losses, and in many valid ways the United States and a majority of the American tropics finished their respective roles in World War II as better friends than we or they have ever been before.

Much the same can be said of several U.S. industries which have poured too much investment capital too rapidly into tropical areas which at the time were not able to absorb the investment capital, but with additional time and productive work were eventually able to. Honduras is a first-rate example. Beginning about 1910 this smallish and frontierish Central American country was all but drowned by successive deluges of capital investment by banana companies. Honduras now begins to swim on its own power, even if upstream. So does Costa Rica, another one-time "banana republic." So does Cuba, despite its still tremendous investments by U.S. sugar companies.

For a quarter-century Venezuela remained a somewhat bleary example of a remote, oil-rich tropical frontier wholly unable to absorb or balance the aggressive deluges of capital investments by U.S., British, and Dutch oil companies. Today Venezuela clearly is becoming a sovereign nation. Its government and at least part of its people are benefiting from petroleum royalties which total perhaps one-third of the combined profits of the oil companies. Venezuela's labor market is exceptionally strong. In terms of public debt, or the comparative lack thereof, Venezuela has become one of the more solvent nations. Furthermore, living standards of most Venezuelans have risen markedly during the past quarter-century, and though still direly underpopulated, Venezuela is one of the healthier and happier of the tropical nations.

No doubt the thanks here are due far more to God than the oil companies, though, to speak objectively, the oil companies have not done too badly by the country or its people, granting that they could have done better in the past and that the odds stand that they will have to do better in the future.

Similar odds apply to most other types and calibers of capital investment in the tropics. Speaking generally, both the patterns and the specific works are improving. Thus far the actual losses of U.S. business in the tropics, owing to expropriation or civil strife, are remarkably slight, quite regardless of the fact that most U.S. business firms which are now successful in tropical work have been content with, or at least have accepted, routine contracts with the sovereign governments in whose territory they operate. It is notable that even in Mexico, where Mexican government expropriation of "foreign" petroleum properties aroused such a prolonged and bitter hullabaloo, U.S. petroleum companies are again operating effectively and amicably.

## WE CAN GET ALONG

COMMENTATORS, official and otherwise, keep pointing out that because of possible and future controversies with other governments, U.S. business will require just and vigorous support from the U.S. State Department and other federal agencies. This reporter accepts the foregoing as affably as he accepts the general statement that in the Arkansas Ozarks dogwoods generally bloom in late March, or that almost nothing tastes better to a hungry man than a really good sirloin steak.

One might also make the scintillating reflection that U.S. business now wears breeches and has learned how to take them off and put them on again, or that—and this without any real malice toward the legal departments—contracts of any sort are precisely as good or as bad as the principals who sign them. By way of further inspired revelation, during all my years of tropical work and roving I have yet to see or find a single bona fide tropical enterprise that has flourished entirely in legislative halls or cloakrooms; I have never seen any banana or sugar cane or rice or corn or cocoa or coffee or any other useful crop growing in such places. And despite all the brass spittoons, guard rails, and Yale locks, I have never seen any real mineral or metal production in capitals (I have seen the oil wells on the grounds of the Oklahoma State Capitol, but respectfully submit that these are exceptions which prove the rule here suggested). I have never heard any Congressional oratory or read any governmental directives which could actually make the soil one whit richer, and in general I have noted that private business still excels government business.

The really pertinent fact is that U.S. business already has blazed good and durable trails into the tropics and already has set many able and excellent precedents for getting along and for prospering beyond U.S. boundaries. All these are superbly important to us and to what remains of or may presently become a free world. For business pioneering in the tropics brightens the hope of freedom while facing realistically the now unavoidable U.S. need for new frontiers of enterprise and trade, a need as truly American as washday, cornbread or the corner filling station.

U.S. business requires expansion. The tropics as a whole need much more of U.S. business. In the tropics, as here, government is necessary; but investment capital and devoted private enterprise are even more necessary. As already noted, too, U.S. business has already gone into the tropics and has already proved ways and means of getting along and prospering when arrived there.

One way is that of becoming minority shareholders in local companies duly incorporated and otherwise authorized in the country or countries where the work proceeds. Another is to become owners of one-half interest in foreign companies. Another is the role of concessionaire with long-time management contracts or agreements. Another is to operate as subsidiary companies, financed in the United States but incorporated and duly accredited in the country or countries where the work is done.

There are many specific examples of U.S. partnership capital now valuably at work in the tropics. An excellent one is Sears, Roebuck, which recently has opened several superb retail stores in Mexico, Cuba, and Brazil, on a partnership-owner-and-management basis and with the determination already realized to sell locally made goods at reduced profits and with improved merchandising.

International General Electric is carrying on highly successful partnerships with citizen manufacturers and producers in at least seven tropical countries. Pan American World Airways, Westinghouse International, National Cash Register, International Business Machines, Swift, Armour, Goodyear, and about fifty other principal industrial corporations have developed and are succeeding with partnership-capital investments throughout the western tropics and in substantial areas of the eastern tropics as well.

These, and others more or less like them, are preponderantly sound and prosperous businesses. During 1950, a fairly typical (and much troubled year), U.S. investments in tropical oil properties earned at the rate of about 20 per cent; in manufacturing enterprises about 15 per cent; in agricultural enterprises an average of 7 to 10 per cent; public utilities about 8 per cent—all prior to currency conversion.

There is nothing new about earning or otherwise getting money in and from the tropics. The vast eloquence of history supports the common knowledge that the tropics have already provided sources of wealth to all wealthy nations. The United States is no exception. U.S. business has gone to the tropics to make money, and in great part is has succeeded. In general, the prospects for continuation are good and getting better. The theme of mutual benefit in business keeps gaining accent. Somewhat more than three-fourths of the current total of U.S. foreign investment is in the tropics. Thirty years ago the proportion was less than one-fifth.

The tropics as a whole require much greater quantities of partnership capital and along with it, or ahead of it, many more technicians and technical skills. Thus far, U.S. business, with its world-leading resources in technical talent, has done most to accommodate these needs.

But the needs are still nowhere near fulfilled, and more intently than ever before, and as rather clearly suggested by the Point Four doctrine, the tropics look to the United States for technical advisors and technicians. The U.S. public, in turn, has built and supports, by taxes and in other ways, the largest, best-equipped, best-led array of technical schools, colleges, and universities in the world, a reality which tends to portray the U.S. technician as a public and international resource as well as a useful private citizen.

In one way or another, the U.S. government and the U.S. public, including tens of thousands of the technicians concerned, are tending to accept the latter point of view. At the present time the United States has more than a third of a million citizen technicians and scientists on public payrolls. Currently, the armed services have at least half that number, with many more coming. And the overall roster of U.S. technicians is increasing at the rate of somewhere near half a million per year.

Already several departments of the U.S. government (the U.S. Department of Agriculture is the largest integrated technical and scientific organization in the world today) have assigned, lent, or otherwise dispatched about four thousand technicians—including plant explorers, pathologists, engineers, physicians, surgeons, map makers, geologists, soil analysts, livestock experts, foresters, nurses, chemists, laboratory technicians, and many others—to various tropical places to work as individuals, advisors, teachers, or in official or quasi-official groups or "missions."

Already the good accomplished is monumental, all the more so because technicians employed by companies or serving churches and other institutions had previously pioneered in many tropical countries. These men, in growing numbers, remain at work: medical missionaries; physicians, surgeons, and others employed by medical departments of major American companies now operating in the tropics; medical missions recently or currently assigned by the U.S. Public Health Service to Liberia, Ethiopia, Egypt, Iraq, and other disease-ridden tropical places. The medical corps of the U.S. Army and Navy, have attended tens of thousands of tropical people and thereby won for the United States many more million of tropical friends. Such scientific and philanthropic groups as the Rockefeller Foundation, International Health Board, American Foundation for Tropical Medicine and many others have done a great deal.

Here again the list of workers keeps growing. The tropics are benefiting immensely from the services of U.S. technicians and scientists. And vice versa. For the tropics, in turn, comprise the most vast and revealing of all laboratories; they are great, lush green frontiers for learning.

The current and total personnel of U.S. medical workers, and all other scientists and technicians now in the tropics on public or private work, now numbers somewhere near sixty thousand. Rarely, if ever have so few given so much to so many. For the tropics now and tomorrow must have technicians and scientists, and they must have help in training and leading their home-raised ranks of these. More than any other nation, the United States has these great facilities to offer—on a forthright basis of reasonable and proper returns.

For all these causes the United States holds advantages in terms of tropical relations that are favorable beyond all precedent. We can enact give-and-take policies. We can afford liberal reciprocity, since we need greater and greater quantities of tropical goods which cannot be grown or mined or otherwise produced within home boundaries. Because so many hundreds of millions of tropical peoples require U.S. goods, we can gain by providing tropical countries a better chance to put more of their goods on U.S. markets and in turn to supply them with a greater proportion of U.S. goods and capital as now exportable.

## LOOKING FORWARD

OUR motives for accomplishing all this far transcend the workings of cash registers and profit sheets. In many ways by so doing we are helping others, and in more than one way we are helping ourselves.

For all around the equator the spotlight of the common man's hope plays to and on the United States as the global fountainhead of business (a good word in any language, not excepting the Russian) and the mighty bellwether of democracy, also a good word in any language which is permitted to use it.

Democracy is a rather beautiful word as well as a wishful one. Also it is a "taking" word in virtually all tropics today. The inevitable desire of tropical peoples to better themselves, however much frustrated, pummeled, and beaten, is rising. It is battered and bleeding, but it can become invincible.

This reality is our particular cue for action and very likely for survival. The global show is on. From the tropics as from other places many other spotlights are on us. The world is our stage, the tropics our most decisive audience and our best hope for victory in an immensely dramatic contest between ourselves and a vast foe who could win that audience, or the most animate part of it, and thereby destroy both us and the globe-circling hope for democracy.

The play is on, and we, the United States, are living and acting one of its two major roles, Soviet Russia the other. Far more literally than most of us realize, we are also playing for our lives and more importantly for the survival of a free world, which includes all the democratic concepts which the United States of Thomas Jefferson's time and thereafter has done most to engender and pass along to others. Soviet Russia, heavily walled and reinforced with satellites and other servile states, is playing both for the survival and the unlimited power of the Kremlin dictatorship.

The United States and Soviet Russia are the great powers of the world today. Inevitably the tropics will have most to do with deciding which one will lead the world tomorrow. For at least twenty years past, the views and strategies of the Comintern have tended to accept this truth.

Determinedly and audaciously Stalin's Kremlin has sought to penetrate the tropics and win them, not by costly trade lines nor costly conquests, but rather by words, gestures, and implications, by exploitations of grievances, prejudices, and emotion, and by other superbly skillful devices of play-acting.

The curtain has risen, lights and sounds are going at full blast; the immensely important tropical audiences are listening and watching more intently than ever before. The dictatorship of the U.S.S.R. know this, and their roles have long been in rehearsal. They know the placing of the audiences and more than a little about its moods, emotions, and prejudices; also they know the seating diagram.

They are well aware that the temperate-zone powers not already in the Soviet camp can now be brought in only by way of expensive conquest, and in the "colossal" show now in progress they know that the audience—the world—can be won most easily and cheaply by way of the tropics and, quite probably, in no other way.

This credo is not original or new. Napoleon believed it though, except for his unsuccessful Egyptian campaign, he apparently "caught" the idea too late. Much earlier, the Caesars looked south for world conquest because they saw the tropics, particularly great Africa, as eternally prolific and resourceful: *Ex Africa semper aliquid novi.* Hitler gambled his chances for winning World War II in an African and a near-tropics "encircling" campaign which he barely lost. Despite all its huffings and puffings and propaganda lines, the basic foreign policy of the U.S.S.R. bears impressive similarity to that of Czarist Russia, which also and on many occasions looked slyly and lustfully to the south and southeast.

The Kremlin has never been content merely to look south and to covet. Since the early 1930's, perhaps earlier, the Kremlin has directed much of its most fervent propaganda and diplomatic efforts into the tropics, both east and west. At a time when the United States was still assigning conspicuous drips, droops, and other ineffective younger brothers or not-too-bright sons or boring brothers-in-law of political machine leaders to tropical diplomatic posts, the Kremlin was assigning its best and first-line diplomatic talent to tropical duty.

This reporter has met several Soviet representatives in the tropics—from Ethiopia to Mexico City. Without exception I have found them shrewd, diligent, and dangerous to us. I have heard such Kremlin moguls as Molotov and Ahrens boasting of the superiority of Soviet diplomacy in the tropics, and I have never been able to regard these boasts as idle. From its beginning, the Lenin School of Moscow has featured the "training" of tropical citizens and Party members.

Beginning in the very early 1930's, the Kremlin opened a long-range program to disrupt and upset the strategic Caribbean and Panama Canal regions and to plant Sovietism at our tropical doorway.

Moscow has long worked by way of Mexico City and Havana and continues to crowd alumni of the Lenin School into and out of both "centers." As this page is written Radio Moscow continues to broadcast nightly (on wave-bands 19-25) propaganda programs in excellent Spanish especially beamed to the lands of the Caribbean. Their activities have gone far beyond mere propaganda handouts. They have penetrated the once-mighty (but now abating) Toledano labor movement in Mexico and Central America. With varying effectiveness they have bored and burrowed into at least a dozen governments in the American tropics, one of the latest victims being the José Arévalo government of Guatemala.

In the person and the work of the late Constantine A. Oumansky, Soviet Ambassador extraordinary to Mexico and Costa Rica (Oumansky died in an airplane wreck in 1945), the Kremlin put at work one of the most brilliant diplomats who ever toiled and conspired. Oumansky arrived on the then magic carpet of U.S. recognition of Soviet Russia (the basic terms of which the Kremlin had violated from the start), the illusion of the U.S.S.R. as a comrade against the Nazis, and the winking, come-hither, smart-to-be-pinko tolerance (possibly intolerance) of the late and in many ways great Franklin D. Roosevelt and his then invincible mentor, Eleanor.

This reporter knew Oumansky. He was far and away the most astute politician I have ever met, not excepting Molotov or F.D.R. He had tremendous personal charm and almost uncanny understanding of people. He was a rabble rouser extraordinary, ruthless, and devoid of any regard for truth. Yet he could play on a group of Latin politicians as adroitly as the virtuoso with a harp and far more commandingly.

Promptly and with almost demoniac skill Oumansky set out to establish and make effective a "program" to reduce or break down completely U.S. influence and to frustrate U.S. investments throughout the Caribbean; to weaken and eventually rub out defense structures there maintained by the United States; to neutralize U.S. procurement of important raw materials; and to implant Soviet ideology and to link "cells" of Communism throughout the Caribbean.

After Pearl Harbor, Oumansky, who boasted of being a "faithful Stalin slave," increased his already too effective labors. During 1944 I interviewed him in Mexico City. He was affable and momentarily firmly attached to a bottle of vodka. I asked him how he justified his intrigues and damaging connivances against the United States with the fact that his nation was fighting for its life and that the United States was its most powerful and generous ally. The great conspirator laughed heartily and said: "In the Soviet Republics we also have proverbs. The best one I know is, 'Yesterday the Russias; tomorrow the world.'"

The U.S.S.R. has gone far in changing that proverb to reality. But even more significantly, the U.S.S.R. has not yet completely won its tropical audience or any principal part thereof.

As this book has noted, tropical trends toward democracy remain real and they continue to increase. Since the sudden death of Constantine Oumansky (one of the luckier days for the United States), "Communism" has lost ground in the Caribbean and throughout most of South America. It has infiltrated into many Latin American governments, but repeatedly such governments have been overthrown or, as in Guatemala and Chile, the Soviet hirelings have been used as mere stepping stones for the ascendancy of more adroit native politicians.

The U.S.S.R., in the guise of international Communism, maintains headquarters in both Havana and Mexico City. But during the past five years it has lost ground both in Cuba and Mexico, as well as in Colombia, Venezuela, Brazil, and throughout most of Central America. Not entirely by coincidence, during these same years, as previously, the mortality rate among tropical dictatorships has been heavy. Since 1930 at least sixteen of the eighteen nominal republics in or nearby the American tropics have been dictatorships. But the majority have wavered, tottered, and fallen on their never too pretty faces. Today only five of the eighteen are clearly dictatorships, and even Perón of Argentina feels obliged to profess a "medium status" between a "socialist state" and a "near democracy" (such as the United States).

Thus far a great and increasing portion of the tropical audience is either on our side or clearly tending toward it, in considerable part because it has begun to spot our primary cue which is constructive, mutually beneficial business. More emphatically, more obviously than ever before, trade means a better life for the tropics; more and more hundreds of millions of tropical peoples know it.

If not by the hundreds of millions, then certainly by millions, the audience in the far south balcony knows that the tropics are actual or potential producers of hundreds of commodities which the United States and our "allies" (that word is becoming almost as accredited in most tropics as "okay" or "ciglette" or "ice cream"—*iz crim*) require and will and must buy, and that we are producers of thousands of commodities which the tropics need and would like to buy.

This audience also knows that the Iron Curtain has shut off from world trade no fewer than 650,000,000 people and at least eleven million square miles of inhabited lands, a fact which greatly emphasizes the importance of the remaining more or less free peoples and the remaining more or less free lands.

They know that the balancing value of tropical trade, always notable, is now nothing short of momentous. Neither Britain, Europe, nor the United States has ever really achieved satisfactory trading balances within home boundaries, and there is no real reason to believe that any of them (us) ever will. In Europe the east-to-west flow of trade is now barricaded by Soviet walls. Quite evidently in the world tomorrow, tropical trade is the one remaining restorer of world trade.

Trade and business, our best and strongest cue and punch line for and in tropics, remains Soviet Russia's weakest. Kremlin propaganda techniques far exceed and perhaps excel those of the United States, but Soviet tropical trade remains weak, vacillating, and conspicuously inferior to ours, which is nowhere near as good as it ought to be.

Even so, the United States maintains accredited trade pacts with about forty tropical nations or colonies. As this page is written the U.S.S.R. has only four—with India-Pakistan, the Malay Federation, Siam, and Ethiopia. The Kremlin has long since ceased to make public the Soviet volume of exports and imports. There are indications that the latter totals are somewhere near those of Sweden and are tending to dwindle rather than increase. We know that Soviet Russia currently purchases rubber and tin from Malaya, petroleum from Iraq and perhaps indirectly from Venezuela, chrome from the Belgian Congo, and so on. But the totals still appear to be pipsqueak, and repeatedly during the past ten years Kremlin spokesmen have stated that Soviet resources require no substantial complements from any tropical countries. Meanwhile the "economic nationalism" of the U.S.S.R. remains iron-fisted. Furthermore, it has long been common knowledge that the afflictions of tropical dictatorships are rarely if ever of the Stalin type. Pigs are not precisely like all other pigs.

Turning from the theme of swinish dictators and Marxian swill, it is fitting and proper that a player know his audience. It is completely impossible to say in a few words or even in a five-foot bookshelf what a billion people are thinking. For the tropics as a whole, a mere fifty million votes, as might be counted in a U.S. Presidential election, is not even a "preliminary" Gallup Poll, and thank God for that.

Even so one can gather from playing to and mixing with tropical audiences at least a relevant glimmering of what they are seeing and what they are thinking. One can be certain that tropical peoples are in an era of mutation and self-liberation and that their eyes and ears follow the United States at least as much as they follow Soviet Russia, and with substantially greater warmth.

From us, the tropical onlooker sees and hears more of himself or, more precisely, more of what he would like to be. Somewhat abruptly, United States viewpoint has become interesting to him. Man's awareness of the basic and dramatic struggle of democracy versus the totalitarian state has penetrated farther and more intensively into the tropics than most of us realize. For throughout most of the tropical earth the slow trend toward democracy has gained momentum out of the humbly wistful belief that the everyday man or woman has most to gain from democracy.

Granted, of course, that democracy in the tropics cannot live on a diet of dreams; granted also that in the tropics, as elsewhere, democracy is a creed of development and production of goods as well as of ideas. Granted, too, that thus far no great number of tropical peoples have actually attained or even approached real democracy. But more and more are heading toward it, and many more are pondering democracy in intuition, emotion, and hope, the last still shackled and partly blind.

Also the everyday man and woman of the tropics is absorbing inklings, frequently vague and whimsical, of what the United States is like. He remains rather deeply bewildered about what Soviet Russia really is. If the U.S.S.R. means merely another and bigger dictator, the tropical citizen has doubts. For he has already awakened to the fact that the dictator and his mirthless states have too many ways of giving too little and taking too much.

The foregoing is inferential, but it is supported by a great deal of rather specific news. Between 1945 and 1951 the would-be tropical penetrations of the U.S.S.R. have stumbled and floundered considerably more and worse than during the warring years 1940-45. They have not halted the globe-circling trend toward democracy, however much they have confused and impeded it. Since V-J Day, three great tropical republics have been born; Greater India, Indonesia, and the Philippine Republic, with combined populations of at least 460,000,000 people, much more than the combined populations of all the other republics on earth. The Republic of Israel has become a significant reality of the borderline tropics, and comparatively independent dominions, such as Ceylon, have lately emerged. Some 80,000,000 people of immense French Africa have been made citizens of the French Republic. Since 1940, at least twenty-four tropical countries, including thirteen in the Western Hemisphere have "liberalized" their constitutions so that they will be better adapted to democracy and democratic practices—this, more or less evidently, on a when-and-if basis.

All of these developments can be listed as gestures or moves to open doors to democracy. Inevitably, and on Kremlin orders, Soviet propagandists deny this. They chortle and shout that the moves just mentioned are desperate, hopeless withdrawals of the "white imperialist." But the provable facts are that virtually all the "white imperialists" are getting closer to the tropics. The United States is. Britain is. France is. Denmark, the Netherlands, even Spain and Portugal are. Even Belgium shows a tendency of liberality toward the so magnificent and so long crucified Belgian Congo; and that, like man biting dog, is news.

## LOOK SOUTH AGAIN

IN PLAYING, perhaps the most definitive omen of success is the ability to take advantage of "breaks"—the opportune happenchances. In tropical terms Soviet Russia has the pre-eminent "break" of all history: it is the immense and potentially decisive tropical peninsula of South Asia which remains the world's most immense concentration of poverty, sickness, and mortal wretchedness along with the most bitter resentment of the "white imperialist"; also, as in so many other tropics, South Asia has great undeveloped resources and a geography which would make the area virtually unassailable once it was absorbed by the U.S.S.R.

Strategically, all this immense concentration of tropics and tropical underprivilege and misery is in the Soviet's front yard. The Khyber Pass has become the twentieth-century Suez. Basic geography is obviously and immensely in the Soviets' favor. By sheer force of isolation, the strange and wondrous kingdom of Afghanistan has been pushed into the Soviet fold. For the same reason, far-removed Tibet has fallen to the outermost dog packs of Chinese Communism. Pakistan, disrupted politically as well as religiously, has waited for years as an easy pushover for Communism. Siam, long a phony, ill-used kingdom, has now stumbled into the beartrap of a particularly shoddy dictatorship. Malaya, one of the more heavily losing victims of Japanese invasion and long a principal tropical victim of abortive cartels and rapacious power politics from afar, staggered weakly out of World War II as an easy prey for Communism. Indo-China still puffs and gurgles above smoldering fires of revolution and profound human distress.

Indo-China, as this page is written, is the one wedge of earth's crust that is most vulnerable to Communist attack. It is the great, wet, sagging sill to Southeast Asia. If it should collapse the Soviet-China tides could sweep readily into India and without a struggle. Soviet Russia would have a good half of the human race in its camps. Already the 23,000,000 people of Indo-China are at close grips with a virulent local ogre of Communism known as Ho Chi Minh. In the past the French usurpation of Indo-China has been both ungracious and punitive. The best of the French Army remains there, and it is obliged to keep fighting, a mere 150,000 men, preponderantly good soldiers, against potential millions of aggressors. The present Minh forces are terrorists, Lenin-School-of-Moscow style. They far outnumber the French.

Indo-China is one of the more primitive of tropical countries and for that reason one of the more revealing. I met the Viet Namese four years ago when revolution seemed inevitable and bright. I found them land-loving and peace-loving farmers. They wanted to remain so. They wanted to raise and market their crops without rapine and usurpation by the "colony men." They spoke the unboundaried language of the tropics, and they dreamed the dreams of all men.

Communism has seeped over the land. Communism has levied still more punitive taxes, stolen more rice and oxen, and raped more wives and daughters than all the "colony men" together. Accordingly, the preponderantly good people of Indo-China, crucial still to Southeast Asia, in overwhelming majority are not Communists, and the chances are easily ten thousand to one that they will never be so at heart or in mind.

They talk of "Communism" and "Capitalism," of the Kremlin and of democracy. One hears such talk all over South Asia today, as for several years past. It is thoughtful talk. Quite evidently the people are pondering, and they have not yet had opportunity to decide. Meanwhile, quite unavoidably, they have looked to Soviet Russia. Now they look toward us. And they look toward God—their own names and interpretations of God. They must have God. At minimum we can tolerate Him. Apparently the U.S.S.R. cannot. Therein waits still another profound and dramatic impetus. Indo-China is likely to remain a significant tropical land surface.

Nearby land surfaces are also of strategic importance. The extremely new republics of India, Pakistan, Indonesia, and the Philippines, and the oven-warm Dominion of Ceylon, for example, are in the same momentous sphere. All, conspicuously, are in infancy, with the inevitable pukings, bed-wettings and other babyhood frailties of infants, not excepting vulnerability to political kidnapings.

Soviet Russia has had motivation and the superb opportunity for taking over and sealing off all this immensely resourceful and populous tropical sphere of lower Asia. Propaganda-wise, and at least by the strategies of power politics, Soviet Russia has tried hard to take over. It may yet succeed. But the decisive time is passing.

The great show goes on. U.S. appreciation of the tropics is not new, however much it has drowsed and slumbered. U.S. appreciation of the tropics is awakening. We have made momentous mistakes regarding the tropics, and the chances are that we will make more. But we can win far more effectively and durably on the stage and facing south than on any literal battlefields.

We are powerful and great as soldiers. We are learning to be an able conqueror. But very definitely we are greater as players and as leaders. The audience is before us, and it is the decisive factor of the world tomorrow.

On stage or off, we are also experimenters and frontiersmen. The tropics are the great remaining frontiers of the earth, and the drama of democracy lives from frontiers. Democracy is our role. It is not an easy one, and neither is the role of benefactor and user of frontiers. New and better lines are essential. The dire old cliché of taking over the tropics first by sending missionaries, then traders, and finally governors and armed constabularies has died a reasonable, natural, and unmourned death.

The play is on and it is now. The tropics are watching and listening to us versus Soviet Russia, and the tropics will do most to decide between us. In turn, that decision will do much or most to shape the world tomorrow, and it will do this inevitably because the tropics, cradles of life, of sun, rain, and earth, have been yesterday and they can and will be tomorrow. Accordingly, now is the time to play well, and look south.

# BIBLIOGRAPHY

As a rule, bibliographies are free of the impediment of forewords. In this particular instance, however, some manner of foreword appears necessary. Since the times of Columbus no fewer than eighty thousand books of one or another sort, size, and language have been published in or about the earth-circling subjects of the tropics. The Library of Congress and the New York Public Library together hold about fifty thousand volumes about or pertaining to the tropics.

The estimate of eighty thousand is an approximation based on many hours of checking library files and many days and nights of reading. In jotting the names of various volumes, old and new, which I have read while writing this book, a procedure covering about three years, I find the total is above one thousand two hundred. Indeed, without half trying I have acquired somewhat more than one thousand nine hundred books about the tropics, past or present. From the total list, I have tried here to assemble a reasonably compact bibliography which I sincerely hope will be helpful to those who wish to read further in this magnificent realm of part-knowledge and invincible wonderment.

Books about the tropics are written in most of the great languages of man. The majority of the works here listed are in English and are obtainable from American sources. As tokens of very real respect I am, however, including at least a sampling from the great literatures of Spanish, French, German, Portuguese, and Dutch. These tokens are suggested with deference toward the immensely greater and worthy total.

Some of the titles that follow are old or ancient. This choice is also deliberate; there is relevance and enlightenment in noting the ever-changing views of the tropics as felt and recorded by people of the temperate zones and/or people of the tropics. Marked with an asterisk are titles which, as one student, I feel are particularly apropos of present-day interest, though all and many more are much worth while.

ANDERSON, AUGUST MAGNUS. *African Jungle.* Anderson, Indiana: Gospel Trumpet Company, 1928.

BALDWIN, CHARLES. *African Hunting: from Natal to the Zambesi, 1852–1860*. New York: Harper and Brothers, 1863.

BALFOUR, SIR ANDREW. *War Against Tropical Disease*. London: Bailliere, Tindall, and Cox, 1920.

BANNER, HUBERT S. *A Tropical Tapestry*. London: T. Butterworth, 1929.

* BARRETT, OTIS W. *The Tropical Crops*. New York: Macmillan Company, 1928.

BATTEN, THOMAS R. *Problems of African Development*. London: Oxford University Press, 1940.

* BEALS, CARLETON. *Pan America*. Boston: Houghton Mifflin Company, 1940.

* ———. *Rio Grande to Cape Horn*. Boston: Houghton Mifflin Company, 1943.

BEEBE, W. C., and Others. *Tropical Wildlife in British Guiana*. New York: New York Zoological Society, 1917.

BENNETT, HUGH H., and ALLISON, R. V. *The Soils of Cuba*. Washington, D.C.: Tropical Plant Research Foundation, 1928.

BLACKLOCK, D. B. *An Empire Problem: The House and Village in the Tropics*. Liverpool: Liverpool University Press, 1932.

BLACKMAN, WILLIAM F. "White Men in the Tropics." In *The Independent*, Vol. LI (New York, 1899), pp. 670-73.

BRAYNE, F. L. *Better Villages in India*. London: Oxford University Press, 1937.

BREINL, ANTON. *The Distribution and Spread of Disease in the East*. Melbourne: McCarron, Bird, and Company, 1914.

* BUCK, JOHN LOSSING. *Land Utilization in China*. Chicago: University of Chicago Press, 1937.

CASTANDEA DE RENARO, JULIO E. *La Granga Guatemala, por el agronimo*. Ciudad Guatemala: Ramirez, 1939.

CHERRY, THOMAS. *Victorian Agriculture in Australia*. Melbourne: D. W. Patterson Company, 1941.

CHORIS, LOUIS. *Vues et paysages des regions équoxiales, reçueillis dans un voyage autour du monde*. Paris, 1826.

CILENTO, RAPHAEL W. *The White Man in the Tropics*. Melbourne: H. J. Green, 1925.

CLERK, A. *Tropic Sketches and Other Poems*. London: Leggatt and Neville, 1840.

CLINE, ISAAC MONROE. *Tropical Cyclones*. New York: Macmillan Company, 1926.

Clute, Robert L. *Practical Lessons in Tropical Agriculture.* New York: World Book Company, 1914.

Coope, Richard. *A Letter to the Proprietors of the South Seas Company.* London: A. Dodd, 1739.

Copeland, Edwin Bingham. *Elements of Philippine Agriculture.* Manila: World Publishing Company, 1910.

* Courtnay, Roger. *Africa Calling.* London: G. G. Harrup and Company, 1935.

Crawford, David L. *Paradox in Haiti.* Boston: Stratford Company, 1937.

* Crow, John A. *The Epic of Latin America.* New York: Doubleday and Company, 1946.

Cudahy, John. *African Horizons.* New York: Duffield and Company, 1930.

* De la Selva, Solomon. *Tropical Town.* New York: J. Lane Company, 1918.

De Lisser, H. G. "The White Man in the Tropics." In *New Century Review,* Vol. VII (London, 1900), pp. 117-24.

Desiré, Adam. *El Dorado.* Paris: LaRose, 1936.

Dobson, James O. *Ronald Ross: Dragon Slayer.* London: Student Christian Movement Press, 1934.

DuBois, W. W. Burghardt. *The World and Africa.* New York: Viking Press, 1947.

Edge, P. Granville. *Vital Statistics and Public Health Work in the Tropics.* London: Bailliere, Tindall, and Cox, 1944.

Eliot, G. F. Scott. "Primary Conditions of Tropical Production: An Introduction to Economic Botany." In *Scottish Geographical Magazine,* Vol. XIV (Edinburgh, 1898).

Engel, F. *Nacht und Morgen unter den Tropen.* Berlin: Samuel Virchou, 1875.

* Enock, Charles Reginald. *The Tropics: Their Resources, People, and Future.* London: G. Richards, Limited, 1915.

Euleh, Margaret S. *White Mother in Africa.* New York: R. R. Smith, 1939.

* Fenn, George M. *The Khedive's Country: The Nile Valley.* London: Cassell and Company, 1904.

Fisher, Stephen Sargent. "Variability versus Uniformity in the Tropics." In *Scientific Monthly,* Vol. XV (New York, 1932), pp. 22-34.

*Foreign Slave Trade: A Report to the House of Commons.* London: African Institute of London, 1821.

FOSTER, HARRY L. *A Tropical Tramp with the Tourists.* New York: Dodd, Mead, and Company, 1925.

FRASER, DONALD. *In a Central African Mission Station.* London: Seeley, Service, and Company, 1923.

FROBENIES, LEO. *African Genesis.* New York: Stackpole Sons, 1937.

* FURNAS, J. C. *Anatomy of Paradise.* New York: William Sloane Associates, 1949.

GERRY, T. GERALD. *African Doctor.* London: Book Club of London, 1939.

GESSLER, CLIFFORD. *Tropic Landfall: The Port of Honolulu.* New York: Doubleday and Company, 1942.

———. *Tropics Earth.* Reno, Nevada: Wagon and Star Publishers, 1944.

GHOSH, BIRENDA NATH. *A Treatise on Tropical Hygiene and Health.* Calcutta: Hilton and Company, 1924.

* GILL, TOM. *Tropical Forests of the Caribbean.* Washington, D.C.: Tropical Plant Research Foundation, 1931.

* GORGAS, WILLIAM CRAWFORD. "The Conquest of the Tropics for the White Race." In *Journal of the American Medical Association,* Vol. LII (Chicago, 1909), pp. 1967-69.

GRAHOMES, GEORGE WALTER. *Some Factors in Thermal Sanitation in the Tropics.* Cambridge, England: Cambridge University Press, 1927.

* GREGORY, JOHN W. *Inter-Racial Problems* and *White Colonization in the Tropics.* London: British Association for the Advancement of Science, 1925.

———. *The Menace of Colour: A Study of the Difficulties Due to the Association of White and Colored Races.* London: Service and Company, Limited, 1925.

GRUGER, KARL. *Tropentechnik: Kolonialtechnik im Luerschnitt.* Berlin: O. Elsner, 1939.

HARDING, ALFRED. *Tropical Fruit.* New York: Duffield and Company, 1928.

HARTFORD, CHARLES F. *Outfits for Travelers in Tropical Countries.* London: Royal Geographic Society, 1911.

HARTWIG, GEORGE LUDWIG. *The Polar and Tropical Worlds.* Springfield, Mass.: Nichols and Company, 1871.

———. *The Tropical World: A Popular Scientific Account of the Natural History of the Animal and Vegetable Kingdoms in the Equatorial Regions.* London: Longmans, Green, 1863.

———. *The Tropical World: Aspects of Man and Nature in the Equatorial Regions of the Globe.* London: G. Richards, Limited, 1863.

* Heiser, Victor. *An American Doctor's Odyssey.* New York: W. W. Norton and Company, 1936.

Higgenbottom, Sam. *The Old Gospel and Modern Farming in India.* New York: Macmillan Company, 1921.

Hubbard, Margaret Carson. *African Gamble.* New York: G. P. Putnam's Sons, 1937.

* Hudson, W. H. *Green Mansions: A Romance of the Tropical Forest.* London: Duckworth, 1934.

Hunt, Virginia L. *How to Live in the Tropics.* New York: Harcourt, Brace, and Company, 1943.

Hunting, Ellsworth. *The Nature and Possibilities of Tropical Agriculture.* Philadelphia: Special Bulletin of the Geographical Society of Philadelphia, 1919.

*Informe de la Comissión especial de Petroleos,* Nombrade por la honorable Camera, segun proposición numero 392 de 1935. Bogotá: Petroleos Comissión, Republica de Colombia, 1935.

Ireland, Alleyne. "European Experience with Tropical Colonies." In *The Atlantic Monthly,* Vol. LXXXII (Boston, 1898), pp. 729-35.

———. "Is Tropical Colonization Justifiable?" *Journal of the Academy of Political and Social Sciences,* Vol. XIX (Philadelphia, 1902), pp. 331-39.

* ———. *Tropical Colonization.* London and New York: Macmillan Company, 1898 and 1899.

Ireland, Gordon. *Boundaries, Possessions and Conflicts in South America.* Cambridge, Mass.: Harvard University Press, 1938.

Keating, Gerald F. *Agricultural Progress in Western India.* London and New York: Longmans, Green, 1921.

Keyser, Arthur Locus. *People and Places: A Life in Five Continents.* London: J. Murray, 1922.

Kidd, Benjamin. *The Control of the Tropics.* New York: Macmillan Company, 1899.

Kirk, J. Balfour. *A Manual of Practical Tropical Sanitation.* London: Bailliere, Tindall, and Cox, 1937.

Kohn, Hans. *World Order.* Cambridge, Mass.: Harvard University Press, 1942.

Labat, Jean Baptiste. *Voyage du Chevalier des Marchias en Guinee.* New York: Ford Collection, 1731.

Latham, G. C. *The African and the Cinema.* London: International Mission Council, Edinburgh House Press, 1937.

* Leake, Hugh M. *Land Tenure in the Tropics.* Cambridge, England: W. Heffer and Sons, 1927.

* LEE, DOUGLAS H. K. *Human Climatology and Tropical Settlement.* Brisbane: University of Queensland, Australia, 1947.

LONG, J. ALDEN. *African Adventure Stories.* Foreword by Theodore Roosevelt, New York: Charles Scribner's Sons, 1914.

LUKES, SIR CHARLES P. *Tropical Hygiene.* Calcutta: Thatcher, Spink, and Company, 1918.

LYDELL, DENNIS B. *African Adventure.* London: J. Murray, 1935.

MACKENZIE, JEAN K. *African Clearings.* Boston: Houghton, Mifflin, and Company, 1924.

MACKINDERS, HALFORD J. *Democratic Ideals and Reality.* New York: Henry Holt and Company, 1942.

MACMILLAN, HUGH F. *A Handbook of Tropical Gardening, with Special Reference to Ceylon.* Colombo: H. W. Cave and Company, 1914.

* MACMILLAN, WILLIAM M. *Africa Emergent.* London: Faber and Faber, 1938.

MANSON-BAHR, PHILIP H. *The Life and World of Sir Patrick Manson.* London: Cassell, Limited, 1939.

MARKHAM, CLARA L. "The South Sea Islanders in English Literature." (Thesis.) Chicago: University of Chicago, 1937.

MARTENS, OTTO, and KARSTEDT, O. *The African Handbook and Traveler's Guide.* London: Allen and Unwin, 1932.

* MARTINDALE, C. C. *African Angelus.* London and New York: Sheed and Ward, 1933.

MELVILLE, LEWIS. *The South Sea Bubble.* London: D. O'Connor, 1921.

MILLS, DAVID. *The English in Africa.* Toronto: G. N. Morang and Company, 1900.

MILNE, A. H. *Sir Alfred Lewis Jones.* Liverpool: H. Young and Sons, Limited, 1914.

MITCHELL, P. CHALMER. "The Future of the Tropics." In *The North American Review,* Vol. CLXXVI (New York, 1903), pp. 711-18.

MOSELEY, BENJAMIN. *A Treatise on Tropical Disease.* London: G. G. and J. Robinson, 1795.

MUERHEAD, W. J. *Practical Tropical Sanitation.* New York: E. P. Dutton, 1925.

NELSON, T. and SONS (comp.). *Tropical Nature.* New York, 1841.

NICHOLLS, H. A. ALFORD. *A Textbook of Tropical Agriculture.* London: Macmillan Company, 1900.

* NIGGLI, JOSEPHINA. *Mexican Village.* Chapel Hill: University of North Carolina Press, 1945.

NORTHCATE, WILLIAM. *Marine Practice of Physic and Surgery.* London: W. J. Richardson, 1770.

OLSON-STEFFER, P. H. *La Agricultura en varios paises tropicales y subtropicales.* Mexico City: Imprente de la Secretaria de Fomento, 1910.

* ORIJU, ALWIEKE A. *Without Bitterness: Western Nations in Postwar Africa.* New York: Creative Age Press, 1944.

"Pamphleteer, The." *Reasons for Establishing a Registry of Slaves in the British Colonies.* London: J. Hatchard, 1815.

PARRISH, SAMUEL L. "Self-Government in the Tropics." In *Journal of the National Institute of Social Sciences,* Vol. I (Boston, 1915), pp. 52-62.

PILLET, ALBERT. *The African Fabiola—the Church of Carthage.* New York: D. and J. Saddler, 1887.

POIVRE, PIERRE. *Travels of a Philosopher.* Philadelphia: Robert Bell, 1778.

PRICE, A. GRENFELL. "Refugee Settlement in the Tropics." In *Foreign Affairs,* Vol. XVIII (New York, 1940), pp. 659-70.

———. *White Settlers in the Tropics.* New York: Publication No. 23, American Geographical Society, 1941.

PULESTON, FRED. *African Drums.* New York: Farrar and Rinehart, 1930.

RAPHAEL, LOIS A. C. *The Cape to Cairo Dream.* New York: Columbia University Press; London: P. S. King and Son, 1936.

RENNER, GEORGE THOMAS, JR. "Primitive Religion in the Tropical Forests." (Thesis.) New York: Columbia University Library, 1927.

REYHER, REBECCA H. *Zulu Woman.* New York: Columbia University Press, 1948.

* RICHIE, ERIC MOORE. *The Unfinished War.* London: Eyre and Spottes-wood, 1940.

RICHWOOD, M. *The South Sea Fortune.* London: J. Wren, 1758.

ROOSEVELT, THEODORE. *African Game Trails.* New York: Charles Scribner's Sons, 1910.

ROSSI, VITTORRIO G. *Tropici del Senegal all' Angola.* Milan: V. Bompiani, 1934.

SAFRONI-MIDDLETON, A. *South Sea Foam.* London: Methuen, and Company, 1919.

* ———. *Tropic Shadow: Memories of the South Seas.* London: Richards Press, Limited, 1927.

SAMPSON, HUGH C. *Report on Development of Agriculture in British Honduras.* London: His Majesty's Stationery Office, 1929.

SAPPER, KARL P. *Die Tropen.* Stuttgart: Stretter and Schroeder, 1923.

* SCHWEITZER, ALBERT. *On the Edge of the Primeval Forest and More from the Primeval Forest.* New York: Macmillan Company, 1948.

SCOTT, J. W. ROBERTSON. *A Free Farmer in a Free State.* London: W. Heinemann, 1912.

SHIPLEY, SIR ARTHUR E. *West Indian Islands.* London: M. Hopkinson, Limited, 1924.

SIMENON, GEORGES. *Tropic Noon.* Translated by Stuart Gilbert. New York: Harcourt, Brace, and Company, 1943.

SIMPSON, W. J. *The Maintenance of Health in the Tropics.* New York: Wood and Company, 1905.

SJAHRIR, SOETAN. *Out of Exile.* Translated by Charles Wolf, Jr. New York: John Day Company, 1949.

SMILANSKY, MOSHE. *Jewish Colonization and the Fellah.* Tel Aviv: Mischar a' Tassia Publishing Company, 1930.

Staff of the Department of Agriculture, Uganda. *Agriculture in Uganda.* London: Oxford University Press, 1940.

* SUNSBROEN, E. S. *A Summary of Some Studies in Tropical Acclimatization.* Melbourne: A. J. Mullette, 1924.

———. *Contribution to Tropical Physiology.* Berkeley: University of California Press, 1926.

SUTTON, CHARLES W. "Irrigation and Public Policy in Peru." In *American Scientific Congress* (Washington, D.C., 1917), pp. 840-54.

SUTTON, RICHARD L. *An African Holiday.* St. Louis: C. V. Mosby Company, 1924.

* SZEKELY, LADISLAO. *Tropics Fever: The Adventure of a Planter in Sumatra.* London: H. Hamilton, Limited, 1936.

TENSENT, JOHN. *Physical Enquiries.* London: T. Gardner, 1742.

THURSTON, ARTHUR B. *African Incidents.* London: J. Murray, 1900.

* TILBREY, AUBREY W. *Britain in the Tropics, 1527–1910.* London: Constable and Company, Limited, 1912.

* TOMLINSON, EDWARD. *The Other Americas: Our Neighbors to the South.* New York: Charles Scribner's Sons, 1943.

* TORCHIANS, H. A. VAN COENEN. *Tropical Holland . . . Birth, Growth and Development of Popular Government in an Oriental Possession.* Chicago: University of Chicago Press, 1923.

TORRANCE, ARTHUR. *Jungle Mania.* New York: Macaulay Company, 1933.

* ———. *Tracking Down the Enemies of Man.* New York: J. H. Sears and Company, 1928.

TOWNE, RICHARD. *A Treatise of the Diseases Most Frequent in the West Indies.* London: J. Clarke, 1726.

*Tropical America* (a periodical). San Juan, Puerto Rico, February, 1941–January, 1942.

*Tropical Life: A Monthly Journal.* London: Bale, Sons, and Danielsson, 1910–34.

*Tropical Products of Scientific Reliability*. Cleveland: Tropical Paint and Oil Company, 1944.

*Tropical Recipe Book, The*. West Palm Beach, Fla.: Tropical Book House, 1935.

TRYON, THOMAS. *Friendly Advice to the Gentlemen Planters of the East and West Indies*. London: A. Soule, 1684.

*Unvikeli-Thebe, The African Defenders: A Paper for Bantus*. Cape Town: M. M. Kotane, 1936–39.

United Fruit Company. *International Conference on Health Problems in Tropical America*. Kingston, Jamaica, 1924.

* VERRILL, A. HYATT. *Thirty Years in the Jungle*. London: J. Lane, 1929.

WALCOX, E. VERNON. *Tropical Agriculture*. New York: D. Appleton and Company, 1924.

WATSON, MALCOLM. *Rural Sanitation in the Tropics*. London: J. Murray, 1935.

WATT, RACHEL S. *In the Heart of Savagedom*. London: Pickering and Inglis, 1912.

WEST, F. A. F. C. *Suriname na 22 Jaar*. Amsterdam: J. H. de Bussy, 1923.

WICKENS, C. H. "Vitality of White Races in Low Latitudes." In *Economic Record*, Vol. III (Melbourne, 1927), pp. 117-26.

WILLIAMS, A. B. *The Remarkable Expedition: Stanley's Rescue of Emer Pasha*. London: W. Heinemann, 1947.

WILLIAMS, FRANCIS E. *The Reform of Native Horticulture*. Port Moresby: W. A. Bock, 1937.

* WILSON, CHARLES MORROW. *Ambassadors in White*. New York: Henry Holt and Company, 1942.

———. *Liberia*. New York: William Sloane Associates, 1947.

———. *Middle America*. New York: W. W. Norton, 1944.

———(ed.). *New Crops for the New World*. New York: Macmillan Company, 1945.

* ———. *One Half the People: Doctors and the Crisis of World Health*. New York: William Sloane Associates, 1949.

WOODROW, G. MARSHALL. *Gardening in the Tropics*. London: A. Gardner, 1910.

WOODSON, CARTER GODWIN. *African Heroes and Heroines*. Washington, D.C.: Associated Publishers, 1939.

WYLLARDE, DOLF. *Tropical Tales and Others*. New York: J. Lane, 1910.

* ZAUALA, SILVIO. *New Viewpoints in the Spanish Colonization of America*. Philadelphia: University of Pennsylvania Press, 1943.

# INDEX